Edited by DOUGLAS RIMMER

Action in Africa

The Experience of People Involved in Government, Business & Aid

The Royal African Society
IN ASSOCIATION WITH
James Currey
LONDON
Heinemann
PORTSMOUTH (N.H.)

The Royal African Society
SOAS, Thornhaugh Street
Russell Square, London WC1H 0XG

in association with

James Currey Ltd
54b Thornhill Square, Islington
London N1 1BE

Heinemann
A Division of Reed Publishing (USA) Inc
361 Hanover Street
Portsmouth, New Hampshire 03801-3912

First Published 1993

1 2 3 4 5 97 96 95 94 93

British Library Cataloguing in Publication Data
Action in Africa: Experience of People
Involved in Government, Business and Aid
I. Rimmer, Douglas
330.96

ISBN 0-85255-373-0 (James Currey Cloth)
ISBN 0-85255-372-2 (James Currey Paper)

Library of Congress Cataloging-in-Publication Data
Action in Africa : the experience of people involved in government, business & aid / edited by Douglas Rimmer.
p. cm.
Papers originally presented at a conference held in Oxford, Mar. 1993, and organized by the Royal African Society.
Includes index.
ISBN 0-435-08098-9 (Heinemann)
1. Africa, Sub-Saharan--Economic conditions--1960---Congresses.
2. Africa, Sub-Saharan--Politics and government--1960---Congresses.
I. Rimmer, Douglas. II. Royal African Society.
HC800.A5424 1994
339.967'032--dc20 93-38558
CIP

Typeset in Eric Gill's Joanna
by Opus 43, Cumbria
and printed in Britain
by Villiers Publications Ltd, London

Action in Africa

Other titles on
Development Economics from
James Currey LONDON
Heinemann PORTSMOUTH (N.H.)

Africa 30 Years On
The Record & the Outlook After 30 Years of Independence
DOUGLAS RIMMER (ed.)

World Food Aid
JOHN SHAW & EDWARD CLAY

Liberalizing Tanzania's Food Trade
Public & Private Faces of Urban Marketing Policy 1939–1988
DEBORAH FAHY BRYCESON

Saving for Economic Recovery in Africa
JONATHAN H. FRIMPONG-ANSAH & BARBARA INGHAM (eds)

The Challenge for Tanzania's Economy
C. GEORGE KAHAMA, T.L. MALIYAMKONO & STUART WELLS

Agricultural Development in Southern Africa
Farm–Household Economics & the Food Crisis
ALLAN LOW

National Development Planning in Nigeria 1900–92
P.N.C. OKIGBO

Modernising Hunger
Famine, Food Surplus & Farm Policy in the EEC & Africa
PHILIP RAIKES

Manufacturing Africa
Performances & Prospects of Seven Countries in Sub-Saharan Africa
ROGER C. RIDDELL

Contents

Contributors

Professor **Adebayo Adedeji** is Executive Director of the African Centre for Development and Strategic Studies at Ijebu-Ode, Nigeria. He was Executive Secretary of the United Nations Economic Commission for Africa from 1975 to 1991, and served from 1971 to 1975 as Commissioner for Economic Development and Reconstruction in the Federal Military Government of Nigeria.

Dr **Elliot Berg** is Vice-President, Development Alternatives Incorporated, at Bethesda, Maryland. In an influential career as development economist and consultant, he is most widely known as principal author of the World Bank publication *Accelerated Development in Sub-Saharan Africa*, often referred to as the Berg Report.

Dr **Kwesi Botchwey** is Minister of Finance in the Government of Ghana. He served as Secretary of Finance in the administration of the Provisional National Defence Council from 1982 to 1992. Previously he had lectured in law at the University of Ghana.

The Rt. Hon. **Baroness Chalker of Wallasey** has been the UK Minister of Overseas Development in the Foreign and Commonwealth Office since 1989, having previously served as a Minister of State. She was Member for Wallasey in the House of Commons between 1974 and 1992.

Dr **Stephen Ellis** is Director of the Afrika-Studiecentrum at Leiden in The Netherlands, having previously been Editor of the newsletter, *Africa Confidential*. He has been a teacher in Cameroon and a university lecturer in Madagascar. His most recent book is *Comrades Against Apartheid* (London: James Currey, 1992).

A. C. Faraji is with ACF Holdings Ltd of Arusha, Tanzania. Nearly all his career has been spent in business in the private sector, but he was Tanzanian Ambassador in Paris from 1970 to 1973 and he has sat on the board of the Tanzanian Central Bank.

Bobby Godsell is an Executive Director of the Anglo-American Corporation of South Africa, with responsibilities for industrial relations and public affairs. In 1992 he became President of the South African Chamber of Mines.

Dr **Ishrat Husain** has been in the service of the World Bank since 1979. He led the Bank's mission which preceded the launching of the Economic Recovery Programme in Ghana in 1983, and was Resident Representative of the Bank in Nigeria when the structural adjustment programme was begun in that country. He is now the Bank's Chief Economist, Africa Region.

Dr **Richard Jolly** has been Deputy Executive Director of UNICEF since 1982. From 1971 to 1981 he was Director of the Institute of Development Studies at the University of Sussex. He has been a consultant to the UN, the International Labour Office and various other organizations and governments, and has worked in Kenya, Uganda and Zambia.

Sithembiso Nyoni is Co-ordinator of the Organization of Rural Associations for Progress in Bulawayo, Zimbabwe.

Douglas Rimmer is an Honorary Senior Research Fellow and former Director of the Centre of West African Studies, University of Birmingham, and a Vice-Chairman of the Royal African Society.

Patsy Robertson has been on the staff of the Commonwealth Secretariat in London since its establishment by the Commonwealth Heads of Government in 1965. She has been its Director of Information since 1987. She was formerly in the Jamaican Foreign Service and served in the London High Commission. In 1988 she received the premier award of the Commonwealth Press Union, the Astor Award, which is given for outstanding contributions to Commonwealth understanding.

N. N. Susungi trained as a geophysicist. After working with Shell, he joined the African Development Bank in 1977 and occupied several positions at the headquarters in Abidjan. He is now resident European representative of the Bank, based in London.

Sir **Roger Tomkys** joined the British Foreign Service in 1960 and acquired extensive experience of the Middle East and North Africa. In 1989–90 he was Deputy Under-Secretary of State in the Foreign and Commonwealth Office, and in 1990–92 High Commissioner in Kenya . He is now Master of Pembroke College, Cambridge.

Dr **R. Z. Zoukpo** is Head of the Debt Management Unit, Development Research and Policy Department, of the African Development Bank in Abidjan.

Abbreviations

ACP	African, Caribbean and Pacific countries (i.e. those related to the European Community through the Lomé Conventions)
BCG	An anti-tuberculosis vaccine
CAP	Common Agricultural Policy (of the European Community)
CCM	*Chama cha Mapinduzi* (Tanzanian political party)
CEAO	*Communauté économique de l'Afrique de l'ouest*
CEPGL	*Communauté économique des pays des Grands Lacs*
CFA	*Communauté financière africaine*
DPT	An anti-diphtheria vaccine
EC	European Community
ECA	Economic Commission for Africa (of the United Nations)
ECOWAS	Economic Community of West African States
ERP	Economic Recovery Programme (of Ghana)
FCO	Foreign and Commonwealth Office (UK Government)
FDI	Foreign direct investment
G7	Group of seven economically advanced countries (Canada, France, Germany, Italy, Japan, UK, USA)
GATT	General Agreement on Tariffs and Trade
GDP	Gross Domestic Product
GNP	Gross National Product
GSP	Generalized System of Preferences
HMG	Her Majesty's Government (UK)
IBRD	International Bank for Reconstruction and Development (i.e. the World Bank)
IDA	International Development Association
IFC	International Finance Corporation
IFPRI	International Food Policy Research Institute
IGOs	Inter-Governmental Organisations
IMF	International Monetary Fund
KANU	Kenya African National Union
LPA	Lagos Plan of Action (of the OAU)
MMD	Movement for Multi-Party Democracy (Zambian political party)
NGOs	Non-Governmental Organizations

NICs	Newly industrializing countries
NPAs	National Programmes of Action (for implementation of objectives agreed at the World Summit for Children, New York, September 1990)
OAU	Organization of African Unity
ODA	Official Development Assistance (i.e. international aid)
OECD	Organization for Economic Co-operation and Development
OPV	An oral anti-poliovirus vaccine
PRE	Policy Research and Economics (series of World Bank working papers)
PTA	Preferential Trade Area for East and Southern Africa
SAPs	Structural Adjustment Programmes
SDRs	Special Drawing Rights (of the IMF)
SPA	Special Programme of Assistance (by World Bank, for Africa)
SSA	Sub-Saharan Africa (as used by the World Bank and more generally, a political rather than a geographical concept, including the Indian Ocean islands of Madagascar, Mauritius and Seychelles, but excluding the Republic of South Africa).
TT2	An anti-tetanus vaccine
UCI	Universal Child Immunization
UDEAC	*Union douanière et économique de l'Afrique centrale*
UN	United Nations
UNCTAD	United Nations Conference on Trade and Development
UNDP	United Nations Development Programme
UNESCO	United Nations Educational, Scientific and Cultural Organization
UNFPA	United Nations Fund for Population Activities
UNHCR	United Nations High Commission for Refugees
UNICEF	United Nations Childrens' Fund
WFP	World Food Programme
WHO	World Health Organization

1 DOUGLAS RIMMER

Introduction
The Agenda of Reform

Outside powers have long had a special interest in Africa south of the Sahara, or have acknowledged a special responsibility for that region. In the late nineteenth century and during the first half of the twentieth, this interest or responsibility was chiefly expressed through imperial rule. Then it took the form of guidance in the building of new nations and promotion of the economic development by which they were to be sustained. Nowadays attention has shifted towards reforming the independent states, both in their economics, through the 'adjustment' of economic structures, and in their politics, through the substitution of 'good governance' for bad and of democracy for regimes that had become exclusive and illiberal.

People in Africa have not been passive spectators of this external concern for their affairs. There were 'colonial collaborators', and there were resistants. Decolonization was fought for in several territories, and owed something to domestic pressures in all. And the current agenda of reform are controversial. Structural adjustment is undoubtedly unpopular in some, if not all, countries, and is regularly denounced by politicians, journalists and academics who regard themselves as spokesmen of the people. 'I am not allowed to finish a sentence', Dr Ishrat Husain has said of his attempts to justify structural adjustment at Nigerian universities. But these economic reforms have not been without African advocates, one of the foremost of whom writes in this volume. Democracy, in the sense of the free electoral competition and legislative representation of parties formed by voluntary association, has won many supporters; but it is also opposed, usually on the grounds that parties in Africa tend to be ethnically based, and so aggravate divisions in national society. Good governance, on the other hand, is an ideal difficult to argue against, even if there are few governments, either in or beyond Africa, that wish to be entirely accountable for their actions, wholly transparent in their dealings, and altogether tolerant of free expression in the media of mass communication.

The papers in this volume are addressed to these current agenda and the context of affairs in which they are debated. They originated in a conference of the Royal African Society, held in Oxford in March 1993, the title of which listed governance, business and aid as the headings of discussion. The invited speakers, whose contributions form the substance of this volume,[1] were persons directly engaged in African affairs in governments and multilateral institutions, in business and, in one case, in a non-governmental organization. As actors, or practitioners, they were chosen in contrast with the academic speakers at the Society's conference of 1991 whose views of developments in Africa were more detached and retrospective.[2] The objects of the 1993 conference were to focus on current issues in Africa and on the ideas and judgements of persons who had some direct responsibility for, or strong influence on, the ways in which those issues were being resolved.

About the time of the 1991 conference, it seemed to the present writer that the time was nearly ripe for abandonment of the political fiction that the African continent, or the region of Sub-Saharan Africa, does not include the Republic of South Africa.[3] This expectation was premature. Participants in the 1993 conference continued to generalize about an Africa that might or might not include the countries of the Mediterranean littoral but invariably terminated, at least by implication, on the Limpopo. An exception, of course, was the speaker from South Africa. For the most part, discussion of economic reforms, of debt problems and investment flows, of political transitions and of human development continued to be confined within the politically correct geographical limits laid down by the multilateral institutions. These limits detract, in the opinion of the present writer, from the value of speculations about action in Africa, and it is to be hoped, once again, that they will not much longer endure.

Economic Liberalization

In the first group of papers that follow, a common attachment to economic liberalism is shown by the Minister of Overseas Development in the UK Government, a leading South African businessman, and the Ghanaian Minister of Finance. There is agreement that the scope of government should be limited, and reliance placed less on public administration than on market forces. The proper role of government, according to Lynda Chalker, lies in 'establishing the framework for private sector activity, and ensuring that services are provided in areas where markets fail'. The framework should protect property rights; it should provide 'stable, predictable conditions in which to do business'; it should minimize administrative discretion. The areas where markets fail, and public provision is therefore justified, are identified as 'basic health and education services, and the physical infrastructure needed to support economic activity'. Consistent with these prescriptions is Bobby Godsell's characterization of good governance. According to Mr Godsell, the evidence is conclusive that 'governments are very bad at creating wealth and running businesses ... The best governments can do is to facilitate the market.' The views of Kwesi Botchwey were formed, like Mr Godsell's, in reaction from a highly politicized and counter-productive economic order in his own country. His paper is restricted to one aspect, albeit the most critical aspect, of the liberalization of the Ghanaian economy from 1983, namely, the processes by which the determination of access to foreign exchange was taken from the official classes and entrusted to the market. In oral discussion at the conference, Dr Botchwey was as vigorous a free marketeer as any participant. Attention may be drawn, however, to the cautionary note on which his paper ends. History may appear to have spoken irrevocably in favour of a liberal economic order, and a certain 'triumphalism' has become evident in debates on national economic management; but deregulation should be considered as a means, not as an end in itself.

Economic liberalism, it may be suggested, was an idea whose time had come in the Africa of the 1980s. The shortcomings of allegedly planned and publicly controlled economic structures were dreadfully exposed by the coincidence of deteriorating terms of trade, and falling export revenues, with heavy debt-servicing obligations that had been acquired in happier times. African governments became vulnerable to pressure from creditor governments and the multilateral agencies, whose thinking was newly informed by ideologies that had become hegemonic in the United States, the United Kingdom and other economically advanced countries, and that were soon to be reinforced by the collapse of the planned economies of the Soviet bloc. It is rather revealing that Dr Botchwey, in discussing the first phase in 1983 of deregulating the foreign-exchange market, does not acknowledge that the 'home-grown and simple' device of export bonuses and import surcharges had been used before in Ghana (though much less comprehensively) as a preliminary to a previous devaluation of the cedi. In retrospect, the push toward economic liberalism in that country during 1970-71 may be judged to have been premature. Economic conditions then may have been such as to make it desirable, but they were not bad enough to make it inescapable; not nearly as bad as they were to become by 1983.

Has history spoken irrevocably? Lady Chalker suggests a need to learn from a forthcoming study by the World Bank of the remarkable economic advances that have been made in countries of East and South-East Asia during recent decades. This study originated, however, in Japanese complaints that the Bank was stressing excessively the importance of the deregulation and privatization of economic activity. And it is believed that the completed study will cite high investment ratios, the hiring of foreign technology, and flexibility in labour markets, rather than any regularity in the division between private enterprise and public intervention, or between market mechanisms and government controls, as the proximate causes of the rapid growth of productivity in Asian countries.[4] Governments in several of those countries have in fact regulated and participated directly in economic activity to an extent hardly compatible with the policy prescriptions that are now orthodox in Africa.

The lesson, however, is that triumphalism is unwise, not that the unreformed African economies were on the right lines after all. Notwithstanding donor opposition and a lack of private interest, the Government of South Korea created a steel industry that has become highly competitive. But it would be rash to assume that as much success awaits the steel industry that has been established by the Federal Government in Nigeria. Models of development have little international transferability, and we understand the causes of economic progress in any place much better after it has happened than before. 'There is no single pattern', Rostow remarked, perhaps a trifle ruefully, of his famous take-off into self-sustained growth. 'The rate and productivity of investment can rise, and the consequences of this rise can be diffused into a self-reinforcing general growth process by many different technical and economic routes, under the aegis of many different political, social and cultural settings, driven along by a wide variety of human motivations.'[5] Explanations of failure to take off could presumably be no less various.

Structural adjustment has disappointed expectations in Africa, though this does not mean that it has made economic performance worse than it would otherwise have been. One disappointment is conspicuous by its absence from Dr Botchwey's paper. He describes the processes of freeing access to foreign exchange in Ghana between April 1983, when the official value of the US dollar was 2.75 cedis, and 1990, by the end of which year the dollar exchanged for about 340 cedis in the unified foreign-exchange market. These reforms removed the overvaluation of the cedi, which had led to a conjunction of rapidly falling external earnings with an insatiable demand for foreign exchange. But the removal was not a once-for-all event, and the cedi continued to depreciate beyond 1990. By March 1993 it was quoted at 600 to the dollar. Thus there had been a further fall of over 40 per cent in less than two-and-a-half years. As in several other African countries undergoing adjustment, an exchange value for the domestic currency, fixed at an artifically high level, had been replaced by one that appears likely to fall indefinitely. It has seemed a poor exchange to many of the people affected by it. Because of strong dependence on imports, a consequence has been rising prices, so that the deregulation of foreign exchange has become popularly associated with the erosion of real living standards. In its origin, however, the inflation is the cause, not the consequence, of the falling exchange rate, and is attributable in turn to failure or inability to contain domestic monetary demand, and in particular the fiscal deficit. Structural adjustment programmes have generally been frustrated by the intractability of public expenditures – notwithstanding which, the governments concerned are frequently criticized, by outsiders as well as by their own peoples, for not spending more on health care, education and the other 'areas where markets fail'.

A second disappointment has lain in the less-than-expected responses to adjustment of private investors, both domestic and foreign. 'We need to develop a deeper understanding of the reasons', writes Lady Chalker. Although the case she goes on to cite of Machakos district in Kenya is less a case of unsatisfactory response to adjustment than of successful reaction to adversity, it perhaps points in the right direction, which is towards informal or unenumerated economic activities. In Nigeria, as Ishrat Husain observes in his paper in this volume, and as he stressed in his conference presentation, there has been a strong response to adjustment in the export of manufactures to other African countries. Because these exports are largely the work of relatively small businesses, using channels of trade which are informal, if not actually illegal, their importance is less than adequately recognized in official records. Thus the unresponsiveness of the private sector is in some degree a statistical illusion.

Perhaps it is to be expected that reaction to changing economic circumstances will be quicker in small businesses than in large. Enterprise, in the strict sense of finding and exploiting new economic opportunities, has always been strongly associated with newly established businesses, which tend also to be small businesses. Bobby Godsell rightly points to the significance for enterprise – whether it thrives or is suppressed – of the administrative regulation of small businesses, and of the cultural attitudes that underlie such regulation. All public authorities tend to look askance at small-scale enterprises, but the distrust has been strongest in those African countries containing populations of European descent.

World Markets or Collective Self-Reliance?

This question was put to two authorities from whom different answers were confidently expected. As Executive Secretary of the UN Economic Commission for Africa, Adebayo Adedeji has been the champion of African regional integration and the promotion of African economic self-reliance. As principal author of the World Bank's famous report of 1981, Elliot Berg had become foremost among the critics of policies in Africa that discriminated against exporting to world markets.

'Countries do not prosper unless they are integrated with world markets', writes Mr Godsell, who adds that few notions have done more harm in the Africa of independent states than those postulating the value of national economic autonomy. These views are perhaps better tolerated in South Africa, which became more autonomous not out of choice but because self-reliance was thrust upon it, than they are elsewhere south of the Sahara.

'Africa produces what it does not consume, and consumes what it does not produce', complained one speaker at the conference – as if such commonplace behaviour was economically abnormal. Many reasons lie behind the animosity that is so often expressed towards trade external to Africa. Until the middle of the nineteenth century, this trade was strongly connected to the traffic in people; it became abhorrent to civilized opinion, and was perceived, retrospectively, to have impoverished Africa. Subsequently, transoceanic commerce became associated with colonial rule. Exports generated the revenues that colonial administrations needed; they were necessary also to the viability of non-indigenous businesses, and of some white settler farmers; they helped integrate African societies with the economic life of imperial powers in Europe. External trade consequently acquired a political complexion, offensive to anti-colonial sentiment. Furthermore, in the 1950s and 1960s, when many people who were to become prominent in African policy-making first encountered development economics, among the ideas in vogue was the perception that the exporting of primary products was unrewarding because of the instability of the prices of those products, or an inexorable decline in the prices relative to those of manufactures, or the absorption of resources that would certainly be better used for producing manufactures in substitution for imports. Grounds of these sorts for a lack of confidence in 'the beneficial workings of international trade' are encapsulated in the quotation made in this volume by Adebayo Adedeji from a paper by Stephen R. Lewis,[6] and some are amplified by Professor Adedeji himself.

A change since the 1970s has been the urging of import substitution for food as well as manufactures. Referring to the World Bank's forecasts of commodity price movements in the remainder of this century, and the productive efforts that would be required, on the basis of these forecasts, to restore real export earnings to the levels attained in 1980/81, Professor Adedeji suggests that the same efforts would be better directed to the production of foodstuffs for domestic consumption. He has nothing to say, however, about movements in the prices of foodstuffs in the remainder of the century, although those prices relative to the prices of export crops would obviously be relevant to the profitability of production decisions – and, indeed, would determine those decisions in the absence of the policy restraints he favours.

There is no questioning the desirability of African economies becoming more diversified or structurally transformed, so long as the changes are economically driven. These changes would then be equivalent to enrichment. But would enrichment follow from transformations that were contrived by policy interventions? Empirically, this question has already been answered, since policy-contrived structural changes have been tried in Africa – for example, in Ghana in the early 1960s and Madagascar in the late 1970s – and the results have been impoverishing rather than enriching. It may be that the policies were imperfectly conceived or executed, or that the time was not ripe for them. Nevertheless, it might be thought prudent in these matters to give some regard to past experiences.

Professor Adedeji's case for remaking African economies by policy interventions rests not on any lessons of experience but on a characterization of African economic life such as to exclude the possibilities of progress except by the policy interventions. According to this characterization, economic life in Africa is marked by 'basic structural rigidities'. Markets for goods and factors are imperfectly competitive and inflexible. Monopolies abound. Financial institutions are not well developed. Non-monetized activities predominate. It is futile, therefore, to rely on spontaneous reactions to economic inducements and deterrents.

This teaching was the common coin, some forty years ago, of analyses of 'underdeveloped countries' and how they might be economically developed. Included in this category were the countries of Asia, Latin America and the Middle East as well as those of Africa. Since then the world has moved on and the received opinion of the 1950s looks distinctly *passé*. Many of the formerly underdeveloped countries are now anything but backward. Policy contrivances have played a part in this global reordering, more so in some countries than in others, and not always positively. But it may also be argued that people in poor countries, by reason of their poverty, have all along been more strongly motivated economically than those in rich countries; and that rigidities, far from being a peculiarity of societies that are materially deprived, can be as readily perceived in those that are relatively prosperous and comfortable. Only in Africa, it seems, does the notion linger that there is a species of countries so economically distinctive as to require an economics of its own.

Elliot Berg's paper considers what is to be gained from export of the commodities customarily supplied from Africa to world markets. As he observes, this issue is another with a long history, pessimism about these trading prospects having been a principal consideration underlying the early prescriptions of development. Since the exports result from comparative advantage, there is nothing to be gained from ceasing their production – from cutting down all the cocoa trees, as Kwesi Botchwey put it at the conference. But ought this production to be encouraged, in spite of the possible adverse consequence for prices, or discouraged in the expectation that higher prices will then more than offset smaller volumes? Encouragement has become associated with the programmes of structural adjustment, and it has been argued that, even if the additional exports of a commodity by any one country do not decrease its net earnings, the combined additions of all the countries following SAPs will reduce the combined net earnings. Dr Berg examines the evidence for this argument (the 'fallacy of composition' argument, as it is often known) and finds it plausible for cocoa,[7] and possibly for coffee, but not for the other African agricultural exports.

Ought producers in any one country to feel constrained by the harm their actions may do to producers in other countries? Even if the other countries are also African? Dr Berg observes that the rising trend in Ghanaian cocoa production after 1983, while it may have damaged the interests of other producing countries, was advantageous – indeed, necessary – from a Ghanaian standpoint. Ishrat Husain argued vigorously at the conference for an aggressive stance in markets for which Africans were the lowest-cost suppliers; for recovering, and then increasing, the market shares that were lost in the 1960s and 1970s; for 'beating the others at their own game', as he put it. Is this stance wrong when 'the others' are such as Brazilians and Malaysians, or if they are even fellow-Africans? Solidarity among commodity producers may be politically appealing, and sometimes it promises short-run economic gains, but competition is an economic law of life, which everyone disregards at his peril.

A general discouragement of Africa's traditional exports is criticized by Dr Berg as excessively indiscriminate, pessimistic and hazardous. He is also sceptical (as is Dr Husain) of the value of selectivity in policy regarding exports. Too often policy prescriptions assume in governments (not only African governments) powers of foresight, administrative capacities and disinterestedness way beyond what they can possibly possess. Neutrality in policy regarding tradeables is better, with decisions guided by market signals rather than by the hunches, conventional wisdom, political needs or purchased goodwill of public authorities. Genuine self-reliance, Dr Berg suggests, is to be perceived in such developments, made through private initiatives, as the entirely unexpected export of cowpeas from Niger and the equally unplanned production of rice from commercialized smallholdings in Mauritania.

As an alternative to dependence on external markets, sources of supply and factors of production, self-reliance imposed by policy would be highly unattractive in countries as small as are many African countries. Hence the substitution of regional for national self-reliance. But not a vast deal of difference is made. According to the estimates published by the World Bank, the combined GDP in 1990 of the countries of Sub-Saharan Africa was a little less than the GDP of Austria. Adding the North African countries gives a total approximating the GDP of the Netherlands. South Africa, which the Bank does not include in Sub-Saharan Africa, had a GDP somewhat less than that of Norway. Can it be true, then, that beyond the borders of each African country lies a 'vast potential' awaiting realization, as Raymond Zoukpo suggests in his paper in this volume?

Austria, the Netherlands and Norway may be in many ways more self-reliant than Africa but their dependence on external trade is even greater; their ratios of exports of goods and services to GDP in 1990 were 41, 57 and 44 per cent respectively.[8] Moreover, those countries occupy tiny areas relative to the huge terrestial mass of Africa, and are equipped with means of transport and communication far superior to those available in Africa. So the distributive costs of supplying domestic markets from domestic sources are far less for them than they would be for the African continent; yet their dependence on external trade is actually greater.

A visionary quality must therefore be recognized in the objective of an African economic community, originally scheduled for achievement in the year 2000 by the Lagos Plan of Action, since amended to 2025 by the Treaty of Abuja. The integration of the African economies is nevertheless advocated not only by the UN Economic

Commission for Africa, with the endorsement of African governments, but also commended by the multilateral agencies and bilateral aid donors. One reason is the usual diplomatic propensity to humour governments in what they say they want. Another is the view that progress in Africa would indeed be helped by freer movements of products and factors across boundaries, co-operation among governments in developing natural and human resources, and co-ordination in the policies of neighbouring countries. But this view is rather beside the point, if the object of African integration is to disengage from the outside world by contriving the substitution of African markets for foreign, and of African for imported goods, inputs and factors. The gains from trade creation will then be outweighed by the losses from trade diversion, and the productive possibilities arising from intra-African dependence dwarfed by the loss of those that are present in extra-African dependence.

From an economic standpoint, African integration with a protective or insulating purpose has nothing to commend it. It is therefore unsurprising that schemes of integration with this purpose have so far made so little headway, as Dr Berg details and Professor Adedeji concedes. Fundamentally, these schemes have failed not so much for want of political will as because they are economically inappropriate.

Debt and Interrelated Issues

The external sovereign debt of most African countries is generally acknowledged to be oppressive both of their living standards and their chances of economic recovery. How this debt burden originated, what can be done to provide relief from it, and what borrowing should be countenanced in the future are among the questions considered in the papers by Ishrat Husain, N.N. Susungi, Raymond Zoukpo and A.C. Faraji.

Dr Husain takes as his starting point, however, the interrelatedness of the debt and other external elements in the Sub-Saharan economies.[9] The capacity to import is critical if those economies are to grow and be developed; indeed, there has long been a fairly stable relationship in African countries between imports and GDP. While debt service reduces the capacity to import, that capacity can be enhanced by growth of exports, by international aid, and by foreign direct investment.

Dr Husain begins, therefore, by surveying the arguments that have been raised against an outward, foreign-exchange-earning, orientation of the African economies. These arguments include rigidities postulated in the structures of production, which have not been such, however, as to prevent remarkable surges in export production in the past;[10] the deterioration in the commodity terms of trade after 1981, which followed, however, a long trend of improvement, and was not peculiar to African countries but experienced also by others that managed nevertheless to increase their export earnings; the 'fallacy of composition' argument, also discussed in this volume by Elliot Berg; the disruptions that follow from liberalizing trade regimes, some of which Dr Husain considers to be illusory, others controllable and the rest transitory; and the impeding of African exports by protection in the markets for which they are destined.

The last point deserves some emphasis because protectionism against the exports of Sub-Saharan Africa is so often supposed, in the popular literature, to be important. In fact, the industrialized countries have nothing to protect, so far as the African exports are of distinctively tropical produce; and other exports, including manufactures, are favourably treated under the Lomé Convention or the Generalized System of Preferences. (South Africa, however, has been a different case.) This is not to say that commercial policy in the industrialized countries is entirely benign so far as Sub-Saharan Africa is concerned. The conference was told of how an abattoir in Côte d'Ivoire managed by the Commonwealth Development Corporation had been rendered unprofitable by shipments of subsidized beef from the European Community. Paradoxically, large sums have been expended from the European Development Fund to improve livestock production in the West African Sahel, while markets for this production are concurrently being demolished by the effects of EC domestic policy.

Dr Husain treats international aid within the context of net resource flows (long-term debt, official grants, foreign direct investment and transactions with the IMF) and net transfers (net resource flows less interest payments on long-term debt and profits on FDI). He shows that both these aggregates increased greatly in the late 1980s, in current dollars and in real terms, almost entirely as a result of a steep rise in official grants.

In contrast, Professor Adedeji states in his paper that 'Sub-Saharan Africa had in 1990 become a net transferor of resources', and he presents figures to show a 'reverse flow of resources' in all 'major sources of foreign aid and investment' except the International Development Association. These statements would mislead, if they were taken to imply a drain from Africa in the totality of financial resources, since they exclude from the account international aid in its most absolute form, namely grants. The point must be stressed, since much is made in the popular literature, in consequence of an exclusive concern for debt transactions, of an alleged negative flow of assistance to Africa. It is, of course, just because of the loss of creditworthiness by most African governments that grants have become the predominant way in which they are supported externally.

Aid is a boon somewhat adulterated. It can have untoward consequences, as several contributors to this volume observe, in instilling dependence in a recipient government, lessening domestic savings, appreciating the exchange rate, or even, as Dr Botchwey notes, counteracting liberalization. Abdul Faraji is especially critical of aid performance in his paper on Tanzania, whose government has a long record of strong, but remarkably ineffective, external support. While conceding that there are many explanations of this failure, Mr Faraji complains particularly of the influence on policies and projects of the foreign advisers and consultants provided through technical assistance. He argues that these outsiders cannot be as thoroughly acquainted with local conditions and possibilities as locals would be, and that their performance is judged by the launching rather than the outcomes of projects.[11] On the other hand, it could be argued that outsiders have the advantage of detachment from sectional interests and pressures within the country being aided.

Mr Susungi considers aid to be a dimension of the donors' foreign policies. While this judgement is unlikely to be disputed, it may be added that aid is also geared to the domestic politics of each donor country, within which there are sectional interests and lobbies – commercial, professional and charitable – keenly concerned with the volume, structure, destinations and purposes of the national aid programme.

The origins of the current burden of African external debt are mentioned briefly by Dr Husain and Dr Zoukpo, while Mr Susungi gives a longer, and more racy, account. Dr Zoukpo is forgiving. Since 'investment is the key to economic growth', African governments were right to borrow externally in the 1970s, 'and in the short run their borrowing was quite rewarding, being accompanied by impressive economic growth.' But difficulties arose when the external economic environment deteriorated, and, in addition, because the borrowings had not always been used efficiently – 'in ways that would generate sufficient income to service the debts'.

An alternative view is that in Africa since the Second World War growth has been the key to investment, rather than investment the key to growth. Governments have spent heavily on capital works when they were flush with revenue as a result of increases in the value of external trade. They have borrowed heavily for investment purposes when they were creditworthy, this attribute deriving from actual or anticipated growth in the value of external trade and public revenues. So there were big investment pushes in the 1970s when the commodity terms of trade were moving favourably for many countries, and when there were booms in such principal exports as mineral oil, the beverage crops, groundnuts and phosphates; and, even when revenues fell, these pushes continued for a time on the strength of borrowings and of trust that the reversal would be short-lived. The public investments did not lack justification, but they were often wasteful, and it is now all too apparent they did not unlock a process of growth in aggregate real output.

Such is Dr Zoukpo's conviction of the importance of increased investment that he advocates further external borrowing by African countries; to choose otherwise would be 'to accept continuing economic decline in Africa'. But opinion at the conference was contrary to this view. It was stated emphatically that Sub-Saharan Africa could not afford any more loan financing, except on the most concessional terms such as are given by the IDA. Not only does this judgement reflect the gravity of debt situations in Africa; it also expresses implicit assumptions about investment opportunities in the region, and about the ability of African governments to use investment funds productively.

Mr Susungi dwells on the folly of the commercial banks in recycling the surpluses of oil-exporting countries in the 1970s to governments whose security was the myth that they could not become bankrupt. The banks were not, however, either alone or most conspicuous in their folly so far as Sub-Saharan Africa is concerned, since creditor governments appear in retrospect also to have been careless, both in their lending and in the insurance they provided for credits on exports from their countries. A further factor encouraging international financial flows at that time was the persistence of negative real interest rates in global markets, a consequence of lax fiscal and monetary policies in the capital-exporting countries; in these conditions a bias in favour of borrowing, relative to saving, is understandable.

As the external long-term debt of Sub-Saharan Africa has increased with transference of export credits to the insurers, with reschedulings and the capitalization of arrears, and with resort to support from the IDA and the IMF, so the private component of the debt has shrunk. By the end of 1991, as Dr Husain shows, only 25 per cent of the long-term debt was owing to private creditors (including 13 per cent to commercial banks). Among the 26 countries which are 'low-income', 'debt-distressed' and covered by the World Bank's Special Programme of Assistance, the proportion of long-term debt privately held was only 9 per cent.

Private debt takes a bigger share – 40 per cent in 1991 – of long-term debt service actually paid; but some three-fifths of that private debt service originate from two countries, Nigeria and Côte d'Ivoire, which, unlike many others in Africa, have not abandoned hope of securing new loans from private sources. Those same countries along with Kenya, Zambia and Zimbabwe account for two-thirds of all debt service actually paid. Actual payments in recent years have been about one-half of the debt service due from Sub-Saharan Africa. The multilateral institutions are treated in practice as preferred creditors, while arrears accumulate on payments due to official bilateral and private creditors.

Dr Husain adds that ten out of 47 countries south of the Sahara account for two-thirds of the total debt outstanding. These ten include four – Nigeria, Côte d'Ivoire, Cameroon and Congo – which are regarded as 'lower-middle-income' rather than 'low-income' countries, though Nigeria appears to owe its inclusion to its status as an oil exporter, not to the estimate of its GNP per head, which puts it firmly into the low-income category.

The variety among Sub-Saharan countries in their debt situations has been a factor impeding schemes of debt relief. Nearly all are distressed by debt. But the debts of some are big relative to the debts of others. Many are judged poor both in their incomes and their prospects; others appear not so poor. Some are distressed chiefly by their debts to the multilateral institutions, payments on which cannot be avoided without prejudicing all external support. A few have substantial debts owing to private creditors. Some become disqualified for relief because they fail to adopt, or keep to, programmes of reform approved by the multilateral agencies. An individual creditor government, for reason of its own politics, may wish to indulge some debtors but is indifferent to others; another creditor has different favourites. While, therefore, much of the literature on the debt is concerned with comprehensive schemes of relief, the creditor governments themselves continue to favour treatment of the sovereign debtors case by case.

A second obstacle is that debt relief cannot be costless. Loan loss provision by private lenders diminishes their profitability. Debt forgiveness by official lenders, or the conceding of easier repayment terms, becomes a charge on aid budgets. Either aid must be increased in total or some of it must be diverted to purposes and countries different from those that would otherwise be favoured. These necessary consequences cannot be disregarded. As with every other proposal for extending public largesse, the questions have to be asked: Who are to pay? Will they pay?

Dr Husain revises projections made in the World Bank's long-term perspective study of 1989 to arrive at a total of US$30 billion per annum (in 1990 prices) as the 'requirements of external financing' for an average growth in consumption per head of 1 per cent in Sub-Saharan Africa during the rest of the present decade. These requirements are also stated as debt relief sufficient to keep scheduled service payments down to the level of actual payments in recent years (about $9 billion p.a.), together with an increase in gross official development assistance (ODA) of about 4 per cent p.a. in real terms. Dr Zoukpo, whose frame of reference includes North Africa, writes of 'needs to mobilize external resources of about $60 billion annually', and to increase the domestic saving ratio to more than 20 per cent, in order to achieve annual GDP growth of about 5 per cent in Africa during the 1990s.

Plus ça change, plus c'est la même chose. Such statements of the 'requirements' or 'needs' of investment and aid that must be met in order to achieve targeted rates of growth have been familiar in prescriptions for development as long as those prescriptions have been offered. In 1981 Hirschman called them 'the only game in town' for 'a generation of planners and foreign aid officials'.[12] The second generation appears no less devoted. Yet, as this introduction has already suggested, and as past experience shows only too well, the connection betwen investment spending and the rates of growth in income or consumption, or between infusions of aid and those growth rates, is problematic at best in Africa. Many investments have proved to be liabilities rather than assets. Much aid has been ineffective in its declared purpose. Yet the hypothesis is still advanced with confidence that quantities of investment finance have a determinate numerical relationship with rates of increase in income or consumption per head. It seems that the charms of economic model-making override empirical observation.

Of course, the explanation is more than the intellectual attraction of simple growth models. The sources of economic growth lie mostly beyond the grasp of politicians and officials in the donor agencies, development banks and planning ministries. Even where they are apprehended, they are difficult if not impossible to quantify and manipulate. Investment totals, on the other hand, can be measured and they do appear capable of manipulation, partly by domestic policy and partly by the beneficence of foreign donors. They lend themselves to planning, targeting and mobilization. It is for these administrative reasons, rather than because of their effects on growth, that they are identified, necessarily, as the key to that process.

While the need for increased flows of aid and relief of debts was urged at the conference, there was general agreement that the most valuable form of external support was commercially-driven direct investment from abroad, which incorporated managerial capacity and technical knowledge as well as finance, and which became a charge on the foreign-exchange budget only when, and so far as, it bore fruit. Foreign direct investment remains a bogey, perhaps somewhat dormant, in African popular opinion, but most governments are now anxious in principle to attract it, and disappointed that its falling trend in the 1980s has not been reversed by the programmes of structural adjustment. As one cause of this disappointment – though surely not the only cause – Dr Husain cited the debt overhang. So long as the debt obligations of African countries were so greatly in excess of their ability to pay, so long there would be uncertainty that exchange transactions would remain free enough, or the rate of exchange stable enough, for foreign investors to remit profits and repatriate capital, and so long, therefore, would FDI be deterred. In this connection, Dr Zoukpo points to the experience of Mexico, where FDI was increased, borrowing from private sources resumed, and Mexican capital brought home from abroad, by the success of the Brady Plan.

Capital transactions have been most free in the CFA countries, because of the linking of their currency to the French franc, but the consequence in recent years, as Mr Susungi notes, has been disinvestment from those countries rather than the encouragement of FDI. In such conditions it is tempting to believe that government controls on the export of capital would be advantageous, and many governments outside the CFA zone have at times so believed. But in practice, as Bobby Godsell observes, these controls are less effective in conserving domestic resources than in deterring the entry of foreign resources. The choice for developing countries, a recent World Bank report argues, is not whether to integrate financially with the outside world, but whether to integrate both ways, allowing both outflows and inflows of capital, or only one way through capital flight.[13] So far as foreign direct investors are concerned, the acid test of policy, it was remarked at the conference, is whether they can both 'enter liberally and exit honourably'.

Political Liberalization

Stephen Ellis contributes to this volume a survey of the causes and the outcomes so far of the current movement toward democratization of the African states. Roger Tomkys writes on political reform in Kenya, which he observed until late in 1992 from the vantage point of the UK High Commission in Nairobi. Patsy Robertson deals, on the basis of extensive first-hand experience, with the international monitoring of recent elections in Africa.

The current trend toward democratization was precipitated, Dr Ellis suggests, by events late in 1989: the collapse of Soviet power, most dramatically symbolized by the breaching of the Berlin Wall and the overthrow of Ceausescu, and the publication of the World Bank's long-term perspective study of Sub-Saharan Africa.[14] The former event revived desires to institutionalize new forms of political accountability in Africa; the latter introduced the notion of placing new conditionalities on international aid to Africa.

The collapse of Soviet power was instrumental not only because of the powerful demonstration effect it exerted on African opinion. In addition, it changed the attitudes of aid donors. The Soviet donors were no longer able, and the Western donors no longer felt obliged, to bolster corrupt and tyrannical regimes on the ground that those regimes were friends and allies. Equally, the tyrants could no longer count on such support.

A variant of this point is that in the West the time had come to find a new basis of public support for aid. In Africa, at least, aid had signally failed to propel economic take-offs. Now it was no longer needed to hold communism at bay. What then was it for? The answer, particularly agreeable to American opinion, was to promote democracy and civil rights.[15]

Possibly disappointed with the results so far of structural adjustment in Africa, the World Bank discovered in 1989 the necessity of 'good governance'. Governance was eventually to be defined as 'the manner in which power is exercised in the management of a country's economic and social resources for development'.[16] Good governance required both a greater aptitude for and a cleansing of such management – both the building of capacity and the removal of corruption. Corruption could be removed, it was suggested, 'by setting a good example, by strengthening accountability, by encouraging public debate, and by nurturing a free press'.[17]

The authors of the 1989 study argued for selectivity in donor support, but the governments to be favoured were those following 'sound programs' and making 'good use' of the assistance they had already received, governments whose economic performance compared well with the targets that had been set for them.[18] As Dr Ellis notes, explicitly political criteria were not invoked. The concern of the Bank was with the quality of macroeconomic policies, parastatal enterprises and public services, not with parties and elections. 'Good governance' was essentially the expression of a desire in the Bank to treat with people who were, so to speak, on its own wave-length. Such people might be administrators working for avowedly 'non-political' military regimes; members of the Bank's staff have, at times, found them more comfortable to deal with than politicians preoccupied by the need to retain popular or sectional support. Of course, it is pleasing to believe that democratic institutions prevent mismanagement and deter corruption, but the relevant empirical evidence is hardly convincing.

The requirement of good governance might therefore be interpreted as a refinement of the economic conditionalities attached to aid. Those conditionalities are long-established. At the micro level they have stipulated what projects should be initiated and how they should be built. With the launching of programmes of structural adjustment, they became macro-policy requirements concerning such matters as the exchange rate, the import regime, the fiscal deficit, the money supply, and the composition of public expenditure. Both the requirements and the transgressions from them were fairly clear-cut: for example, aid was not being spent on the purpose for which it had been given, administrative controls had not been removed, performance targets were not being met.

Stanley Please, a co-author of the 1989 study, told the conference that the idea of placing explicitly political conditions on aid to Africa was initiated several months after publication of that study, when Douglas Hurd, the UK Foreign Secretary, addressed a conference organized by the Overseas Development Institute in London.[19] In the same month, June 1990, occurred the francophone 'summit' at La Baule, mentioned in Dr Ellis's paper, at which President Mitterrand, while conceding that 'it is for Africans to know who should govern them and how', referred also to a French expectation that 'true democracies with multi-partyism, free elections and respect for human rights will be established'. Many further instances could be cited of the favouring of political reform both by donors and African governments themselves. For example, Patsy Robertson refers to the Harare Declaration of October 1991, by which the Commonwealth Heads of Government resolved to promote 'the practices of democracy, accountable administration and the rule of law'. In May 1993, the US Secretary of State, Warren Christopher, promised American leadership in providing support for the South African economy, once a transitional executive council was installed and a firm date for elections set.

Political conditionalities are more uncertain than the economic in their application. Competitive party formation may be allowed and elections held. But what if the elections are less than 'free and fair', and so merely confirm a former single party in its possession of power? And what if government after the elections behaves much as government before the elections – imprisoning opponents, closing down newspapers, denying justice, declaring a state of emergency? Whether the conditionalities are sufficiently satisfied must be a matter of judgement. There is no simple measurement like the money supply or the fiscal deficit that can settle the matter.

Furthermore, what would follow from an adverse judgement? External creditors and donors have felt able to insist that the fiscal deficit be reduced or the foreign-exchange market unified in order to recover eligibility for aid. They have not yet stipulated that a government resign or fresh elections be held. The election results by which Paul Biya was returned to office in Cameroon in October 1992 were dubious, to say the least. In Ghana, not only was the previously self-appointed Head of State returned in the election of November 1992, but the paradoxical outcome of instituting multi-party competition was the election of a single-party legislature. In the case of Kenya, 'the events on nomination day', writes Patsy Robertson, 'cast a pall of suspicion over the entire election' of December 1992, and this pall was to thicken. But the political conditionalities in such cases seem to have been judged sufficiently satisfied. Democracy may not have been established, but that 'the process of democratization' had begun was deemed enough. And elections are, as Mrs Robertson observed at the conference, a rough game everywhere: people living in glass houses should not throw stones.

Uganda gives further cause to doubt the efficacy, or even the reality, of political conditionalities. The government of the National Resistance Movement allows little scope for party activity and shows no inclination to hold multi-party elections, yet continues to receive aid and is esteemed by the multilateral institutions. President Museveni takes the view that sovereignty belongs to the people and that party government would therefore be a usurpation. Again, Nigeria was at odds with the IMF and its official creditors from 1991 not because its extraordinary two-party system was incompatible with freedom of association and greatly detracted from real political competition, nor because of the frequent and arbitrary changes in the rules of the protracted transition to civilian government, but because the military administration failed to control its deficit.

It is a fallacy to suppose that aid is given grudgingly. As has already been suggested in this introduction, there are strong political interests supporting the aid programme of each donor country. While there is difficulty, because of overall budgetary considerations, in increasing the total of aid, any reduction in or suspension of aid is deplored by those who depend for their profits or livelihoods on its continuation. Consequently, as Roger Tomkys mentions in the case of Kenya, the donor governments keenest to penalize the transgression of conditionalities tend to be those whose nationals have least material interest in the country concerned.

Conditionalities are therefore enforced with difficulty, and the more so when they require a united front of donors and creditors. The political variety, because of the uncertainties surrounding their satisfaction, and perhaps of a less than complete conviction that they *can* be satisfied, are likely in many cases to be weakly applied. Both Stephen Ellis and Roger Tomkys consider democratization to have depended much more on internal pressures than external inducements, and the relative strength of those factors is unlikely to change.

Good governance, as the World Bank's definition of governance makes clear, is justified by its supposedly positive effects on economic development. Development must surely be advanced by greater competence and less dishonesty in the management of national resources. When good governance is translated as democracy, democracy is justified in the same way. Institutions by which the conduct of government is subjected to continuous critical scrutiny will promote accountability, dispel corruption, keep governments on their toes. As a result, economic performance will improve.

There is a lack of systematic evidence in support of these hypotheses. The lack might be explained, so far as Africa is concerned, by the rarity of good governance and the novelty of the current democratization. But it occurs also in the wider context of developing countries since that category came into existence in the 1950s. Economic performance, whether measured by crude rates of growth or by finer criteria, correlates neither with political liberalization nor with authoritarian government.[20] The obvious reason is that governance is not the only, and usually not the most important, determinant of economic performance. This is, of course, a conclusion unpalatable to both policy-makers and would-be policy-makers.

It does not follow that we should be indifferent between good governance and bad, or between political freedom and tyranny. Political liberalization may well have positive effects on development, even though those effects be overwhelmed by determinants beyond the reach of policy and politics. And efficiency and honesty in public administration, and freedom of political expression and association, may well be considered goods in themselves, regardless of what they do or fail to do to the GDP. Stephen Ellis writes of the 'deep therapeutic effect' of the national conference in Togo in 1991, and Roger Tomkys of the replacement of 'sullen hostility' by fresh political commitment when multi-partyism was allowed in Kenya in 1992. There are many African countries where the value of democratization has lain primarily in personal freedom to say publicly what one thinks, and others in which this freedom is still to be won.

Human Development

At the opening of the conference from which this volume has resulted, Lynda Chalker suggested pessimism about the condition of Africa to be not entirely justified. Her principal reason was the effect on economic growth of the programmes of economic liberalization – a matter on which opinion is by no means unanimous. But she pointed also to 'a disaster which did not happen' – to the success of governments and other agencies in southern Africa in combating the severe drought that region underwent in 1992. The paper by Sithembiso Nyoni that is printed here discusses the effects of and responses to that drought in Zimbabwe, and emphasizes the role of one local NGO and the importance of self-help. When so much is said of the dependence of African societies and administrations on succour from outside, there is a danger of forgetting that the resources for coping with adversity are largely found locally, through national governments, home-bred voluntary institutions and the adaptations made by households and communities. The 1992 drought was not the first whose effects were substantially moderated by local initiative in at least some African countries.[21] And other remarkable African achievements in managing cataclasm could be cited: for example, Ghana's absorption of about one million of its nationals expelled from Nigeria in 1983. If development has for the most part to be a do-it-yourself activity, as Bobby Godsell argues, so too has the weathering of calamity – even in Africa.

Other grounds for resisting pessimism are considered by Richard Jolly. In spite of the economic retrogression of recent years, the declining trend in infant and child mortality is believed to continue, there is evidence from a few countries of falling fertility, access to clean water has greatly increased, and the immunization of children against prevalent diseases has grown rapidly relative to the population as well as absolutely. The validity of the statistics on which these statements are based is not considered, and it is unfortunately true that much so-called data in Africa are the outcomes of demographic models rather than real empirical measurements. There can be no doubt, however, that life expectancy in Africa overall has trended upward for many years and that a principal explanation is reductions in infant and child mortality achieved through measures of public health. Dr Jolly observes that not all the credit belongs to governments; here again the initiatives of local communities have been important.

Dr Jolly lists the targets set at the World Summit for Children organized by UNICEF in 1990, and cites the estimated annual costs of achieving these targets by the end of the decade. He suggests that these costs could be met by changes in the composition of African national budgets (more particularly, the substitution of social for defence expenditures); by increasing the proportion of international aid that is allocated to the 'social priority sectors'; and by the relief of African indebtedness. In the second of these proposals, emphasizing the reallocation of aid rather than more aid, the difficulty is recognized of securing increases in the total flows. But, as previously observed in this introduction, debt relief also has implications either for the total of aid or for its allocation – and, in this case, its allocation among countries rather than among objects. Readers will also notice the parallel between Dr Jolly's connecting of specified financial outlays to specific changes in mortality and literacy rates, nutritional standards and the incidence of certain diseases, and the relationships posited no less confidently by Dr Husain and Dr Zoukpo between specified investment expenditures and specific rates of growth in GDP or consumption per head. It must be questioned whether the means of human development can be so simply formulated, any more than can the conditions of economic growth. But this caveat does not, of course, deny that reductions in disease, malnutrition, illiteracy and the like will cost money, and that there is some value in estimating how much.

It is salutary that the discussions in this volume of action in Africa should end with human development. Many of the real advances made in the human condition in Africa are overlaid by our fondness for estimations of GDPs, the tendency of political affairs to engross our attention, and the news values of the media of mass communication. Social betterment through advances in public health or education is gradual and usually apparent only over the long term. It is seldom the stuff of daily or weekly reportage. It impinges only occasionally on the world of affairs. Increases in the coverage of antigens are not newsworthy. Improvements in water supply excite less interest than deficiencies in food supply. Growth in the numbers of people as mortality rates fall is regarded, somewhat perversely, as an indication of threatening disaster rather than as evidence of success. But progress of these kinds has been made and continues to be made, even in Africa, at least where armed conflict has been avoided, and even in Africa it is on improvements in the health and the physical, intellectual and moral capacities of the human population that development will principally depend in the long run.

Notes

1. The papers published here are substantially what the conference received. The exceptions are as follows.
   1. Two sections have been excerpted from N.N. Susungi's paper. In the complete paper, the first excerpt printed here was preceded by a discussion of European direct investments in Africa, more particularly in the Congo, South Africa, the Rhodesias and Cameroon; and it was followed by accounts of the various plans proposed in the 1980s for resolving the debt crisis, more particularly in relation to Latin America, and of episodes in the recent debt histories of Mexico, Brazil, Zaïre, Côte d'Ivoire, Zambia, Venezuela and Peru. The second excerpt printed here is the concluding part of the complete paper.
   2. Raymond Zoukpo, like Mr Susungi, attended the conference as representative of Babacar Ndiaye, President of the African Development Bank. But his paper was not available for presentation at the conference, and the version printed here is an abridgement made by the editor.
   3. Abdul Faraji presented two papers at the conference. They have been combined here.
   4. Patsy Robertson was a very late addition to the conference programme. She was able to give only an oral presentation, and the paper printed here and based on that presentation was written after the conference.
   5. The titles have been chosen by the editor.
2. See Douglas Rimmer (ed.), *Africa 30 Years On* (London and Portsmouth, N.H.: Royal African Society with James Currey and Heinemann, 1991). A decision not to include academics among the invited speakers at the 1993 conference could not be fully kept. Salim Ahmed Salim, the Secretary-General of the OAU, who had been asked to give the general survey of democracy in Africa, was obliged to withdraw from the conference by his necessary participation in attempts at that time to secure national reconciliation in Somalia, and his place was filled at short notice by Stephen Ellis. It may be added that Roger Tomkys had become head of a Cambridge college by the time of the conference, although he had been invited while head of the UK diplomatic mission in Kenya.
3. See Rimmer, *Africa 30 Years On*, p. 2.
4. See Michael Prowse's article, 'Miracles beyond the free market', in the London *Financial Times*, 25 April 1993, p. 15.
5. W.W. Rostow, *The Stages of Economic Growth* (Cambridge: Cambridge University Press, 1960), p. 46.
6. However, the rest of Lewis's paper provides little support for Professor Adedeji. Thus, Lewis devotes only one short paragraph to African regional integration, and among his conclusions (the paper was published in 1986) are that 'African countries need to adopt reforms of exchange rates, import controls, and agricultural pricing systems to remove the extremes of subsidies and penalties inherent in their current arrangements', and that their future policies must 'maximize the opportunities inherent in international trade', (Stephen R. Lewis, Jr., 'Africa's Trade and the World Economy', in Robert J. Berg and Jennifer Seymour Whitaker (eds), *Strategies for African Development* (Berkeley and Los Angeles: University of California Press, 1986), pp. 496-7).
7. Elliot Berg cites econometric work by J.R. Coleman, T. Akiyama and P.N. Varangis on the effects on cocoa prices and export volumes and values of the SAPs in Ghana and Nigeria. This study is utilized also by Ishrat Husain in his paper in this volume. Note, however, that while the results of the model are given by Dr Berg for the year 1989/90 only, those given by Dr Husain refer to the period from 1982/83 to 1989/90.
8. The export ratio for Sub-Saharan Africa is put at 29 per cent in 1990; for South Africa, Algeria, Morocco and Egypt less than that: World Bank, *World Development Report 1992* (Washington, DC, 1992), Tables 3 and 9, pp. 222-3 and 234-5.
9. Note that Dr Husain, following the practice of the World Bank, analyses data for Sub-Saharan Africa, a concept that excludes South Africa, however. On the other hand, Dr Zoukpo, following the practice of the African Development Bank, defines Africa in his paper to include the North African countries (while still excluding South Africa). This difference accounts for discrepancies between certain aggregates cited by Dr Husain and those to be found in Dr Zoukpo's paper.
10. Classic cases include Gold Coast cocoa and Northern Nigerian groundnuts before the First World War and Ivorian coffee and cocoa after 1950.
11. In the World Bank, criticisms of this kind appear to have struck a chord. The unpublished Wapenhans

report of 1992 is reported to have attributed shortcomings in the performance of the Bank's loan portfolio to a tendency for the Bank to judge success by the volume, rather than the results, of its lending, and to the arrogance of Bank staff in imposing their own schemes on borrowers rather than responding to borrowers' needs. And Edward Jaycox, the Bank's Vice-President for the Africa region, was reported in May 1993 to have said that the Bank would stop dictating to African governments their needs and how those needs should be met, and would support the preparations of plans and projects by Africans themselves. See also criticisms in the UNDP *Human Development Report 1993* (New York: Oxford University Press, 1993) of the use in technical assistance of foreign instead of indigenous personnel.

12. Albert O. Hirschman, *Essays in Trespassing: Economics to Politics and Beyond* (Cambridge: Cambridge University Press, 1981), p. 61.
13. World Bank, *Global Economic Prospects and the Developing Countries 1993* (Washington, DC, 1993). Flight capital from SSA is estimated in this report to amount to 80 per cent of the region's GDP. It is argued that this capital is likelier to return, and other investment from outside likelier to be induced, if the owners of the capital are confident that they can get it out again if they wish.
14. World Bank, *Sub-Saharan Africa: From Crisis to Sustainable Growth* (Washington, DC, 1989).
15. See Carol Lancaster, 'Governance and Development: the Views from Washington', *IDS Bulletin*, 24, 1 (January 1993).
16. World Bank, *Governance and Development* (Washington, DC, 1992), p. 1.
17. World Bank, *From Crisis to Sustainable Growth*, pp. 5-6.
18. *Ibid.*, pp. 183, 193.
19. 'To Africa', because precedents for tying financial assistance to political reform had already been set in Eastern Europe. The significance of Douglas Hurd's speech was also stressed at the conference by Sir Roger Tomkys, who was despatched to Kenya shortly after it was made.
20. See John Healey and Mark Robinson, *Democracy, Governance and Economic Policy: Sub-Saharan Africa in Comparative Perspective* (London: Overseas Development Institute, 1992), Part III.
21. Specifically those that were spared the devastation of war. See the discussion of Kenya and Botswana by John Borton and Edward Clay, 'The African Food Crisis of 1982-1986', in Douglas Rimmer (ed.), *Rural Transformation in Tropical Africa* (London: Belhaven Press, 1988). The effects of the drought of the early 1970s in the West African Sahel were also less serious than was initially expected.

PART I ECONOMIC LIBERALIZATION

2

LYNDA CHALKER

The Proper Role of Government

My purpose is to discuss the changing roles of government, business and aid donors in the economic development of Sub-Saharan Africa. I shall suggest the need for a more active and co-operative relationship among these three if sustained progress is to be secured.

Is Pessimism about Africa Justified?

Before turning to my main theme, however, let me comment on the deep pessimism of some recent press articles about Africa.

The problems of Africa are undeniably serious. The continent has more than a fair share of the world's disasters. Some are man-made as in Somalia; others have natural causes, as in the southern Africa drought of 1992. There is the depressing spectacle of continued civil war in Angola; of a corrupt dictatorship presiding over a breakdown in law and order in Zaïre; of chaos in Liberia. This is the Africa that catches the headlines.

Nevertheless, the picture is not all gloom. Economic reform programmes *are* contributing to a modest revival of economic growth. The 20 African countries benefitting from the World Bank's Special Programme of Assistance achieved economic growth of nearly 4 per cent a year in the period 1988–90.[1] This was faster than before the reforms were introduced, and faster than population growth, leaving room for some modest increase in average incomes.

Countries which have a longer-term record of consistently sound policies have done better. Since 1986 Ghana has achieved 5 per cent per annum growth, reversing two decades of decline. In Zambia a democratically elected government was able in 1992 to weather the worst drought in living memory, avoid famine, and continue to implement a challenging economic reform programme. Indeed, the overall handling of the southern African drought by the countries of the region showed what can be achieved. It was the disaster which did not happen, thanks to prompt action by governments, and constructive partnerships with donors and the private sector.

This brings me back to my theme: the roles of government, business, and the aid donors in the future economic and social development of Africa.

The Role of Government

A changed perception of the role of government in Africa is neatly summarized by John Healey and Mark Robinson, who write:[2]

> There has been a perceptible shift in the literature since the 1960s, when the state was treated as the principal agent of economic development, to a situation in the 1980s when the state was seen as the main obstacle to progress.

The reasons are well-known. African economies were dominated by large, inefficient public enterprises. Private sector activity was heavily regulated. Failures of macro-economic management – especially public sector deficits – caused debt problems and inflation. Excessive controls and regulations encouraged corruption. Economic activity became distorted. The biggest profits were earned not from production, but from gaining access to favours from the bureaucracy.

Establishing an enabling framework

Many of the activities undertaken by African governments are still harmful to economic growth. But there will always be a positive role for government in establishing the framework for private sector activity, and ensuring that services are provided in areas where markets fail.

A legislative framework with effective sanctions is needed to protect property rights. Contracts should be enforceable through the Courts. The regulatory and taxation framework should be consistently applied, with minimal scope for arbitrary decision-making by officials. Business needs to be confident that the state will guarantee reasonable standards of law and order.

Above all, government must provide stable, predictable conditions in which to do business.

Political and economic reforms reinforce each other. Corruption and mismanagement grow best in the dark. They wither in the light of close scrutiny by elected assemblies or a free press. Liberal economic reforms are therefore most likely to be sustained when there are parallel developments on the political front.

Providing services where markets fail

Policy is important, but policy alone is not enough. Government must also ensure that necessary services are provided where markets fail to provide them – especially basic health and education services, and the physical infrastructure needed to support economic activity. African governments have not been able to do this. Less than half the African population has access to health services. Only 40 per cent have access to safe water supplies. Nearly 18 per cent of African children die before the age of five, and only half of the 6–11 year-olds are enrolled in school. Transport and energy systems are underdeveloped.

A major challenge for the 1990s is to find ways to improve these services, with the limited resources which will be available. In some countries more revenue could be raised from general taxation; Uganda, for example, collects only 7 per cent of GDP in taxes. Faster economic growth should generate larger revenues for governments – though population growth of 3 per cent per annum will leave little scope for raising expenditures per head.

Africa already receives aid equivalent to nearly 10 per cent of GNP, or $34 per head as compared with $5 in South Asia. It may be neither feasible nor desirable to raise the already high level of dependence. The bulk of the extra resources will therefore have to be found by cutting out less essential activities, using resources more efficiently, and developing new and creative approaches to funding.

Smaller and More Efficient Government

Governments also need to reduce their ambitions. They must try to do less, but to do better what they continue to do.

Reductions in public expenditure have too often been achieved by across-the-board cuts in investment spending and in non-salary operating costs. The result is low efficiency in all public sector activities. Poorly paid and motivated staff lack the tools and materials to do their jobs.

Governments have started the process of selling, closing, or reforming public enterprises. White elephants are not yet extinct in Africa, but they are becoming more rare as governments trim their public investment programmes and concentrate on high-priority projects – including rehabilitation of assets which had deteriorated due to past neglect.

Civil service reform is reducing excessive government employment. It leaves more money for operating costs and for paying a living wage to those who remain. Ghana, for example, raised real salaries and tripled real expenditure on non-wage goods and services between 1984 and 1989, helped by significant staff reductions.

Progress is also being made in reducing defence expenditure – notably in Uganda, where donors are helping both to fund demobilization, and to strengthen the financial management systems in the Ministry of Defence.

Governments should further review the scope for private-sector alternatives to public utilities such as electricity supply, telecommunications, water and sewerage, and transport services. A recent World Bank Working Paper reviewed the experience of the Bank Group's lending for privatization. It is worth quoting at some length:[3]

> The main lessons of experience are clear: First, private ownership itself makes a difference. Some state-owned enterprises have been efficient and well managed for some periods, but government ownership seldom permits sustained good performance over more than a few years. There is a higher probability of efficient performance in private enterprise....
>
> Second, the process of privatization, though not simple, can and has worked; this is true for a variety of enterprises in a variety of settings, including in poor countries.

Within the key social sectors of health and education, more responsive and effective services require the development of partnerships between the public and private sectors – and also the NGOs, which are often already major providers of services. There is also a strong case for strengthening cost-recovery to supplement the resources available.

The Role of the *Aid* Donors

The donor community has recognized the difficulty of moving from a public-sector-dominated economy to an environment more supportive of the private sector. The Special Programme of Assistance for Africa was set up to ensure that reform programmes in low-income African countries did not fail for lack of balance-of-payments finance. The United Kingdom has been a strong supporter of the SPA: its commitment of £550 million since 1988 represents 10 per cent of bilateral donor pledges to support reforms in SPA countries. The UK has also provided, and continues to provide, a wide range of technical assistance for purposes including tax reform in Uganda, privatization in Zambia, and civil service reform in Ghana.

African reforms have received generous support from the donor community, with few strings attached. Most of the balance-of-payments support to SPA countries is untied – three-quarters of it in the British case. It is generally sold on free foreign-exchange markets. Moreover, revenues from the sale of donor programme aid – known as counterpart funds – are increasingly used to give *general* support to the budget of the recipient country. Restricting these counterpart funds to specific projects causes problems.

However, donor willingness to sustain high levels of aid in very flexible forms cannot be taken for granted. The economic returns so far, though encouraging in some countries, are less than were hoped for. The pace of reform in some key areas has been sluggish.

In low-income African countries that are implementing reforms, the World Bank estimates that 60 per cent of government expenditure is financed directly or indirectly by donors. This is a sobering figure. What meaning can sovereignty have when aid dependence is so high? Remember too that the donors have responsibilities to their own taxpayers. They must be confident that the allocation and management of public expenditures are appropriate.

The donors must also ensure that their own priorities do not distort public spending. Too many capital projects of doubtful value are started because donors are willing to finance them. Too little is spent on the operation and maintenance of projects. Many collapse when donor finance ends.

Public expenditure reviews are proving a valuable tool for identifying and beginning to resolve these conflicting priorities. The World Bank is undertaking reviews in most African countries. The UK has helped. In Ghana and Nigeria, the work of the Overseas Development Administration on public expenditure reviews has led to programmes of UK support to the health sector.

Donors need to shift their focus to the support of deeper policy and institutional reforms at the level of individual economic sectors. Projects cannot be considered in isolation: they need to be part of a coherent, sustainable strategy for the sector as a whole. Examples of the sectoral approach in which the UK Overseas Development Administration is involved include support for the wildlife service, for forest conservation and for agricultural research in Kenya; health sector development in Ghana; and primary education in Zambia.

Donors are increasingly looking at possibilities for bypassing failed public sector structures entirely. Where public sector services have effectively broken down, they have to consider how they can effectively direct more support to NGOs or the private sector, to strengthen self-help efforts at community level.

Encouraging the Private Sector

This brings me finally to the role of the private sector. The pursuit of private profit will be the ultimate source of economic growth and development in Africa. We need to understand how best to enable the business sector to thrive.

We know a lot about the negative effects of misguided government policies on private enterprise. We know something about the importance of infrastructure and of a healthy, well-educated labour force. These problems are beginning to be addressed, though it is a long, slow haul and needs financial support. But donors and Africans are also asking what more can and should be done directly to encourage the private sector. This is not easy. Aid bureaucrats are used to dealing with governments, and tend to have what Kim Jaycox of the World Bank has called a 'public sector mind set'. But the response from the private sector to the changes so far has been more limited than had been hoped. We need to develop a deeper understanding of the reasons, and we may need to develop new skills in responding to them.

A recent study of the Machakos district in Kenya provides some insights.[4] The area is one of low rainfall. Experts were predicting environmental degradation fifty years ago. It did not occur. Disaster was avoided by the remarkable ability of the population to adapt to changing circumstances. They invested in conservation; they adapted farming systems; they diversified their sources of income, investing in the education of their children to help secure modern sector jobs. Agricultural growth opened opportunities for investment in off-farm trading and transport activities. Government helped this process by improving the transport infrastructure and enabling farmers to market higher-value crops, and by more liberal marketing arrangements. But much was done by self-help, including community investments in schools, roads, and coffee factories. The authors of this study argue that the investment of people's own labour greatly exceeded the value of support received from government or NGOs. This is not the story of an 'aid-dependent' community.

We need more studies to improve our understanding. There should also be scope for learning from a major study currently being undertaken by John Page in the World Bank of the East Asian experience, where the role of foreign investment in providing capital, technology and management skills, and export markets have been so important. The UK Overseas Development Administration is participating with the World Bank in a major regional study of private enterprise development in Africa. We hope these studies will begin to produce answers to some of the key questions:

- What is needed to achieve the major increase which Africa needs in non-traditional exports?
- How can private investment (local *and* foreign) be increased?

We should also continue to experiment with new forms of assistance to the private sector. I do not believe in subsidizing private enterprises. Nevertheless, there may be a direct role for donors and governments in helping overcome market failures, which, for example, inhibit access to finance. The Commonwealth Development Corporation is supporting the development of venture capital funds in several African countries. This is an innovative and potentially valuable approach to alleviating both financial and management constraints. There may also be a case for technical assistance; recent work in Zimbabwe by Price Waterhouse achieved substantial productivity improvements by applying modern management concepts to African businesses.

Conclusions

Summing up, I draw three main conclusions:

First, the pessimistic view of Africa as a hopeless case is *not* justified. In much of Africa political and economic reform is taking hold. The policy environment has improved. There are some signs of economic revival and increased investment, especially in natural resource-based activities.

Second, the private sector response so far has nevertheless been disappointing. We need to look more carefully at ways to step up private investment in the short to medium term.

Third, and looking further ahead, Africa will need to develop a capacity to diversify beyond natural resource-based sectors. It does not at present possess the necessary skills or infrastructure to support a major development of the manufacturing sector. Acquiring them will need much larger, and more productive, investments in education and health, in transport and communications, in electrical power, and in water supplies. Progress will require more active partnership between government, business, and the donor community.

Notes

1. See Ishrat Husain and John Underwood (eds), *African External Finance in the 1990s* (Washington, DC: World Bank, 1991), p. 16. The World Bank's Special Programme of Assistance (SPA) was begun at the end of 1987 to provide highly concessional and quick-disbursing finance to African governments following programmes of economic reform approved by the Bank and the IMF. The SPA was made up of additional disbursements from the IDA, concessional co-financing from other multilateral agencies and bilateral donors, concessional debt rescheduling, and concessional financing of interest due on World Bank loans.
2. John Healey and Mark Robinson, *Democracy, Governance and Economic Policy: Sub-Saharan Africa in Comparative Perspective* (London: Overseas Development Institute, 1992), p. 42.
3. World Bank, *Privatization: the Lessons of Experience* (Washington, DC, 1992).
4. Mary Tiffen and Michael Mortimore, 'Environment, Population Growth and Productivity in Kenya', *Development Policy Review*, 10, 4 (December 1992).

3

BOBBY GODSELL

Six Strategies for African Development

A growing number of newly industrializing countries, mostly in Asia, have achieved rapid economic development without either socialist central planning or programmes of economic restructuring imposed by the IMF. Elsewhere decades of development aid, expert outside advice, and concessional trading arrangements have produced little success. It seems increasingly as if development is a do-it-yourself activity.

What strategies are to be followed if in Africa we are to do it ourselves? Six are suggested in this paper. They are informed by South African experience, but may well be thought no less germane to other African countries. The chances that they will be followed – in South Africa, or anywhere else – must be judged problematic. That does not detract from their importance.

Good Governance

Good governance underpins and promotes development. How should we characterize it?

First is the quality of certainty. Government actions should be predictable within the framework of known and dependable laws and regulations. In all areas of policy, citizens should be able to rely on constancy in the actions of public authorities.

Second, policies should be administered objectively or disinterestedly. The manner of their implementation should be bound by constant rules, and therefore be independent of the identity of the persons responsible for implementation. Good governance means government by law rather than government by men.

The third characteristic is transparency. Laws, administrative practices and the uses made of public resources should be known or accessible to all citizens. Appeals against, or reviews of, governmental decisions should be public. Public servants no less than other citizens should be clearly subject to the law.

Fourth, participation improves the quality of policy decisions and also promotes transparency. Societal interest groups should be involved in policy formation through public hearings and through standing consultative bodies (such as, where appropriate, tripartite meetings of government representatives with those of organized labour and business associations). Good governance requires regular, formalized interaction between state and society.

Fifth is accountability. Every exercise of power invites corruption. The only effective control is sustained public accountability of politicians and civil servants for their actions. Freedom of the press, including freedom of access to official sources of information, is one means of securing accountability. Another is multi-party democracy, i.e. the presence of parties alternative, and opposed, to the government, and having both the means and the incentive to scrutinize government actions and to publicize those that are aberrant.

Market-Friendly Economic Management

At the end of the twentieth century, the evidence has become conclusive, both worldwide and over time: governments are very bad at creating wealth and running businesses. Wealth is created in the market place, not the cabinet room or the civil servant's office. The best governments can do is to facilitate the market. But often their economic management in fact obstructs it. That economic management should be market-friendly is particularly important in the following areas.

First, prices. Nowhere else do markets manage better than governments than in setting prices. An illustration of the contrary view is South African agriculture, which could not be in worse shape after decades of 'price stabilization' and 'market management', and for most of whose products consumers are paying prices significantly higher than world market prices.

Second, taxes. Governments run on money, and the tax system is their fuel tank. The structure of the system and the levels of tax may either inhibit or encourage markets and entrepreneurship. Whenever the relative merits of tax systems are debated, one lesson emerges clearly: a good tax system has the broadest possible base, the simplest and most effective methods of collection, and the lowest rates compatible with public spending objectives.

Third, monetary policy. The currency of economic life is publicly controlled – if not directly by government, then at least by a public institution. Three points deserve emphasis in this context:

- that exchange control is less effective in keeping domestic resources in an economy than in shutting foreign resources out of it;
- that negative interest rates not only deter savings but also destroy the savings habit;
- that independence in the central bank is much to be desired.

Fourth, administrative regulation. From trading on sidewalks to techniques of building, choices have to be made of what is allowable and what should be prevented. Valid restraints on economic behaviour arise from requirements of public safety and concern for the quality of life. But such restraints also impede market access and are often so motivated. A reasoned balance has to be struck between allowing markets to work and serving other social objectives.

Investing in Human and Social Infrastructure

Much of the contemporary debate abstracts from people. A policy dilemma is commonly posited – between using resources for capital formation or for redistribution, between production or welfare, between growth or equity. Markets are conceived as if they were structures derived from natural philosophy.

Yet people make or unmake markets – including people in government. And capital consists of people as well as of the physical assets they create. The use of resources to enhance the effectiveness of people as economic actors is growth-promoting. It constitutes capital formation just as much as the building of roads or dams. Aspects of a strategy to develop human infrastructure include the following:

First, industrial literacy and numeracy. Technology, broadly defined, is the most important single propellant by which value is added and wealth created. Access to novel and changing technologies requires an industrially literate and numerate workforce.

Second, skills development. An enterprise seeking a place in domestic or outside markets needs an appropriately trained workforce. Training is appropriate when it delivers the skills to make and keep markets.

Third, urbanization. Although urbanization has many critics, it is a process that can be harnessed to promote economic growth. Not only is housing critical in this context, but also the effective – especially the cost-effective – provision of such other aspects of urban living conditions as water supply, energy, transport and health care.

Global Orientations

Of the many unhelpful notions to have emerged from decolonization and the establishment of new nations in the last few decades, few can have done more harm than those of 'self-sufficiency', 'strategic industries', 'the commanding heights of the economy', and so on. Unlike many other African countries, South Africa has suffered this incubus of ideas not so much voluntarily as because of a long economic isolation externally imposed, and an international economic status that might be ironically termed that of the 'least favoured nation'. From procurement of oil supplies to the local-content programme for motor vehicles, the curtains have been drawn on world markets.

The evidence is, however, unambiguous: countries do not prosper unless they are integrated with world markets. In this connection, four broad observations may be offered.

First, new world markets can be penetrated selectively. Countries seeking to escape exclusive reliance on traditional commodity exports really can find outlets for new products, at least in niche markets. South African experience in the 1980s shows what can be done – even, in this case, in the face of very widely applied external sanctions.

Second, consumers can benefit enormously from reductions in tariffs and other barriers to import trade. But liberalization should be carried out carefully and cautiously. As a recent World Bank report on the South African economy suggests, measures should be taken to raise productivity in the relevant industries to a level of international competitiveness before tariffs are reduced.

Third, the debate on what the 'North' should do for the 'South' needs to move from aid to trade – from philanthropic impulses and guilt assuagement to questions of mutual benefit. Developing countries can gain more from free access to big markets than from the hand-outs of the rich. The international debate needs to focus more on obstructions to free access such as the Multi-Fibres Arrangement.

Fourth, regional integration can help promote global orientations. Taking southern Africa as an example, significant reciprocal benefits can be achieved through regional integration in energy, water supply and transport. A regional approach to agriculture would also bring benefits. Regional tourism, including development of regional airlines, offers distinct possibilities. In all these areas, opportunities for developing wider, global relationships can be built upon regional integration for mutual benefit.

A Culture of Entrepreneurship

In the end value is added and wealth is created not by cabinets and ministries, not by national leaders and national plans, but by a myriad of individual actions performed by a myriad of individual entrepreneurs. That heroic individual who sees a better way of making something, a new service to be provided, a new way of reconciling means and wants - he or she stands at the epicentre of economic development and growth.

Governments can encourage or discourage entrepreneurship; societies can value or devalue the entrepreneur. Is the petty trader, the backyard manufacturer, the taxi operator seen as an asset to the community? Is he or she seen as a resource to be nurtured and protected? Or as an administrative blemish and social hazard that should, if possible, be tidied away? On the answers to these questions turn the possibilities of progress.

One important consideration is the hegemony of established career ambitions. In eighteenth-century England gentlemen without sufficient means of their own looked to the Church, the Navy and the Army. The counterparts in twentieth-century Africa seem to be the Law and Medicine. Somehow we must break the grip that these professional careers have on the minds of the young. They are not the only ways of earning a good living, and from the standpoint of economic development they are not the most useful.

Another consideration is the need to escape a culture of entitlement. Any society worthy of its name will offer entitlement to those of its members unable adequately to support themselves. But this cannot be a justification of the unearned, or very partially earned, incomes accruing to the holders of certain offices or the members of certain racial or ethnic groups privileged by policy. Those who can earn their livelihoods ought fully to do so.

Social Stability and the Social Fabric

Societies may be shaped from the top but they are built up from the bottom. The material with which national leadership works is provided by the fabric of the lives of individual citizens and the communities they have created. There are at least three institutions inherent in this fabric.

First, the family. Possibly, the family is central to all patterns of society; certainly it has been the building block of modern urban-industrial society. The integrity of the family permeates every level of social, political and economic institutions. As also does family disintegration.

Second, the community. In South Africa, crime and violence are the overriding preoccupations of everyone, irrespective of race, class, age or sex. Much can be done by governmental institutions at national level to address this problem, but chiefly the real players are the communities so afflicted. Can the individual communities mobilize to fight crime – both by preventive action (neighbourhood watch and patrols) and by assisting the police in identifying criminals and securing prosecutions? Can they persuade or coerce their more frenzied members to differ in debate and votes rather than with bullets and bombs? Laws may be made in parliaments and courts, but they are enforced, or not, on the streets and by the actions and attitudes of ordinary people living and working in actual, specific, geographic communities. In the end, while politicians propose, the people dispose.

Third, religious organizations. The social fabric depends on social values, and nowhere are African social values shaped more than in religious organizations. It is there that attitudes to life and death, right and wrong, production and consumption, rights and duties have their foundation. The nature and the vitality of these organizations are critical to the strength and adaptability of the social fabric.

Conclusion

The economic development of a society depends on entrepreneurship, expressed frequently as the economic application of advances in technology. Entrepreneurship can be facilitated by wisely chosen policies and institutions relating to governance, markets, human and social infrastructure, and external economic relationships. The society must be held together, however, by a fabric consisting chiefly of families, local communities and the common values deriving principally from religion.

4

KWESI BOTCHWEY

Deregulating the Foreign-Exchange Market in Ghana

Ghana's Economic Recovery Programme (ERP) was initiated in 1983 against a background of unprecedented economic decline spanning a period of over a decade during which real per capita income fell by over 30 per cent. The decade-long crisis, caused by a combination of severe external shocks and wrong domestic policies, was typically characterized by large fiscal deficits which were financed mainly through borrowing from the domestic banking system, with resultant high inflation (close to 120 per cent in 1983) and a highly overvalued exchange rate. Pervasive government intervention in the economy through an intricate web of price, distribution and import controls aggravated distortions in relative prices and weakened incentives for production, savings and investment.

The reform strategy followed a more or less conventional path. Its key elements included (i) a realignment of relative prices in favour of productive activity and exports, (ii) the restoration of monetary and fiscal discipline, (iii) a massive rehabilitation of social and economic infrastructure, (iv) the implementation of wide-ranging institutional and structural reforms, and, most importantly, (v) a deregulation of the economy through a gradual shift from direct controls and intervention to greater reliance on markets.

Ghana's adjustment experience has not been without its problems – among them, a slower than desired private sector response, especially outside the mining sector. Even so, the experience has been very rewarding. Real GDP has grown by about 5 per cent per annum on average, thus allowing gains in real per capita income. Inflation has declined markedly and the overall balance-of-payments position switched from deficits to surpluses in 1991, making possible the elimination of external payments arrears that had totalled about $600 million at the end of 1982.

The record of Ghana's economic performance under the ERP has been well documented in academic writing, and in World Bank and International Monetary Fund documents. My intention is therefore not to duplicate it here; instead, I would like to dwell on one critical dimension in the Ghanaian experience where deregulation proved most challenging and, incidentally, also most rewarding, namely, the area of exchange-rate policy and the whole process of trade and exchange reform. I do so for the added reason that this area, more than any other, mirrors, in a rather interesting way, the dialectical relationship between 'deregulation' as such, and the issues of governance, business and aid; that is, the way deregulation as a policy affects, and is in turn affected by, issues of governance, donor aid policy and business practice.

The Reform Process

Before April 1983 when the ERP was launched, specifically from about August 1978, the exchange rate of the cedi was pegged to the US dollar and fixed at 2.75 cedis per dollar. With the rate of inflation in Ghana exceeding the average trends in its main trading partner countries, the real effective exchange rate of the cedi appreciated by more than 400 per cent between 1978 and 1983. The differential between the official and parallel market rates widened to over 2000 per cent by the end of 1982. There were predictable and dire consequences for exports and the balance of payments; external payments arrears rose to almost $600 million or about 10 per cent of GDP.

The reform process went through four distinct but related phases, all of them accompanied by appropriate monetary and fiscal policies. The first phase saw a series of discrete exchange-rate adjustments; the second, establishment of a foreign-exchange auction market with the exchange rate of the cedi being determined by market forces; the third, 'absorption' of the parallel market through the licensing or legalization of exchange bureaux; and the fourth, unification of the exchange system.

The choice of a 'gradualist' approach was a conscious and important one. It was adopted in place of a 'faster track' or 'bolder step', for economic and political reasons.

On the economic side, the extent of the cedi's overvaluation, and the widespread distortions to which it had given rise, would have suggested that a faster approach in the form of an immediate floating of the currency would be more appropriate. But there were genuine concerns that a precipitate floating of the currency would risk unacceptable short-run costs, especially in the form of losses of output if the floating should get out of hand. Moreover, it was recognized that time was needed to improve the fiscal situation and increase the availability of foreign-exchange resources, among other things, to create more favourable conditions for sustaining a floating rate.

At the political level, the 'gradualist' approach also enabled policy-makers to broaden the consensus within government and in the public generally behind the policy reforms, through debates and public discussions.

The first phase

As already noted, a key element of economic strategy under the ERP was the adoption of a flexible exchange-rate policy. The first phase of this policy reform was the devaluation of the cedi through a series of discrete adjustments from about April 1983 when the ERP was formally launched to the beginning of 1986.

An interesting feature of this first phase was the mechanism employed in introducing it. The mechanism, which was in essence a multiple exchange-rate system with two different rates being applied to specified foreign-exchange receipts and payments, was presented as a system of 'bonuses and surcharges' – bonuses to the earners of foreign exchange, and surcharges on foreign-exchange users. This rather unconventional terminology had its roots in the debates that preceded the introduction of the reform programme, and was meant to implant in the popular consciousness the view that those who earned foreign exchange needed to be given incentives through 'bonuses' and that the most 'appropriate' way of doing this was to impose levies or surcharges on users of foreign exchange; the imagery was home-grown and simple, and the logic compelling.

The discrete rate adjustments made in the framework of this seemingly confusing mechanism led to a depreciation of the currency by about 90 per cent in US dollar terms. The adjustments were done quarterly, with the average exchange rate being moved by reference to an index which measured the inflation differential between Ghana and its principal trading partners.

The system of bonuses and surcharges was abandoned towards the end of 1983 when it was believed to have achieved its main purpose – that of planting the logic of flexibility in exchange-rate policy firmly in the popular psychology. In its place, the official rates were unified with a further devaluation of about 90 per cent and thereafter adjusted quarterly in accordance with the index rule noted above. During this first phase, imports continued to be controlled through an annual import programme and an import licensing system, except for a minor but important modification in 1985 which permitted holders of special import licences – as opposed to specific import licences which gave the holder access to foreign exchange at the official rate – to import a wide range of consumer goods and some capital goods with foreign exchange from their own sources at the parallel market rate.

The devaluations effected in the first phase enabled the extreme overvaluation of the cedi to be corrected to a significant extent. But by mid-1986 it was acknowledged that the devaluations had not gone far enough; the differential between the official and the parallel market rates was still about 100 per cent. Clearly, further depreciation of the cedi was required to improve the balance-of-payments position. Moreover, at the political level, discussions preceding the quarterly adjustments had become increasingly acrimonious, and with the public also getting increasingly weary of the frequent adjustments, it was felt that the time had come for a shift in strategy towards a less politicized and more market-based mechanism for adjusting the exchange rate.

The second phase – floating the cedi

In order, therefore, to bring about the desired further depreciation of the cedi and also to reduce the differential between official and parallel market rates, a floating system was introduced, again cautiously, in September 1986, in circumstances that enabled the Central Bank to continue to manage the bulk of the nation's foreign-exchange receipts while at the same time reducing the risk of collusion among the commercial banks.

A dual arrangement was introduced under which access to foreign exchange could be obtained at two windows – one at a fixed rate and the second at a rate determined by the market in a weekly auction conducted by the Central Bank. Transactions involving debt-service payments on official debt contracted before a specific date, and imports of crude oil, petroleum products and essential drugs were conducted at the first window; all others were conducted at the second window. At the same time export receipts from cocoa and residual oil were to be exchanged at the first window.

Side by side with the introduction of the auction system, this phase of the exchange policy reform process also saw the liberalization of the trade/import licensing system. Under the new system, access to foreign-exchange auction funds, which before was restricted to a relatively limited range of goods and only to those who had specific import licences, was widened to cover virtually all non-consumer goods, while restrictions on the number of licences which could be issued were also removed.

The floating of the exchange rate in the second phase helped to bring about the desired further depreciation of the cedi and a marked reduction in the spread between the official and parallel market rates by the end of 1986 – to between 20 and 25 per cent, compared with about 100 per cent before the establishment of the auction.

The auction system was subsequently modified through unification of the two windows. At the same time, access to the auction was widened through the inclusion of more and more categories of consumer goods and debt-service payments, so that by the end of the first quarter of 1988, just about all consumer goods could be funded through the auction, making possible the abolition of the import licensing system by January 1989. Indeed, by the end of 1989, virtually all restrictions on payments for current international transactions had been eliminated.

The retail auction described above – 'retail' because it auctioned foreign exchange to end-users – worked reasonably well, from the point of view of further cedi depreciation and reduction in the spread between the official and parallel market rates. But, even so, a substantial parallel market remained and continued to bedevil the management of the foreign-exchange market and to erode the efficiency of the auction mechanism.

The third phase – absorbing the parallel market

In order, therefore, further to strengthen the role of market forces in the determination of the exchange rate, a major policy decision was taken early in 1988 to license foreign-exchange bureaux. Under this policy any corporate or natural person licensed by the Central Bank could operate a foreign-exchange bureau. These bureaux were authorized to engage in the business of buying and selling foreign exchange at freely negotiated rates. All import and service payments qualified for funding through the bureaux, provided they could be supported with appropriate documentation. On the other hand, the bureaux got their funds principally from exporters of so-called non-traditional exports (generally, exports other than cocoa, gold and timber) and private remittances. After a rather halting start, the number of bureaux increased rapidly and, by the end of the second year of their operation, they were disposing of a volume of foreign-exchange transactions close to 50 per cent of the foreign exchange supplied through the formal auction. They now number over 230 and manage a volume of transactions close to a quarter of the total.

The introduction of the foreign-exchange bureaux meant, in effect, the absorption of the parallel market and the facilitation thereby of further rationalization of the exchange markets. But the system had one major drawback. The two markets – the official weekly retail auction and the foreign-exchange bureaux – remained segmented to the extent that the bureaux were not permitted to purchase foreign exchange at the retail auction. Thus, in spite of the further improvement which the introduction of the bureaux brought to the exchange arrangements, the spread between the bureaux and auction rates remained unacceptably high, even after a dramatic decline by the end of the second year of operation of the bureaux.

The fourth phase – the unification of the exchange system

With the narrowing of the spread between the bureaux and the auction rates already noted, the Central Bank abolished its retail auction in early 1990 – almost exactly two years after the introduction of the foreign-exchange bureaux – and, in its place, instituted a weekly wholesale auction in which *all* authorized dealers, including the foreign-exchange bureaux which met criteria set by the Central Bank, could now participate. With the opening of the official auction to the bureaux, the exchange markets became unified in a composite exchange system which combined a weekly wholesale auction with an interbank and retail foreign-exchange market. The weekly wholesale auction rate applied to official transactions including customs valuation, while to all other transactions the other rates applied.

With the establishment of the wholesale auction, all other restrictions on payments for current international transactions were removed.

Deregulation and Counteracting Policies

An interesting aspect of the Ghanaian experience in deregulation in the sphere of exchange and trade reforms was the way in which some aspects of donor policies affected the liberalization process, often pulling it in the opposite direction.

Let me illustrate my point with some problems of 'tied aid'. An important advantage or effect of a shift from controlled to market-based systems, apart from its general benign effect on economic incentives through the better rewarding of efficiency, is that it removes a major source of corruption and patronage. Public officials engaged in the allocation of foreign exchange administratively have a strong incentive to demand rewards when they know how much of a premium the beneficiary gets from the exercise of their administrative power. The market-based or indirect system of allocation that comes with deregulation deprives them of this power and removes the temptation. But when some portion of donor funds, no matter how small, comes tied to a particular source of supply and is required to be allocated administratively, we are thrown back to a culture of 'regulation', to the delight of its advocates.

The cost of these counteracting influences may not reside only in the malfeasance to which they may give rise. They may also have distortive effects on the m. economic environment. In a situation of relatively unhindered access to foreign exchange through a free market, tied funds need 'sweeteners' to be disbursed. The businessman who needs foreign exchange will, given a choice, understandably prefer free-standing foreign exchange which he can use in the most competitive market. Therefore, when there is pressure to disburse donor funds quickly – even where they are tied – lest the absorptive capacity of the recipient country be impugned, the pressure is strong for special terms to be given to get the funds disbursed. When these terms take the form of preferential interest rates and extended loan repayment periods, they are bound to distort monetary policy. It is important therefore that donor policies, whether from bilateral or multilateral sources, be fully supportive of liberalization or deregulation drives in adjusting countries. It is also important that the business community conducts itself in ways that are equally supportive.

The politics of deregulation

The ignominious collapse of the so-called centrally planned economies of Eastern Europe has given rise to a certain mood of triumphalism in which 'deregulation' or liberalization in economic management is seen in an almost exclusively polemical or ideological sense. It is almost as if history had spoken irrevocably in favour of *market-based* or *deregulated* as opposed to *planned* systems, and that therefore economic and social relations must everywhere be deregulated or liberalized, almost as an end in itself. However, it is important to recognize that efficiency is the fundamental objective of deregulation. This recognition makes it possible to acknowledge the tremendous management challenges that a deregulation programme carries. The relative success of the Ghana programme was made possible by early recognition of these challenges – in particular, the need to reorientate institutions and change the outlook not only of bureaucrats in the administrative machinery but also of the public at large. Indeed, one of the most fascinating aspects of Ghana's experience in deregulation was the attitude of the public and some sections of the business community. For instance, in the first few weeks of the opening of the foreign-exchange bureaux, public patronage was restrained by fear that customers would be arrested. After over two decades of exchange controls, people simply could not believe that they could walk into a shop in any corner of the city and buy foreign currency freely! Again, years after the abolition of import licences, some businessmen would go to the erstwhile licensing authorities and demand import licences.

Conclusion

Deregulating an African economy – any economy – requires a comprehensive macro-economic programme and policy framework. Moreover, its objectives must be properly explained and debated widely so as to build the necessary political consensus. Equally important, the institutional restructuring and management implications of the process must be anticipated and addressed. Finally, the pace and mode of presentation of policy changes must be informed by the real dynamics of the political economy of the domestic situation.

PART II

WORLD MARKETS OR COLLECTIVE SELF-RELIANCE?

5

ADEBAYO ADEDEJI

The Case for Remaking Africa

Introduction: *Governance, Aid and Africa*

The Royal African Society chose three extremely topical subjects – *governance, business and aid* – for its 'Africa 1993' Conference. Undoubtedly, these three factors not only determine the rate of progress – material and non-material – but also critically affect its direction. The way they evolve and develop will continue to determine, by and large, the nature and strength of Africa's polity and economy, as indeed they have done, both positively and negatively, since independence in 1960.

No one in Africa, not even former and contemporary despots, doubts that good governance is the very foundation of civilized society and that neither social and economic progress nor political stability and national cohesiveness and unity are possible unless and until good governance is in place. Good governance should by definition be human-centred, guaranteeing civil and political rights on the one hand and social and economic rights on the other. There is now a general acceptance of the proposition that it is extremely difficult, if not impossible, to launch a process of socio-economic transformation – by means of which genuine and sustained social and economic progress can take place – in a country where good governance is absent. In fact, as I have often argued, we shall never fully comprehend and grasp the current African crisis as long as we continue to assume that it is primarily an economic crisis. What we confront in Africa is primarily a political crisis, albeit with devastating socio-economic consequences.[1]

The right to life and liberty, the security of the person, freedom from torture or cruel, inhuman or degrading treatment or punishment, the right to recognition and equal protection under the law and to effective judicial remedy, freedom from arbitrary arrest, detention or exile, freedom from arbitrary interference with privacy in the home, freedom of association and assembly, the right to nationality and the right to take part in governing – these are essential requirements for a civilized polity. Yet, even today, they cannot all be taken for granted everywhere, nor in many African countries.

How to achieve universally in Africa good governance, democracy, accountability and political empowerment is the challenge that faces all Africans and their friends today and in the years ahead. The *African Charter for Popular Participation in Development and Transformation* (Arusha, February 1990) and the shift from autocracy to democracy in Benin Republic in the same year were hopeful first signs of a budding democratization process. Three years later we cannot but conclude that this process has been largely aborted and subverted, the subversion in some cases master-minded by the very leaders who had proclaimed their commitment to the realization of democracy. Indeed, the past three years have witnessed oscillations between tumult and paralysis, and have shown more clearly than ever before the deep-rooted and systemic weaknesses of current leadership in Africa. There is, therefore, an urgent need to bring the reform process back on track, to put a halt to the ongoing mockery and charade of democracy in many countries, and to embark on the restitution of real democracy. More than ever before, Africa needs good governance and democracy as well as democratically determined development. And in order to foster both popular participation and democratic development, there must emerge a strong civil society with autonomous grass-roots organizations.

Over the years, aid, in the form of foreign grants, loans and investment, has become a dominant factor in Africa's development equation. Cynics may add that it has become the opium of African leaders. Without aid, nothing happens. The aid syndrome is so devastating that it subverts rather than energizes development. This aid dependence developed from the once dominant paradigm that the motive force of economic development was massive capital injection. Arthur Lewis argued that the central problem of economic growth was to understand the process whereby a country moved from being a 5 per cent to a 12 per cent saver and investor of national income.[2] Since a sufficient volume of savings could not be achieved domestically, given the low level of income and thus surplus, various forms of aid and foreign investment were encouraged to complement domestic savings. Yet, the cumulative effect of this development paradigm is the massive debt crisis which today threatens the very survival of most African countries – a crisis that has been further aggravated by high rates of interest, unstable exchange-rate regimes, misdirection and mismanagement of loans and aid, and low rates of return on investment.

Indeed, the heavy debt burden and the stranglehold of debt servicing in the face of collapsing commodity prices offered African countries few options for attracting new resources. This led to a situation in which there was only one game in town: adopt the terms of a Structural Adjustment Programme or perish. One of the most effective means of ensuring that poorer countries adopted SAPs was the promise of continued foreign aid.

> As Zambia, Peru and other indebted Southern countries learned, non-compliance with the terms of SAPs resulted in cuts of donor assistance, if not its complete discontinuation. The World Bank (with the support of Northern governments and their aid programmes) not only chose the game – they also wrote the rules.[3]

As Table 5.1 shows, Sub-Saharan Africa had in 1990 become a net transferor of resources. Apart from the World Bank's International Development Association, all other major sources of foreign aid and investment showed a reverse flow of resources. In other words, the poorest region in the world has been paying more to the richest countries and multilateral institutions than it received from them. No wonder there is so much talk about aid fatigue. The recipient African countries are suffering severely from the fatigue, more than the donors can imagine. But given their present circumstances, they seem to think that there is no way out. Or, rather, that they can buy their way out through international trade.

Table 5.1 New Lending and Debt Servicing for Sub-Saharan Africa, 1990 ($US billion)

Creditor	New lending	Repayments	Net flow
World Bank-IDA	2.04	0.15	1.89
World Bank-IBRD	0.81	1.37	-0.56
IMF	0.73	1.27	-0.54
Private	1.34	2.56	-1.20
Bilateral	2.42	2.60	-0.18
Total	7.34	7.95	-0.59

Source: *World Debt Tables*, 1991–92; Percy S. Mistry, *African Debt Revisited* (The Hague: Forum on Debt and Development, 1991).

Trade and Dependence

Indeed, it is taken for granted that countries must trade. The dominant view in the North is that trade is an equalizing force. But since trade patterns are determined – if not dictated – by those who have maximum leverage, the South's dissatisfaction with the traditional pattern of trade and specialization has remained unabated. As far as Africa is concerned, its relationship with the world economy over the past four centuries has failed to instil much confidence in the beneficial workings of international trade. As Professor Stephen R. Lewis Jr of Williams College has so aptly written:[4]

> The first two centuries were dominated by the human plunder of the slave trade. Then, the 19th-century scramble for Africa by European commercial and political interests began, in some regions, an exceptionally exploitive system. The cash crop economy and African labor's involvement in production for the international market were expanded in the 20th century. But development was limited to primary production: Africa was to provide hewers of wood and drawers of water for the industrial world, and trade and international commerce often was controlled by foreign minorities. In the post-independence period, shocks from the international economy have reverberated more strongly in Africa than in other regions of the world.

In spite of this dismal record of Africa's contact with the world economy, foreign trade plays a dominant role. Moreover, African economies are highly dependent on primary commodities in their foreign trade. In virtually all African countries, one to three primary commodities account for between 50 and more than 90 per cent of total export earnings. The exceptions are South Africa and Zimbabwe (see Map/Chart 5.1 and, for 1987 and 1988 data on a country-by-country and commodity-by-commodity basis, Table 5.2).

Africa is more dependent upon primary commodities for its export earnings than any other region in the world. For example, whereas in 45 out of 51 African countries these commodities make up more than half of total exports, only 8 out of 19 South-East Asian countries show a similar ratio. Similarly, the export concentration ratio for

Map/Chart 5.1

African Exports Concentration Ratios, 1982–6:

Countries where 1, 2, 3 or 4 Products Account for over 75% of Export Earnings

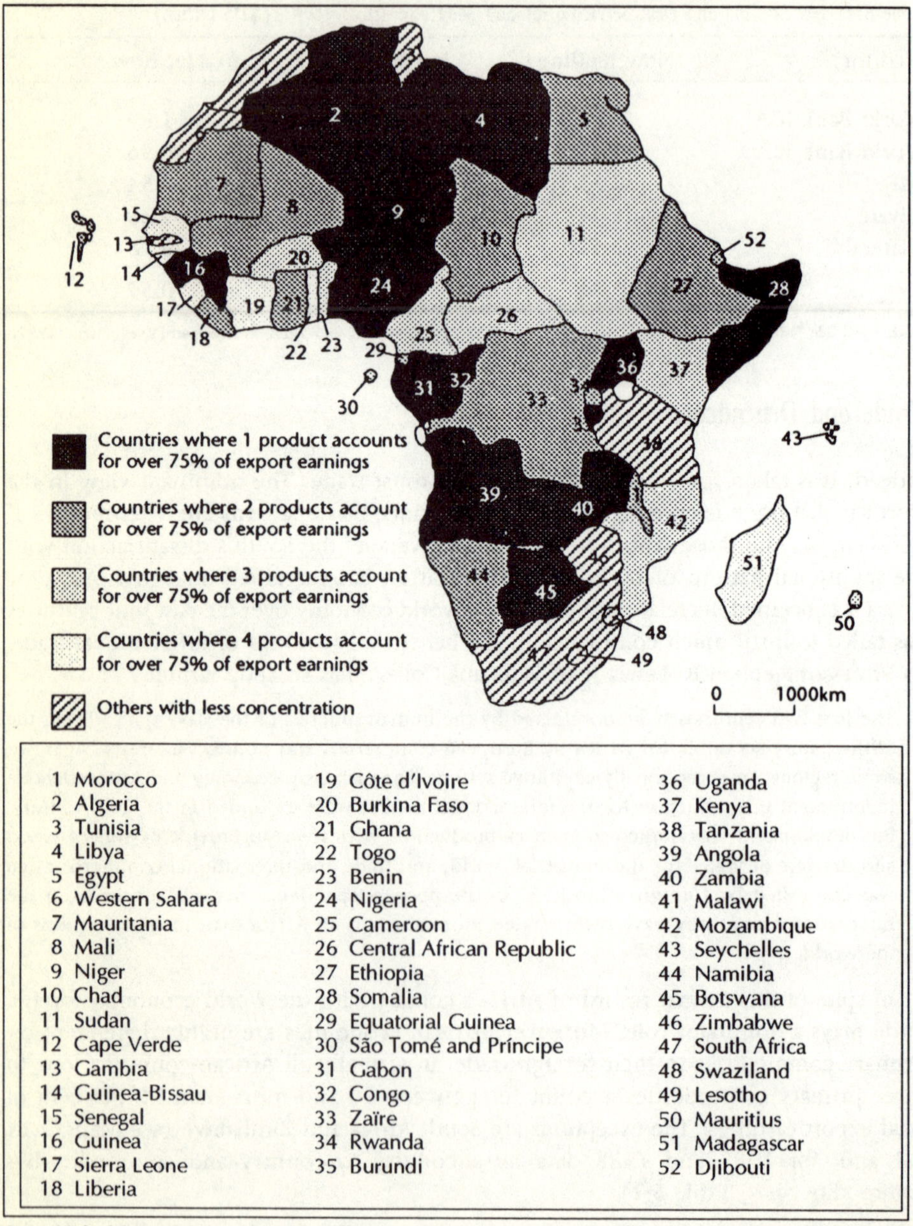

1 Morocco	19 Côte d'Ivoire	36 Uganda
2 Algeria	20 Burkina Faso	37 Kenya
3 Tunisia	21 Ghana	38 Tanzania
4 Libya	22 Togo	39 Angola
5 Egypt	23 Benin	40 Zambia
6 Western Sahara	24 Nigeria	41 Malawi
7 Mauritania	25 Cameroon	42 Mozambique
8 Mali	26 Central African Republic	43 Seychelles
9 Niger	27 Ethiopia	44 Namibia
10 Chad	28 Somalia	45 Botswana
11 Sudan	29 Equatorial Guinea	46 Zimbabwe
12 Cape Verde	30 São Tomé and Príncipe	47 South Africa
13 Gambia	31 Gabon	48 Swaziland
14 Guinea-Bissau	32 Congo	49 Lesotho
15 Senegal	33 Zaïre	50 Mauritius
16 Guinea	34 Rwanda	51 Madagascar
17 Sierra Leone	35 Burundi	52 Djibouti
18 Liberia		

Source: Michael Barratt Brown and Pauline Tiffen, *Short Changed: Africa and World Trade* (London, Pluto Press, 1992), Chart 3.1.

Africa is much higher than for other regions. It is, for example, twice that of countries which are relatively dependent on agricultural exports, like Australia, New Zealand, Denmark or Ireland, or the non-oil producing countries of Asia.[5] Consequently, African primary commodity export earnings loom large as a percentage of GNP – up to 50 per cent for oil-producing countries.

The unequal integration of Africa into the world economy has left a permanent, unwholesome and inhibiting mark on the development process. Africa's problem is not whether to choose between world trade on the one hand and regional integration and collective self-reliance on the other. Its primary and grave problem is that of excessive dependence for export on primary commodities – for which there is little domestic demand – while at the same time being highly dependent on imports of basic manufactures and, worse still, of food for its survival. In fact, today, one out of every four Africans depends on food imports for sustenance.

The non-subsistence sector of the African economy – still in many countries considerably smaller than the subsistence sector – is characterized by a predominance of activities arising from exports and imports. Domestic production plays a secondary role. The services sector – banking, finance, insurance and transport – is largely oriented towards external trade. The production base in Africa is narrow, both in terms of size and in relation to the range of goods produced. Inter-sectoral linkages are fragile and few. The weak production base and the predominantly export-oriented economy, coupled with its openness, have accentuated the external dependence of Africa. The continent also requires massive imports of factor inputs.

Graver still, Africa's relevance in total world trade has been shrinking since the 1970s. Except for sugar, tobacco, tea and fish products, where slight increases have occurred, Africa's world market share has been declining in its major export crops: cocoa, cotton, timber, live animals and meat, groundnuts, rubber, sisal and palm oil. The same holds true for its mineral exports. African exports have fared worse than those of other Third World regions. Whereas the developing countries' combined share of world markets remained at about 20 per cent between 1964 and 1987, Africa's share fell by half, from 4.2 to 2.1 per cent.

A myriad of factors account for this decline. During the 1960s and 1970s, for example, some African primary commodity exports dropped sharply in volume due to political and economic decisions. The deteriorating terms of trade, particularly in the 1980s, with their resulting severe losses in incomes and revenues, discouraged investments and raised the costs of factor inputs. Nevertheless, as shown in Graph 5.1, the volume of exports did increase by some 7.5 percentage points between 1981–86 and 1986–90. But the unit value index dropped by 23.2 points. In 1986 alone, Africa sustained a loss of US$19 billion in foreign exchange from the fall in commodity prices and the dollar depreciation – ironically, this amount approximated the foreign aid which Africa 'received' during the same year. Also between 1981–86 and 1986–90, the unit value of Africa's imports rose by nearly 13.9 percentage points as against a 3.8 percentage points decrease in the quantum index. Consequently, the income terms of trade declined by a third in the course of the decade, thus aggravating Africa's financial situation. The steep decline in Africa's terms of trade and the purchasing power of exports during the 1980s is illustrated in Graph 5.1 (based on data from the UNCTAD Secretariat).

Table 5.2 Relative Importance of Principal Export Commodities 1987, 1988 in African Countries (% of total exports)

Country/commodity	1987	1988
NORTH AFRICA		
Algeria		
Crude petroleum	43.5	42.7
Petroleum products	22.4	–
Natural gas	28.1	31.2
Egypt		
Crude petroleum	25.8	21.7
Raw cotton	8.9	8.0
Petroleum products	9.4	10.2
Cotton yarn	21.6	17.7
Unwrought aluminium	7.9	–
Libyan Arab Jamaniriya		
Crude petroleum	93.4	–
Sudan		
Raw cotton	30.0	42.7
Water melon seeds	3.7	–
Sheep, lambs & goats	2.6	–
Sesame seeds	9.0	–
Natural gums, resins	17.8	10.5
Dura	16.6	–
Tunisia		
Crude petroleum	21.5	13.6
Clothing	25.5	–
Manufactured fertilizer	11.8	11.6
Olive oil	3.7	3.4
Phosphoric acids	4.0	–
Petroleum products	2.0	–
Super phosphates	1.5	1.3
WEST AFRICA		
Burkina Faso		
Cotton in bulk & seeded	48.9	45.3
The Gambia		
Groundnuts shelled	21.9	–
Groundnut oil	11.2	–
Ghana		
Cocoa beans	46.1	45.5
Gold	16.4	–
Cocoa butter	3.4	–
Côte d'Ivoire		
Cocoa beans	33.6	–
Green coffee	12.7	–
Timber	2.6	–
Raw cotton	2.4	–
Liberia		
Iron ore	57.0	–
Raw rubber	22.3	–
Diamonds	2.3	–
Mali		
Raw cotton	74.2	–
Cotton thread & cloth	–	2.4
Groundnut oil	1.0	–
Livestock	–	29.8
Mauritania		
Iron ore	31.1	–
Nigeria		
Cocoa beans	1.9	–
Petroleum	94.2	88.4
Senegal		
Phosphates	5.6	–
Petroleum products	18.8	–
Natural fertilizer	0.7	–
Fish, shellfish	18.6	–
Sierra Leone		
Diamonds	23.0	3.2
Coffee beans	11.5	13.5
Cocoa beans	14.0	11.6
Togo		
Calcium phosphates	45.8	49.7
Green coffee	12.6	9.2
Cocoa beans	11.4	9.1
Cotton in bulk & seeded	11.8	17.3
CENTRAL AFRICA		
Burundi		
Green coffee	64.3	88.8
Tea	5.5	–
Cotton	1.6	–
Cameroon		
Crude petroleum	17.1	–
Green coffee	15.6	–
Cocoa beans	15.1	–
Timber	9.4	–
Raw cotton	3.2	–
Central African Republic		
Timber	20.6	9.3
Green coffee	17.8	20.0
Diamonds	51.8	41.2
Raw cotton	10.3	5.9
Chad		
Raw cotton	39.0	–
Congo		
Crude petroleum	87.1	77.2
Equatorial Guinea		
Cocoa & products	27.8	33.7
Coffee	13.2	–
Gabon		
Crude petroleum	74.4	–
Ruanda		
Coffee	88.9	84.8
Tin	0.7	–
Tea	8.7	14.0
São Tomé and Príncipe		
Cocoa beans	75.0	–
EAST & SOUTHERN AFRICA		
Angola		
Crude petroleum	83.8	–
Coffee	1.0	–
Botswana		
Diamonds	84.6	–
Meat & products	3.1	–
Copper nickel matte	4.4	–
Comoros		
Vanilla	36.5	–
Cloves	44.5	–
Ylang-ylang	17.0	–
Ethiopia		
Coffee beans	56.3	61.2
Hides & skins	16.8	13.9
Petroleum products	–	2.9
Pulses	–	3.5
Khat	–	1.0

Table 5.2 cont.
Relative Importance of Principal Export Commodities 1987, 1988 in African Countries

Country/commodity	1987	1988
Kenya		
Petroleum products	12.4	12.0
Coffee beans	24.6	26.6
Tea	20.7	20.2
Cement	1.2	1.1
Sisal	1.3	1.3
Madagascar		
Green coffee	27.9	–
Cloves	2.6	–
Vanilla	25.6	–
Malawi		
Raw tobacco	60.7	40.7
Tea	9.9	10.6
Sugar	10.3	–
Groundnuts	2.1	3.1
Mauritius		
Sugar	35.8	33.1
Clothing	44.9	–
Molasses	0.6	0.7
Tea	0.7	0.7
Seychelles		
Copra	2.6	1.7
Fish fresh & frozen	6.4	–
Petroleum products	58.5	–
Somalia		
Live animals	67.0	–
Bananas	22.6	–
Swaziland		
Sugar	35.9	–
Wood pulp	18.9	–
Canned fruits	5.1	–
Citrus fruits	4.3	–
Tanzania		
Coffee beans	31.3	26.1
Raw cotton	15.3	23.8
Cloves	1.9	–
Sisal fibres	1.7	1.4
Minerals	3.3	–
Cashewnuts	3.9	–
Diamonds	1.3	–
Uganda		
Coffee	85.4	–
Cotton	1.3	–
Zambia		
Copper	84.9	84.8
Cobalt	5.8	–
Zinc	1.6	–
Zimbabwe		
Raw tobacco	21.7	–
Ferro alloys	13.2	–
Asbestos crude	4.8	–
Cotton linters	6.4	–
Nickel	4.9	–
Sugar, raw & refined	4.2	–
Maize, unmilled	3.4	–

Source: Economic Commission for Africa, *African Socio-Economic Indicators 1988* (Addis Ababa, 1991) Table 26.
Note: – indicates figure not available

During the 1980s, the growing impact of biotechnology, through which process substitutes and new products are emerging, began to be felt – faster-growing coffee bushes, micro-propagation of high-yielding cocoa plants, cloning of oil palms to double yields, etc. This trend will definitely accelerate in the 1990s. Biotechnology will change the whole nature of the market for primary commodities, giving manufacturers much greater flexibility in their choice of inputs.

What, then, is the outlook for the rest of this decade? Judging from the long-term trend in demand and prices, in particular the drastic deterioration in the 1980s, it would appear that African countries have no alternative but to reduce their dependence on primary agricultural and mineral exports. The World Bank projections to the year 2000 support this view.[6] They indicate:

- a fairly strong recovery beyond the 1986/87 price levels for tea, sugar, palm oil, cotton, rubber and logs; but no return to 1980/81 levels for these commodities;
- some recovery for coffee and cocoa (key African commodities) after 1990, but not to 1986/87, 1970/71 or even 1980/81 levels (assuming price increases for coffee at 3 per cent a year and for cocoa at 7 per cent a year).
- an actual price decline for tobacco.

Notwithstanding these projections, the World Bank continues to advocate that African countries should step up their production of export crops and minerals. On the assumption that the current mix of policies under World Bank/IMF SAPs will hold,

Graph 5.1
Africa's Terms of Trade 1981–90
(1980 = 100)

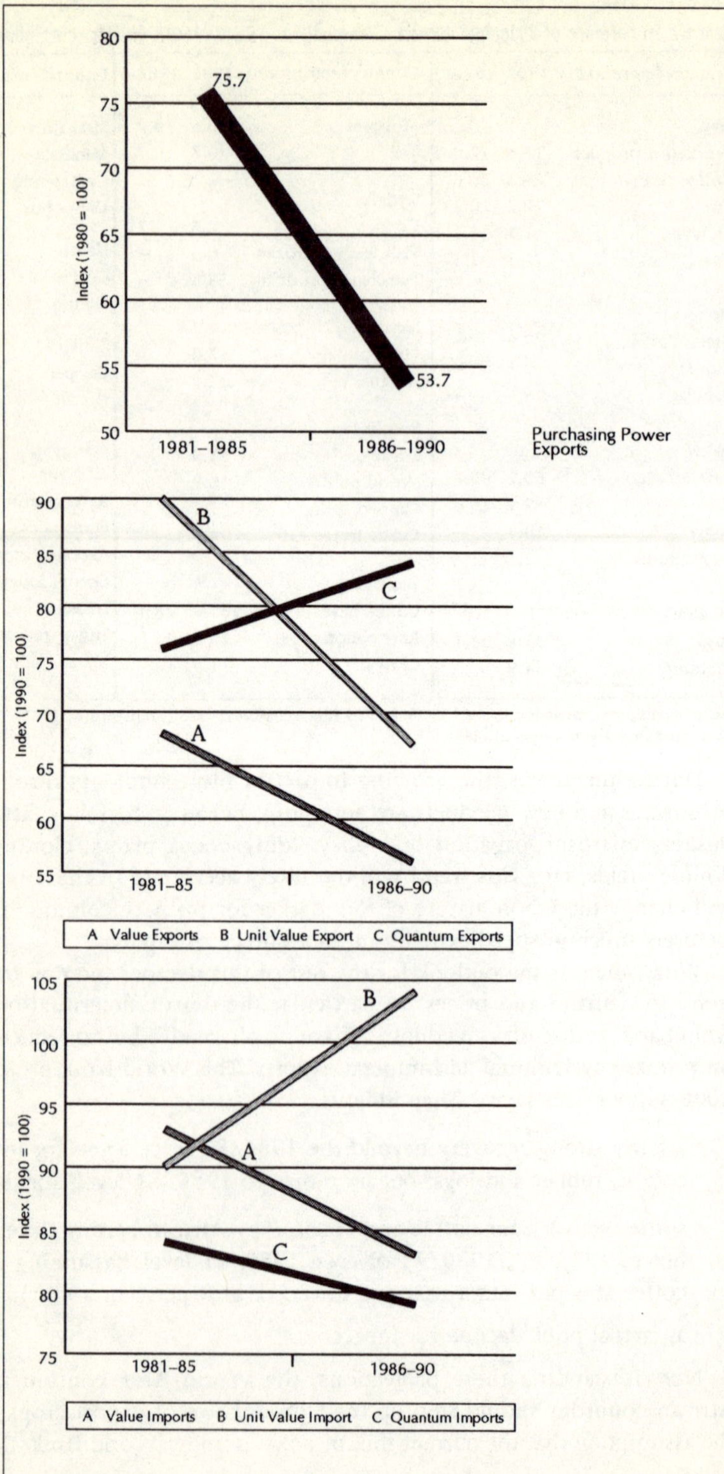

it projects that export volumes for a selected group of commodities (coffee, cotton, tobacco, groundnut oil, cocoa, sugar and tea) in Sub-Saharan Africa will grow on average by some 16 per cent up to the year 2000. It further forecasts a 5 per cent annual growth rate in export earnings.

How realistic is the Bank's assumption that export earnings from these commodities will increase by 5 per cent per annum during the rest of the millennium? The current decline of most export prices and the retracting world market for these commodities certainly appear to contradict the World Bank's projection. Even more important, why cannot the tremendous effort that would be required to increase export production in order to recover the 1980/81 level of revenue in the year 2000 be devoted to transforming Africa's food production? According to the Bank's 1988 forecast of real commodity prices in 1995 and 2000, the aggregate indices for coffee, tea, cocoa, sugar, palm oil, coconut oil, tobacco and cotton, using 1980/81 as the base year, are 60.5 and 70.5, respectively. For coffee alone, the indices are 68.1 and 68.5 respectively, and for cocoa they are 46.4 and 51.3. In other words, a country would need to more than double its cocoa output in order to reach its 1980/81 export earnings in real terms. For the aggregate of products, the required increase in output to achieve the same earnings as in 1980/81 would be 30 per cent. Increased quantities on an already glutted market must necessarily depress prices further. Why not devote the same effort to stimulating African food production? Output would increase by between 30 and 100 per cent and food self-sufficiency could become a reality in spite of the relatively high rate of population growth.

However diversification away from primary commodity production for export, and even within that sector, is the very antithesis of the structural adjustment policies which, under the tutelage of the IMF and the World Bank, the majority of African countries have been implementing for more than a decade. Not surprisingly, therefore, neither the World Bank nor the International Finance Corporation had a single African country among the recipients of loans for export-oriented diversification in the 1980s. To make export production more attractive to farmers, currency devaluation is a major policy instrument in the IMF/World Bank package. So are policies for removing subsidies on food and other essential commodities and policies of import liberalization, sure ways of nipping in the bud any attempts at sustainable local industrialization and food self-sufficiency. Indeed, all the SAP policy instruments exacerbate the openness and external dependence of the African economies.

Equally serious is the lack of effective regional co-operation and of increase in collective self-reliance. In fact, Africa's persistent economic crisis can be said to be due to excessive dependence on foreign markets, foreign goods, foreign factor inputs and even ideas crafted abroad, and too little progress – or none at all – in launching an internally generated process of sustained and sustainable development both at the national and regional levels. Worse still, the international economic environment has been hostile to Sub-Saharan Africa. One of the consequences of the unequal integration of the region with the world economy is that it is always at the receiving end of its inequities and inequalities. And for Sub-Saharan Africa, the global economy means in effect the economy of Western Europe, and particularly the European Community. After all, Africa's contact with the rest of the world was through Western Europe, which is also its neighbour. And even today, the greater part of its international relations

– whether trade, aid and technical assistance or political, social and cultural intercourse – is with Western Europe. This special relationship made possible the Lomé Convention which linked the whole of Sub-Saharan Africa (and the Caribbean and Pacific countries) with the European Community. Yet, in spite of its geographical proximity to Western Europe, its past colonial relations and its post-independence special relationships, Sub-Saharan Africa has been moving from crisis to crisis, its debt burden is excruciating, its commodity markets have virtually collapsed and there is a reverse flow of resources. After more than three decades of independence, Africa's faith in Europe's good intentions to help it get out of the poverty trap has remained unfulfilled. Is it therefore any wonder that alternative strategies are being sought – alternative strategies that will liberate Africa from its dependence syndrome and through diversification wean it from the unenviable monocultural economic system which is its colonial legacy? Should not such alternative strategies put at the centre of their concern regional co-operation and integration, through which Africa could achieve an increasing measure of self-reliance?

Search for Alternative Development Paradigms

An examination of the present socio-economic conditions in Africa, an analysis of the evolution of the African crisis particularly during the past two decades, and an extrapolation of the present trends are enough to force the conclusion of a bleak and unenviable future for Africa – a future of structural crises and permanent emergencies. The World Bank has projected the proportion of people living below the poverty line to fall – in many cases to single-digit figures – in all developing regions except Africa! With 40 to 50 per cent, in some cases even more, of its people living in abject poverty, Africa is almost bound to become synonymous with poverty. What an abhorrent trauma to imagine! How much the more urgent, then, is the imperative of pursuing alternative development paradigms.

The fundamental cause of Africa's recurrent crisis is that it has yet to experience the degree of structural transformation and economic diversification required to move the continent away from inherited colonial economic structures, typified by a vicious interaction between excruciating poverty and abysmally low levels of productivity, in an environment marked by serious deficiencies in basic economic and social infrastructures, most especially the physical capital, research capabilities, technological know-how and human resources development that are indispensable to an integrated and dynamic economy.[7] The low productivity of the African economies, the heavy dependence of domestic production on imports, the failure to diversify both within agriculture and into non-agricultural activities, and the absence of domestic linkages are at the heart of Africa's problems. For example, hardly any African economy has as yet achieved the stage of structural sophistication that enables resources to be shifted fairly easily, depending on changing situations in the world markets, between activities producing for export and those producing goods, including import substitutes, for domestic use.

Thus, as I have often stated, Africa needs fundamental change and transformation, not just adjustment. The change and transformation required are not just narrow, economistic and mechanical ones. They are the fundamental remaking of the polity, economy and society. Nothing less is required to launch the continent on the path of self-sustained and self-reliant development.

The search for an alternative development strategy that would address the structural weaknesses of the African economy and lead to its economic decolonization began in the early 1970s. It culminated in the adoption of the Lagos Plan of Action (LPA) by African Heads of State and Government in April 1980. Among the precursors of the LPA was the ECA's *Revised Framework of Principles for the Implementation of the New International Economic Order*, which came out in 1976.

The *Revised Framework* outlines an alternative strategy built around four pillars: self-reliance, self-sustainment, the democratization of the development process, and a fair and just distribution of the fruits of development. Self-reliance is defined as

- allowing domestic needs and demand to determine the direction of development, economic growth and patterns of output;
- increasing substitution of domestic factor inputs for external factor inputs; and
- increasing the participation of the mass of the people in the production and consumption of the social product.

Self-sustainment means the promotion of mutually supportive and reinforcing structures – with cumulative and multiplication effects – so that the whole system can unleash its own internal dynamics.[8] Such a development strategy is inward-looking rather than externally oriented. It does not make a sacred cow of foreign-exchange earnings and, therefore, does not attach too much importance to foreign trade, particularly the type of foreign trade with which we are familiar in Africa, as the basis for initiating development. It puts the domestic market, including sub-regional and regional markets, at the heart of the development effort. And when it emphasizes indigenous factor inputs, it means African scientists and technologists, African entrepreneurs, indigenous analysts and distributors and indigenous technology. In the new development strategy, external trade is seen as supplementary in character, not as constituting the heart of our development effort.[9]

The LPA carried the argument further and put forward a blueprint of self-reliance, self-sustainment, democratic development and political and economic empowerment. The failure of African governments to translate these ideas into operational programmes and implement them faithfully is one of the major underlying causes of the continent's persistent crisis. The regional strategies and policy frameworks that had been conceived in the 1980s were all too readily abandoned in the face of the crisis and in the rush for quick-disbursing foreign aid and balance-of-payments support. Instead of undertaking the fundamental restructuring of their economies, African leaders opted for a quick fix, for a programme that guaranteed them the almighty foreign exchange and allowed external debt rescheduling. The acceptance of structural adjustment programmes was a condition for financial support and debt rescheduling from the World Bank, the IMF and bilateral donors and creditors.

Thus, instead of putting in place policies and programmes catering predominantly for internal demand and increasing substitution of indigenous for foreign factor inputs; instead of promoting democratic development and rigorously investing in human beings through education, health and manpower development; and instead of unleashing the energies of the people through popular participation in policy-making and implementation, governmental policy became glued to domestic demand 'management' (in the sense of 'belt-tightening'), incessant currency devaluation, import liberalization, privatization of state and parastatal enterprises and freeing of prices. In the course of all this the state itself became privatized.

My own views about the relevance of structural adjustment programmes to the fundamental causes of persistent underdevelopment in Africa are too well known to need further elucidation. As I have argued again and again, the monetarist approach of SAPs (the grand triplet of which is fiscal stabilization, monetary stabilization and exchange-rate depreciation) ignores the basic structural rigidities that are at the heart of Africa's economic disequilibria. By pursuing the symptoms of Africa's persistent crisis, the underlying factors of the malaise have been neglected. As I summarized the matter in a paper which I presented to the Royal Society of Canada,[10] a satisfactory functioning of the policy instruments of SAPs is predicated upon competitive production and exchange and a well-developed institutional framework. Markets for products and factors of production are assumed to be competitive and resources perfectly mobile. Also assumed are well-developed financial institutions and capital and money markets. However, the reality of the African economies exhibits the obvious absence of these conditions. Marked imperfections, with significant monopolistic and oligopolistic structures, technical rigidities, structurally induced shortages, underdeveloped financial structures and the existence of a dominant non-monetized and subsistence sector, invalidate the assumptions of the competitive model in Africa.

SAPs have not led to sustainable development, nor have they even succeeded in meeting their limited objectives of internal and external equilibrium. Nonetheless, they have become, like all received doctrines, the new orthodoxies, propelled and propagated as gospel truths, even after their fallacy has been exposed by running counter to the overwhelming mass of available evidence and empirical verification. This growing gap between theory in the form of received doctrines and orthodoxies, on the one hand, and empirical analysis, on the other, led Nobel Laureate Leontief to lament, more than twenty years ago, the tendency of economics to become concentrated on theoretical constructions to the exclusion of facts, while on the other hand facts accumulated but were not organized as theory; there was an urgent need, he argued, to fill with relevant empirical data the 'empty boxes' of economic theory.[11] Nowhere is this more true today than in the area of development economics exemplified by the experience of the SAPs. There is, therefore, an imperative need for an alternative development paradigm which derives from evidence and empirical verification and analysis – and not from ideology.

Indeed, given the experience of Africa under SAPs during the past decade or so, I am tempted to agree with Simon Jenkins' judgement in a recent article:[12]

> it is in the nature of a novice profession to oversell itself to politicians. It will also tend to claim that bad decisions were a perversion of its advice. . . . If economic advisers were members of a professional body there would surely have been hearings and strikings off: economics shares with architecture a belief that its blunders are due to the idiocy of its clients.

While Simon Jenkins' article will certainly displease the neo-classical economists of 1818 H Street NW, Washington DC, he has nevertheless captured the truth behind SAPs and the Bretton Woods institutions in their impact on Africa.

Collective Self-Reliance

If individual African countries are facing crises of unprecedented proportions and need fundamental restructuring in order to overcome them, the region as a whole is in equally grave condition. It is without doubt the most fragmented region in the world, containing a large number of minuscule states at low levels of income. Of 51 countries, 23 have populations of less than 5 million, including 10 with populations of less than one million. Fourteen are landlocked and 28 are classified as least developed countries – the wretched of the earth. The structural characteristics of African economies, the uneven spatial distribution of population and considerable physical limitations have militated against the expansion of national as well as regional markets for products and factors, and intensified the African countries' dependence on the outside world.

As already noted, the African economies have undergone very little transformation during the last thirty years. One of the reasons, which we have not yet mentioned, is that economic and social transformation can be achieved only where the potential for economies of scale exists. The optimal use of natural resources, the viability of industrial structures, the establishment of appropriate institutional frameworks and the build-up of infrastructure, both at the national and inter-country levels, have been severely limited by the size and structure of the nation states inherited at independence.

As I have already proposed publicly, our leaders, governments and people should have undertaken a fundamental restructuring of the post-colonial states. We would then have today, instead of 51 states with varying degrees of internal strife, border disputes, unviable economies and political independence, some one to two dozen capable of standing up and being counted, economically and politically. We would also have a manageable number of conflicting interests to resolve, and we could thus be light years ahead in our regional integration. The founding fathers, in their wisdom, decided that the game was not worth the candle because it was fraught with too many dangers. But the only way open is to overcome the restrictions and constraints that fragmentation has imposed, through rigorous and relentless promotion of regional co-operation and integration.

True enough, experience of regional co-operation in Africa has been disappointing. But there can be no doubt that multinational co-operation and integration is a necessary condition of the effective pursuit of national socio-economic transformation. As I said to the ECA Conference of Ministers at its February 1977 session,[13]

> there is no viable alternative to intra-African co-operation. Indeed, it is a mistaken belief to regard economic co-operation among African States not as a *conditio sine qua non* for the achievement of determined national socio-economic goals, but as an 'extra' to be given thought to after the process of development is well advanced.

Unfortunately, one of the effects of SAPs is that they make regional integration and co-operation extremely difficult, if not impossible. In addition, the purpose of integration has been seen primarily in terms of the development of intra-African trade through the removal of institutional barriers. However, it has now been generally realized that a programme of collective self-reliance that rests primarily on the establishment of a preferential trading area through the removal of the formal constraints on trade is inadequate because the effects of such removal are long-term rather than short-term. In any case, given the low level of production of goods that would be tradeable in African markets, the volume of intra-African trade cannot but be small in spite of the removal of trade barriers. Hence the growing shift to production-focused integration.

Accordingly, the integration of the African economies and the attainment of full regional collective self-reliance should involve six mutually interdependent dimensions, namely,

(i) the integration of the physical, institutional and social infrastructure;
(ii) the integration of production structures;
(iii) the integration of the African markets;
(iv) the resolution of inter-country conflicts and the prevention of acts of political destabilization by outsiders;
(v) ensuring stability and security – at nation-state, inter-country and personal levels; and
(vi) the creation of an enabling environment for initiative and enterprise, and for across-the-border factor movements.

In other words, success in the integration process will be demonstrated by our ability to construct inter-state roads and railways, to boost inter-state trade, to interconnect electric grids, to exploit, jointly, natural resources wherever they exist, to set up multinational joint ventures in key economic areas (transport, energy and industry) benefiting from economies of scale, to operate cost-effective regional and sub-regional institutions in the fields of science and technology, agricultural research and higher education, and to create currency convertibility with a view ultimately to a single currency as a means of payment throughout the continent. Briefly, the economic restructuring of our states will result from our ability to exercise a common, collective sovereignty in the management of our economy.

Africa and the International Community: Permanent Underdog or Effective Partner?

Africa bears the scars of a long history of spoliation and deprivation, of the ravages of slave trade and foreign aggression and of both political and economic injustices. It has had an even more dismal history since independence. The continent has come to connote crisis, decay and bad governance, lack of human rights and corruption. The imperial notion of Africa as the 'Dark Continent' has returned with a vengeance. There is profound disillusion. In the chanceries of the North, Africa has become a basket case, a permanent *mezzogiorno*.

The choice before Africa is therefore straightforward. It can continue the business-as-usual approach – the historical trends scenario – or it can make a sharp break with its unenviable past and crisis-ridden present and pursue the path of fundamental change and transformation in the political and socio-economic spheres. The challenge that confronts Africa is not between *either* the world market *or* African collective self-reliance. It is rather a struggle to avoid being completely marginalized, if not totally forgotten, and to undertake the herculean task required to launch and sustain the process of transformation so that it can emerge eventually as a true and respected player in the international economy. At present, accounting for only 2 per cent of world trade, Africa is economically insignificant and negligible. Therefore, it has to choose between remaining the economic underdog of the world or evolving to become a true partner.

I have stated in a much quoted passage what future lies ahead of Africa if it persists in pursuing the path of adjustment, monoculturalism, commodity export dependence and an externally oriented and open economy – the historical trends scenario. Put bluntly, such a future will be horrendous.

It therefore becomes imperative for Africa to design for itself another future – the normative development scenario – which enables the region (i) to internalize the development process in the spirit of collective self-reliance and self-sustainment; (ii) to substitute indigenous factor inputs for foreign factor inputs; (iii) to launch a democratically determined process of development so as to facilitate popular participation to the fullest extent possible; (iv) to ensure economic and political empowerment and an equitable distribution of income; and, (v) to strengthen and intensify regional and sub-regional co-operation and integration.

Notes

1. Adebayo Adedeji, 'Promoting Economic and Social Rights within Nations; Thoughts on African Development'. Lecture delivered at the Second Ambassadors' Colloquium on Human Rights in Africa (Lagos, 21 April 1991).
2. W. Arthur Lewis, *The Theory of Economic Growth* (London: George Allen and Unwin, 1955), pp. 225–6.
3. 'Sapping Aid: Aid Money Diverted from Poor to Service Debt', *Economic Justice Update*, No. 5, 12/92 (Inter-Church Coalition on Africa).
4. Stephen R. Lewis Jr, 'Africa's Trade and the World Economy', in Robert J. Berg and Jennifer S. Whitaker (eds), *Strategies for African Development* (Berkeley, CA: University of California Press, 1986), p. 476.
5. Michael Barratt Brown and Pauline Tiffen, *Short Changed: Africa and World Trade* (London: Pluto Press, 1992); pp. 19–23.
6. World Bank, *Price Prospects for Major Primary Commodities, 1988–2000* (2 vols, Washington DC, 1989).
7. OAU/ECA, *Africa's Submission to the Special Session of the United Nations General Assembly on Africa's Economic and Social Crisis* (Addis Ababa, 1986).
8. Adebayo Adedeji, *Towards a Dynamic African Economy* (London: Frank Cass, 1989), pp. 321–50.
9. *Ibid.*, p. 330.
10. *International Symposium on Constraints to Freedom of Scholarship and Science*, organized by the Royal Society of Canada, Ottawa, November 1991.
11. See Wassily Leontief's presidential address to the American Economic Association, 'Theoretical Assumptions and Non-Observed Facts', *American Economic Review* 61, 1 (1971).
12. *The Times* of London, 3 February 1993, p. 16.
13. Adedeji, *Towards a Dynamic African Economy*, p. 235.

6

ELLIOT BERG

Reappraising Export Prospects & Regional Trade Arrangements

Introduction

Confronting the question of world markets or collective self-reliance is like embracing a big balloon: the surface of the issue is so large that it is hard to grasp manageable pieces. The issue is posed in terms of broad strategy alternatives: should countries of Sub-Saharan Africa (SSA) concentrate on trade with existing, non-regional partners or focus on regional trade? But the answer, of course, has to be that both are needed.

Almost everybody who thinks about these issues agrees on several basic points. African economies are small and cannot do without trade, except at extremely high cost. Effective, flexible export sectors are required to provide productive employment and foreign exchange for imports of vital consumer goods (food in much of the continent), inputs and capital goods. Dependence on primary commodity exports that have low price and income elasticities and formidable competitors is a misfortune, and diversification into more promising lines of production is highly desirable. Regional integration within SSA can be a source of mutually beneficial increases in trade, investment, and growth. So the necessity for both world trade and collective self-reliance (regional integration) is universally acknowledged on a general level. The interesting divergences, and the real issues, are about the proper mix or balance of policies, and about the details.

Two sets of issues are at the centre of debate. The first concerns the role of traditional exports. Is it right to encourage their production, as general trade liberalization tends to do, or should more discriminatory policies be put in place that favour non-traditional exports and other growth points? What priority should old exports be given in research and other investment, relative to new exports and import substitutes?

The second set of issues concerns strategies of regional economic co-operation. Market integration through sub-regional trade liberalization within the present preferential trade groupings is the prevailing approach. Such groupings are supposed to be the central instrument of collective self-reliance. Yet regional trade remains small and the approach is widely criticized by its partisans and also by free traders who urge general import liberalization with few or no regional trade preferences.

What Role for Traditional Exports?

Prevailing policies in many countries, including those following formal adjustment programmes, stress exchange-rate realignment and reduction of policy biases against exports – reduced taxation on export crops, deregulation, and privatization of export-related institutions. These policies are widely criticized as being too indiscriminate, too general: they encourage across-the-board expansion of SSA's current export bundle.[1]

The fallacy of composition: how crippling?

Critics give various reasons to explain why indiscriminate export promotion policies are a bad idea. As is well-known, when an exporting country has market power in a given commodity (indicated by a significant share of world exports), demand for this export is not perfectly elastic; as the country increases its sales abroad, the price will fall. Its export earnings may be higher with less output rather than more. Export taxes are appropriate in these cases.

But the major criticism has to do with the 'fallacy of composition' argument: that although individual African countries produce small market shares in most commodities and are therefore price takers (changes in their output do not affect world prices), yet if all African countries expand exports indiscriminately, as urged by the World Bank and the International Monetary Fund, they will cause world prices of many traditional exports to fall. Marginal export earnings will increase at a lower rate than the increase in export volumes, and may actually decline.

The issues raised here have deep roots. They are related to the debates about elasticity pessimism that marked the earliest thinking about development: whether exports could be a sustainable and adequate engine of growth for developing countries. That debate was mainly about the potentials of exports of manufactured goods. Indeed the pessimists, including such notable figures as Sir Arthur Lewis, lost much of the argument because they underestimated these potentials. But they also overlooked the extent to which developing country primary products were competitive with developed country primary products and hence capable of winning greater shares in the developed country markets.[2]

The African case is different, not least because its industrial base is so small and its exports are composed so overwhelmingly (90–95 per cent) of primary products. Moreover, tropical beverages, which have particularly bleak prospects, make up well over half of total agricultural exports. It is useful to review the debate as it arose in the 1980s in relation to SSA.

The 1981 World Bank report on Africa argued that for most African exports there were no serious demand constraints on expansion. The report stated: 'Africa's share of world trade in most commodities could be increased with relatively small effects on prices.'[3] This hypothesis was challenged by Martin Godfrey, among others, as a pure example of the fallacy of composition. In a 1984 article, Godfrey noted that for any commodity in which SSA's share of world exports was greater than world price elasticity of demand, marginal revenues from output expansion would be negative.[4] Using 1982 data, he showed that this was the case for coffee and cocoa: a 1 per cent increase in coffee exports led to a 1.14 per cent fall in world price; a 1 per cent rise in cocoa exports caused a 2.17 per cent drop in the world price. Expanding coffee and cocoa exports would therefore induce a decline in SSA export revenues.

Sugar and tea, according to Godfrey, were on the margin: their market shares and demand elasticities were closely matched. Although no elasticity estimates were available for groundnut oil and sisal, he argued that the large SSA share of world exports of these commodities made them unlikely candidates for revenue-raising volume expansion. He concluded that broad recommendations to expand exports were wrong, and diversification to high-income-elasticity products was essential.

Two questions have to be raised about his analysis. First, is it true, in the sense that the numbers are credible and the underlying analytical framework is right? Second, to the extent that it is true, what policy implications follow?

There are a few problems with the price elasticity–market share measure. First, market shares change significantly over fairly short time periods. Between 1980 and 1987, for example, the African share in total world exports of palm kernels rose from 71 to 84 per cent, groundnut oil from 24 to 67 per cent, and tobacco from 9 to 13 per cent. The sisal share meanwhile fell from 47 to 33 per cent, coffee from 22.2 to 18.8 per cent, and groundnuts from 13 to 6 per cent.[5]

Also, it is not always easy to define the market in question. For example, groundnut oil and palm kernels should probably be considered a part of the oilseeds market, and sisal a part of the wrapping materials market. In both cases, the wider markets are integrated and competitive, so we should expect price elasticities of demand for each of the component commodities to be above those normally cited.

But these are small points. There can be no doubt about the bottom line: most studies find price elasticities of demand to be low for the main African exports – for example, around -0.2 for cocoa, coffee, and cotton, and around -0.4 for tea, sugar, and groundnuts.[6] So declining marginal revenues with expansion of exports is possible even for a single producing country with large market share, such as Ghana and Côte d'Ivoire with cocoa. Expansion in one country can also lead to welfare losses in other producing countries. And where African countries together have large market shares, these negative impacts are accentuated.

The negative short-run results of cocoa export expansion have been underscored in several recent studies. One analysis of African cocoa policies uses an econometric model of the world cocoa market to estimate impacts of higher African cocoa production due to structural adjustment policies.[7] Based on counterfactual simulations (no-reform scenarios), the authors conclude that, if there had been no adjustment in Ghana and Nigeria (and hence no resulting higher cocoa output from those countries), world cocoa production in 1989/90 would have been 6 per cent lower, world cocoa prices 24 per cent higher, and the value of cocoa production worldwide 17 per cent higher.

The Ghanaian economy reaped substantial gains from its expansion of cocoa exports induced by the adjustment programme. Without this expansion, the country would have been even more devastated than it was in 1982; cocoa production, for example, would have been at half its 1989/90 level. Incomes would have been much lower and the budget deficit unsustainable. But other SSA producers lost. The study suggests that there was a 15 per cent drop in their welfare caused by the higher Ghanaian exports, though Ghana (and Nigeria) were small factors in the cocoa price declines of the 1980s, compared to the expanded output in Côte d'Ivoire, Malaysia, Indonesia, and Brazil stemming from high prices in the 1970s.[8]

These results are not surprising, given the low price elasticity of demand for cocoa and the fact that Africa is the world's major producer. But the applicability of these results to other crops is dubious, and even for cocoa the implications are less ominous when account is taken of longer-term effects. The 1990 IFPRI study cited earlier shows that price declines following a production increase are substantial only for cocoa and coffee, and short-term marginal revenues fall only in the case of cocoa. This means that, even if domestic costs of expanding output of cocoa are zero, expansion would be undesirable. And coffee output (in the short run) should be increased only if expected marginal costs are less than half of expected world prices – an unlikely prospect, given world price prospects.

In the longer run (five years in the IFPRI model), taking into account worldwide supply and demand responses to lower prices, the outlook is better, though still grim for cocoa and not happy for coffee. The price declines are smaller and output growth results in marginal revenue increases for all crops, but especially for sugar, cotton, and groundnuts. The results for cocoa and coffee are due mainly to output contraction by non-African competitors.

Policy Implications for the Agricultural Sector

What policy prescriptions flow from these analyses? A universal recommendation is that greater attention be given to export diversification, notably by moving into higher stages of processing, into manufactured goods generally, and into crops (and minerals) with higher income elasticities of demand.[9] We consider only agricultural exports here.

Economically efficient diversification should be (and indeed is) high on national policy agendas in SSA, and progress is being made in many countries. Several issues should be addressed, however. First, to what extent should traditional exports be discouraged, actively or by neglect? Second, is there a case for a contrary position on traditional exports (especially beverages) that calls for aggressive African expansion of output to drive out competitors? And, finally, how much of a role should governments play in picking new exports for encouragement?[10]

Discouragement of traditional exports?

A frequent recommendation is to restrict production.[11] Specifically, this can mean the imposition of an appropriate tax on these exports. But in many statements broader restrictions are suggested, notably a shift of research and investment emphasis away from traditional exports. This seems to be the case in the Economic Commission for Africa's proposed alternative strategy put forward in 1989.[12]

Numerous problems bedevil this recommendation:

- It is too indiscriminate. Although thinkable for cocoa and coffee, given the nature of their markets and their prospects, its appropriateness even for tea is open to question, and for cotton, groundnuts, and sugar, among others, it has little technical justification;[13]

- It is too pessimistic. After all, income growth in developing and developed countries will continue to increase demand for primary products. Also, anti-trade policies in industrial countries may change as world trade liberalization proceeds. But, most important, non-African primary product producers are unlikely to continue output expansion in the face of predicted poor market prospects;

- It is at the same time excessively risky. If any major producer restricts output it is possible or even likely that others will increase production and prices will fall anyway. The restricting country will suffer reduced export revenues and lose market share. Recognition of this evident problem leads to parallel recommendations for collective action among producers, presumably commodity agreements that would impose export quotas.[14] But the prospects for effective agreements of this kind are slim. Aside from the long history of broken agreements in every commodity, the inability to maintain the recent coffee agreement, which had strong consuming country support, is a strong indicator of just how unlikely these agreements are;

- Many proposals to diversify fail to emphasize the need to intensify research and development efforts in traditional crops so as to at least maintain competitiveness and market shares in areas of established comparative advantage. After all, land and labour productivity may be higher in Malaysia than anywhere else, but West African production costs are nonetheless lower.[15] If SSA's traditional exports are discouraged by macroeconomic, trade, fiscal and expenditure policies, the main beneficiaries will be non-regional competitors – Malaysia, Indonesia, and Brazil in the case of cocoa.

Rather than blanket proposals to restrict production and export of traditional exports, much more differentiated policies are called for. For crops like sugar, groundnuts, cotton, sisal and tobacco, considerable scope exists for expansion of output; external demand constraints are slight. For tree crops (particularly cocoa and coffee), the 'orthodox' package seems on the mark:

- Make sure the macroeconomic prices are right, notably the exchange rate. If they are wrong, it is hard to achieve competitiveness via other policies;

- Impose 'optimal' export taxes on countries with large market shares;[16]

- Work hard to raise productivity and reduce marketing costs. With productivity increases, output can grow slightly (enough to maintain market share as demand rises with income growth in consuming countries), and at the same time resources will be liberated for alternative production. Any increases in countries with substantial shares of world output should come via cost reduction not area expansion;

- Do not automatically reject production expansion. Even when production expansion reduces world prices, it still may pay even a big producer to expand. In deciding whether this is worthwhile, marginal costs of expansion have to be compared not with future world prices but with future marginal revenues.

A case for predatory pricing?

Instead of discouraging output of cocoa and coffee, it is possible to conceive of a different, opposite, approach: African producers could expand output and drive down prices with the intention of squeezing out competitors. For countries that have limited alternatives for using the land, labour, and capital now absorbed in cocoa and coffee production, it may be preferable to follow a predatory policy of this kind.

It also may be feasible. In the more developed of the competitor countries (Brazil and Malaysia), alternatives for the use of resources engaged in cocoa and coffee production are more abundant; their crop supply curves, especially with respect to downward movements in world prices, are more elastic than in West Africa. A sustained period of low prices with little expectation of improvement would probably shrink the Malaysian and Brazilian cocoa industries severely. Indonesia is a different story. It is the lowest-cost world producer, has a small share of the market, and considerable scope for expansion.

Whether predatory pricing is desirable is another matter. West African producers would benefit unequally. Ghana and Nigeria are now lowest-cost producers, and would survive, though their trees are old. Cameroon production would probably disappear. Côte d'Ivoire would survive, perhaps thrive, if its exchange-rate situation were improved.

More important, the industry remains contestable, and were prices to rise significantly new producers would emerge. So perennially low prices would be the price for this policy. And finally, it would be unwise to accept this path of despair without much greater effort to diversify agricultural production and exports, and to exploit unfolding potentials in manufactured exports.

What kind of role for public policy?

Here there is much consensus. Government has a major role to play in developing a vital export sector, much of it related to government's general role in creating a suitable enabling environment. Investment in infrastructure and in building human capacity is part of it. Agricultural recovery can be speeded up by better incentives, and by strengthened agricultural services and institutions – from extension and credit agencies to export marketing entities. It is now widely recognized that a dynamic manufacturing export sector demands, above all else, ready access to inputs.

Differences in emphasis and priorities persist. The alternative framework put forward by the Economic Commission for Africa proposes multiple exchange rates and selective subsidy policies, for example, and other measures indicating a substantial role for the state in picking winners. Others justify similar kinds of policies on the grounds that smallholders may be unaware of market prospects for particular exports.[17]

Two broad perspectives can be defined. One favours indiscriminate market signals as the key factor in determining patterns of economic activity. This does not mean 'no government', but rather government policies that are relatively neutral as between exports and import-substitutes and between different kinds of exports. It means a set of signals that are largely market-determined. According to the second view, the state should determine more directly, by selective incentives and disincentives, priority activities and a pattern of imports and exports that is judged likely to meet economic and social objectives.

The right mix of these policy orientations depends on many factors, among which the organizational capacity of the state is probably the most important. It is highly improbable that weak, soft states will be able to maintain an economically efficient differentiation in incentive arrangements and to avoid capture by the firms they are helping or hurting.

That is one reason to fear discriminatory (selective) export promotion and other trade policies. Another, of great importance, is that innovation in production and exports is not likely to be developed by economists or civil servants. Private entrepreneurs will do it, and given a chance they will discover opportunities that nobody has ever thought of.

Government can help, by filling some information gaps and by assuring the right enabling environment. But when governments engage in selective trade interventions, they run risks of unintended negative consequences. Bangladesh offers a good case in point on the import side.[18]

The Bangladesh case

Until the mid-1980s, imports of agricultural inputs were closely regulated in Bangladesh.[19] In the mid-1980s, the government allowed private import of any make or model diesel engine, but only for non-agricultural purposes. The duty was 50 per cent. Importers of diesel engines for irrigation paid only 15 per cent duty, but Ministry of Agriculture approval was needed. Importers began bringing in low-cost Chinese engines, which were a quarter of the price of existing Japanese makes; these took over the non-agricultural market. Using this opening, farmers began buying them, even though it was illegal to use such 'non-approved' engines for irrigation.

The spread of liberalization made this evasion unnecessary by late 1988. Farmers were given duty-free access to the cheap Chinese engines and pumps and to imports in general. Also, restrictions on private installation of wells for irrigation were removed. The cost of shallow tubewell irrigation fell to 60 per cent of the (subsidized) prices offered by the government agricultural agency. Inputs of great diversity and range appeared on the input markets, such as bigger and smaller equipment, lighter pumps, and plastic pipes. The result: irrigated acreage expanded at record rates – 3 per cent a year in the late 1980s, twice as fast as in the past.

African cases

Similar stories exist on the export side in Africa. In Niger, in the mid-1970s, 300,000 tons of groundnut production – the country's main export – disappeared because of disease and other factors. In a few years farmers and traders came up with a substitute export – cowpeas, which found a ready market in Nigeria. Yet a search of planning documents and experts' studies in the 1960s and 1970s gives no hint that cowpea exports to Nigeria had such promise. In fact, private traders had to develop the new export channel illicitly, going around a government monopoly.

And before 1983, no development plan document, no World Bank study, referred at all to privately organized smallholder commercial production of rice in Mauritania. Yet in less than five years a wholly new group of private rice growers emerged along the lower Senegal River and produced some 80,000 tons annually, far more than had ever been produced by the existing, highly structured rice sector. Nor had anybody in Madagascar predicted a few years ago that there might be jobs and profits in crocodile ranching for export.

These are only a few examples. The beauty of a neutral set of incentives is that it allows the really key actors to find opportunities that reflect true prices, not prices distorted by overvalued or administratively manipulated exchange rates and accompanying systems of quotas and licences. Sustainable economic growth in SSA, and genuine self-reliance, are unlikely to come otherwise.

Are Preferential Trading Blocs Right for Africa?

Trade expansion within Africa is central to the achievement of collective self-reliance. The main approach being pursued to achieve this goal is market integration by the creation of preferential trade blocs, the well-known economic communities of which the most significant are the 16-member Economic Community of West African States (ECOWAS); the 7-member West African Economic Community or CEAO; the Central African Customs Union (UDEAC, with 5 member states); the Economic Community of Great Lakes States (CEPGL, 3 members); and the Preferential Trade Area of Eastern and Southern Africa (PTA, 18 members).

The desirability of closer regional economic integration by greater intra-African trade and other means is universally acclaimed in Africa and among most outsiders concerned with the continent's problems. No other idea has had such long and broad-based support among the continent's political leaders, officials, and intellectuals.[20] It is a rallying cry of African and donor organizations alike. The World Bank's 1989 *Long-Term Perspective Study* gave it strong support. And the Economic Commission for Africa states that 'as envisaged in the Lagos Plan of Action, Africa should aim at the establishment of an African Economic Community by the year 2000.'[21] The ECA urges removal of trade barriers and greater roles for the regional trade associations; agreement on 'rationalized product specialization to reduce competition among countries of the same subregion' and 'avoidance of unnecessary duplication of large scale industries by establishing and harmonizing subregional industries'.

A paradox quickly arises. The economic advantages of preferential trading arrangements that will create wider regional markets seem plausible and unambiguous, and the apparent political support for them is very wide. Yet there is little growth of regional trade and the past is littered with failed integration schemes. And the analytical foundations of the case for regional market integration have been attacked from widely different points on the ideological spectrum.

There can be little dispute about the record. After 10–20 years of existence, the intra-group trade of these African market integration communities remains a very small share of their total trade: at the beginning of the 1990s, it was 9 per cent in ECOWAS, 10 per cent in CEAO, under 4 per cent in UDEAC, under 1 per cent in CEPGL, and about 5.5 per cent in the PTA.[22] Experience in developing regions outside of Africa is not much different. Many of the 20-odd recent developing country regional integration schemes that can be identified have broken up, and almost all have experienced stagnating or declining intra-group trade.

In two respects, African integration efforts have been less successful than those elsewhere in the developing world. They have had more explicit goals of collective self-reliance, and yet dependence on external trade has increased since the mid-1960s, which has not happened in other regions.[23] And recorded trade between member countries of most of the African trade groupings expanded less than did member country trade with non-member African countries.

What went wrong? One widely held opinion is that it is all due to deficient political leadership and lack of political will. But this is a dubious or at least an incomplete explanation. After all, these preferential trade blocs have collapsed or stalled everywhere in the developing world, regardless of the dedication and commitment of political élites. Political will is very much a matter of costs and benefits. If the trade-enhancing organizations failed to deliver the expected benefits, or brought unacceptable costs, evaporation of political will is not surprising. This is closer to the real reason for poor past performance on integration.

Criticisms of Regional Trade Arrangements

The African economic communities are involved in a wide range of integration-related activities, from regional investment programmes to projects for the harmonization and simplification of customs procedures. But their main focus is on regional trade. They are essentially preferential trade areas, engaged in encouragement of intra-regional trade.

Doubts about the suitability of African preferential trade schemes arise from three directions. First, the empirical record reveals that they do not set into motion the forces for growth that might be expected from *a priori* analysis. Secondly, some critics fault them for their timidity, the fact that they lead at best to marginal changes and because they increase inequality and foreign dependence. Free-trade-oriented economists, finally, see them as having marginal impacts at best and as basically distortionary – inefficient import-substitution vehicles on a regional scale. Let us consider each in turn.

Minimal growth impacts

The sources of growth that the trade blocs were and are supposed to unleash have not emerged. Growth was supposed to come from five main sources:

- Larger markets would allow import substitution on a regional level, which is more efficient than national-level import replacement and might permit better exploitation of dynamic comparative advantage;
- Increased competition would take place within the preferential trade bloc, as producers of each country took market share from inefficient producers of the same commodity in other countries of the group ('trade creation'). Specialization, economies of scale and scope, and 'learning' would bring increased productivity, lower costs, and increased competitiveness;
- In the industrial sector, 'training effects' would occur. This is a variety of learning effect. It arises from the fact that it may be easier to compete within regional markets than in world markets. The opening up of industrial sectors to regional competition could prepare them for the stronger winds of world competition later;

- Labour and capital would be used more efficiently because of freer cross-border movements of productive factors; and
- Investment, both local and foreign, would be stimulated by the bigger markets.

In the event, not many of the expected advantages were realized. Intra-group trade stagnated. Factors flowed no more freely than before. Investment, for exogenous reasons, shrank, and private foreign investment all but disappeared in much of SSA.

Many explanatory factors exist, among them structural obstacles (for example, the dominance of primary products in output and exports, similar production structures and high transaction costs in regional trade), divergent macroeconomic policies, and widespread controls over foreign trade. Trade liberalization was not, in fact, much implemented. Three aspects merit special mention.

- The preferential trade groups tended to be protectionist; average protection tended to be greater than before, reducing external competition. At the same time governments were unwilling to allow genuine trade creation – region-wide competition that might have led to replacement of less efficient regional producers. African governments, like most elsewhere, showed no willingness to sacrifice local industry (and domestic jobs) in the name of regional integration.
- Much of the trade that did result from creation of the trade groupings failed to lead to efficiency gains via greater specialization, exploitation of scale economies, and learning. Market size within the trade blocs was still too small to allow many scale economies. Integration by particular products and firms (which is the way it was done) was not designed to stimulate competition and hence efficiency. To the contrary, intra-regional competition was systematically excluded. The result was little industrial learning of a kind that could be transferable to external markets.
- The great disparities in economic size and levels of development that exist in SSA exacerbated the deeply vexing problem of unequal distribution of costs and benefits, which plagues all preferential trading arrangements. The more advanced, richer states benefited more, and more quickly, than the poorer states. The latter found their national industrial structures threatened or their fiscal stability shaken, given their dependence on customs duties. So they had to be compensated. But compensation arrangements are hard to work out, reduce the benefits to the advanced members and to the group as a whole, and tend to undermine the economic efficiency rationale that is the main economic justification for the creation of preferential trade areas in the first place.

Trade blocs are too timid, inequitable, and dependence-augmenting

This criticism comes, loosely speaking, from the left. Ironically, the ECA is its chief advocate. The market-integration model is attacked for its modest ambition and excessively market-determined character. Even if regional trade liberalization worked, it could not be a major engine of growth; to go from 5–6 per cent of total trade to 10–12 per cent, which is the most that could be expected, would not change much. And even if it did, it would be undesirable. The pattern of growth it entails brings accentuated disparities between richer and poorer states, favours foreign capital, and leaves the economic structures of the region unchanged.[24]

These critics recommend an alternative approach that puts trade-liberalizing market integration on the back burner and urges instead that priority be given to regionalized investments in infrastructure and industry.[25] The ECA's 1989 strategy statement, the 'African Alternative Framework' paper, does not say much on this matter. However, in setting priorities for 'the production dimensions of regional collective self-reliance', it puts intra-African trade in third place, after regional food security and 'production of intermediate and capital goods, especially iron and steel, machine tools, fertilizers, chemicals and pharmaceuticals, building materials, as well as agricultural, transport and construction equipment'.[26]

General trade liberalization is better

Another avenue of attack on the African approaches to trade expansion via preferential regional trade blocs is used by market-oriented critics. These critics judge that there is too little growth potential in regional trade liberalization, and that in practice the trade groups are too inward-looking, basing their hopes for growth mainly on increased protection and on moving import-substitution to the regional level.[27]

A recent World Bank paper levels a broadside attack on preferential trade blocs not only in Africa but in Latin America as well.[28]

Experience with regional integration between two or more developing countries leaves little doubt that these countries cannot expect big gains by integrating themselves. Integration schemes among developing countries, benign at best, have in many cases been positively harmful. In the benign cases, the potential for trade expansion among the countries simply was not there. In the harmful ones, the arrangements themselves became instruments of protection.

The fact that none of the African trading groups account for as much as 10 per cent of total exports underscores the harsh conclusion: significant growth of exports has to come from external trade. This means that the highest priority in any integration efforts has to be given to trade creation, not diversion. It implies the removal of obstacles to trade in general – moving toward currency convertibility, scaling down non-tariff barriers and, if common external tariffs are set in preferential trade areas, setting low tariff barriers at the level of the least protectionist member, not the most as often occurred in the past. And preferences to members should be modest – something close to 20 per cent at most – and should be quickly phased out.[29]

Conclusions

Two related questions have been addressed in this paper: the role of traditional exports and the development potential of regional trade arrangements. On the first issue three points were emphasized.

The fallacy of composition, which has been so much emphasized in these debates, appears less menacing to African traditional exports than is often argued. It is a clear problem for cocoa exports, and a possible problem for coffee. But modelling of commodity markets suggests that when account is taken of non-African supply reactions to falling prices, and over the longer term, output expansion will bring export revenue gains, even for cocoa, though these are modest.

Secondly, the policy response in any case should not neglect investment, research, and reform efforts aimed at increasing productivity in traditional crops and reducing their marketing costs. To neglect such efforts means further and rapid abandonment of market share to non-African growers.

Finally, attacks on the 'indiscriminate' nature of market-oriented reforms and the related argument that selective government interventions are needed to guide production and export decisions are acceptable in principle but worrying in practice. Few governments in low-income countries have the capacity to fine-tune incentive structures for imports and exports. And there are good reasons to remain sceptical of the argument that, even in low-income primary producing economies, governments can do better than private farmers and traders in discovering new production and export possibilities.

The answer to the second question is that, on balance, preferential trade areas are not good for African development at this stage. The empirical record is not encouraging and analysts of diverse doctrinal persuasion are sceptical, to say the least. These conclusions are of course not shared by everybody. But they are widely held by economists, and not only in connection with African cases.

In any event, there are many alternatives to efforts at building regional markets now – measures that can increase regional economic co-operation with benefit to all parties. These are mostly small and relatively uncontentious: for example, removal of burdensome regulatory obstacles to cross-border trade; increase of trade information and access to trade credits; emphasis on removal of obstacles to factor mobility; concentration on partial trade-enhancing agreements like the removal of obstacles to trade in meat in West Africa; elimination of duplication in regional organizations; and, perhaps most promising, a far more systematic and intensive use of regional co-operation in technical service provision in research and training.

These are small steps, but sure. Not only can they bring broadly shared gains in economic growth, but they are also building blocks for the future, the foundation of tomorrow's integrated continent.

Notes

1. See G. K. Helleiner, 'Structural Adjustment and Long-Term Development', in F. Stewart, S. Lall, and S. Wangwe (eds), *Alternative Development Strategies in Sub-Saharan Africa* (New York: St Martin's Press, 1992), p. 67.
2. The argument in the 1970s and 1980s was that the rate of growth of developing country output depended on the rate of growth of exports of primary commodities to developed countries, which in turn depended on developed country output growth. In his Nobel Prize lecture in 1980, Sir Arthur Lewis argued that, historically, primary exports grew by less than 1 per cent a year for each 1 per cent of GDP growth in the developed countries. Like many before him, he concluded, for this and other reasons, that developing country exports could not grow fast enough to generate a satisfactory rate of economic growth; he estimated that 6 per cent a year was needed, although more than 4 per cent was highly unlikely. In the event, the argument proved over-pessimistic, at least until the mid-1980s, for two reasons: it took developing country market share in primary products as given, although

in reality developing countries could gain developed country market share in all products other than tropical beverages; and it neglected the possibilities for rapid expansion of manufactured exports. Thus, though the average developed country growth rate fell from 4.7 per cent in 1963–73 to 2.5 per cent in 1973–84, the rate of growth of non-fuel primary exports from developing countries to developed countries rose from 2.5 per cent to 4.6 per cent between these two periods. (The food and beverage component grew fastest, rising from 2.1 to 5.9 per cent.) The composition of developing country exports changed radically, with manufactures jumping from 7 per cent of the total in 1963 to 40 per cent in the mid-1980s and almost 60 per cent if fuels are omitted. (W. A. Lewis, 'The Slowing Down of the Engine of Growth', *American Economic Review*, September 1980, pp. 555–64; James Reidel, 'Trade as the Engine of Growth in Developing Countries', *Economic Journal*, March 1984, pp. 56–73; and Bela Belassa, 'The Adding-Up Problem', Background Paper for the 1988 *World Development Report*, July 1988.)

3. World Bank, *Accelerated Development in Sub-Saharan Africa: An Agenda for Action* (1981), p. 23. The emphasis on shares was incidental. The big loss of Africa's share in many commodity markets during the 1960s and 1970s was underlined to show that bad agricultural policies were important in explaining performance, and to suggest that better policies could bring positive changes.
4. M. Godfrey, 'Trade and Exchange Rate Policy: A Further Contribution to the Debate', in T. Rose (ed.), *Crisis and Recovery in Sub-Saharan Africa* (Paris: OECD Development Centre, 1984).
5. UNCTAD Yearbooks for 1987 and 1989, cited in Dean De Rosa and J. Greene, 'Will Contemporaneous Devaluations Hurt Exports from Sub-Saharan Africa?', *Finance and Development*, March 1991.
6. Income elasticities of demand are also low: +0.3 to +0.5 for the six commodities. U. Koester, H. Schafer and A. Valdes, 'Demand-side Constraints and Structural Adjustment in Sub-Saharan African Countries', IFPRI, July 1990, p. 75, and the sources cited there.
7. J. R. Coleman, T. Akiyama, and P. N. Varanges, 'Impacts of Recent Policy Changes in Major Sub-Saharan Cocoa Producing Countries', (World Bank draft, September 1992). See also A. Panagariya and M. Schiff, 'Commodity Exports and Real Income in Africa', (World Bank PRE Working Paper No. 537, November 1990).
8. Another study models the impact of a 100,000-ton increase in Ghanaian production. It caused a world price decline of 3.7 per cent and income losses (defined as the sum of tax revenues and producer surplus) of 8 per cent for Côte d'Ivoire, 12 per cent for Cameroon, and almost 6 per cent for Nigeria. These losses closely matched Ghana's gains (Panagariya and Schiff, 1990).
9. More effective exploitation of import-substitution potentials is also possible and desirable.
10. Markets for non-traditional exports are difficult to win and keep. Minor or non-traditional exports are not immune to fallacies of composition. After all, all developing countries are seeking to diversify, and each searches for new market niches, usually in the same sectors – cut flowers, fruits and vegetables, shellfish, and cassava chips, to name only a few of the usual non-manufacturing possibilities. It is nonetheless true that the elasticities are better and many successes have been registered.
11. For example, see Stewart *et al.*, *Alternative Development Strategies*, p. 33.
12. UN Economic Commission for Africa, *African Alternative Framework to Structural Adjustment Programmes for Socio-Economic Recovery and Transformation* (Addis Ababa, 1989). Under the heading 'Export Re-orientation', this paper calls for 'specific export incentives for processed exports and carefully selected primary commodities . . . differential export subsidies . . . and bilateral and multilateral agreements on primary commodities' (pp. 41–2). And its discussion of agricultural research is focused on food crops and the objective of food self-sufficiency.
13. On cotton, see a study on African cotton export potential (Coleman *et al.*, 'Impacts of Recent Policy Changes').
14. Stewart *et al.*, *Alternative Development Strategies*, propose this, arguing also that the international financial institutions should support such joint restrictive actions. They also urge limiting research and development on traditional crops to demand-increasing activities (p. 33).
15. One recent inquiry estimated per kilogram cocoa production costs at farmgate as follows: Côte d'Ivoire, 40 (US) cents; Nigeria, 45 cents; Cameroon, 60 cents; Malaysia, 70 cents to $1.30; Indonesia, 30 to 80 cents; and Brazil, 'above $1'. But marketing costs and taxes were substantially higher in Côte d'Ivoire, Cameroon, and Ghana, and somewhat higher in Nigeria. In terms of FOB costs, Indonesia is the lowest-cost seller, Cameroon and Brazil the highest. Nigeria, Ghana, and Côte d'Ivoire are competitive with the Asian and Latin American producers. (Caisse Centrale de Coopération Technique,

'Competitivité du Cacao Africain; Analyse du marché mondial et des principaux producteurs', September 1990, pp. 269–70).

16. Coleman *et al.*, 'Impacts of Recent Policy Changes', suggest tariffs of 33 per cent for Côte d'Ivoire, 17 per cent for Ghana, 8 per cent for Nigeria, and 5 per cent for Cameroon, on the assumption that their market shares in the year 2000 will be 26 per cent, 13 per cent, 7 per cent, and 4 per cent, respectively (p. 39).
17. For example, Helleiner, in Stewart *et al.*, *Alternative Development Strategies*, p. 67. It is not clear why in this case the appropriate response is not to inform the smallholders of the information available to government and let them decide on actions to take, rather than government to act directly.
18. The story comes from D. Gisselquist, 'Privatizing Technological Change in Agriculture: Open the Door and Get Out of the Way', draft paper, World Bank Trade Policy Division, June 1992.
19. The aim was to protect farmers and local industry and to reduce costs of managing and maintaining these imports. Thus private fertilizer imports were prohibited; only prescribed brands of pesticides could be imported; seed varieties were screened; private import of diesel engines for irrigation was illegal, except for approved makes and models and with special permission of the Ministry of Agriculture; and no private pumps could be imported except with Ministry of Agriculture and Ministry of Industry permission.
20. Except perhaps the idea of democratic government, which has taken hold in recent years.
21. UN Economic Commission for Africa, 'African Alternative Framework to Structural Adjustment Programmes for Socio-Economic Recovery and Transformation; A Popular Version' (Addis Ababa, 1991), p. 10.
22. Faezeh Foroutan, 'Economic Integration in Sub-Saharan Africa, Past Experience and Future Prospects', paper presented at World Bank Conference on New Dimensions in Regional Integration, April 1992. Conference volume under that title forthcoming.
23. Ali Mansoor and A. Inotai, 'Integration Efforts in Sub-Saharan Africa: Failures, Results and Prospects – A Suggested Strategy for Achieving Efficient Integration', paper prepared for the African Economic Issues Conference, Nairobi, 5–7 June 1990.
24. A 1988 ECA report comments, concerning CEAO and UDEAC, that '[these] market integration schemes, which [give] no priority to the basic industries, reinforce the position of foreign private capital in the African countries and increase economic domination from abroad. They also have the disadvantage of accentuating the disparity between the levels of development of the member countries.' (ECA/UNDP/IGOs, 'Assistance of ECA and UNDP to the Economic Integration Entities and to the River and Lake Basin Organizations in the Preparation of their Project Documents for the Fourth UNDP Project Cycle' (Addis Ababa, March 1988). See also the 1984 ECA report, 'Proposals for Strengthening West African Economic Integration'.
25. 'The subregional economic communities must give less importance to trade liberalization. They must turn to transformation . . . of their national and subregional production systems, by creating a subregional transport and telecommunications infrastructure and developing new products or capacities by the community industries.' *Ibid.*, p. 10.
26. ECA, *African Alternative Framework* (1989), pp. 14–15.
27. See Mansoor and Inotai, 'Integration Efforts in SSA'.
28. J. de Melo and A. Panagariya, *The New Regionalism in Trade Policy: An Interpretative Summary of a Conference* (World Bank and Center for Economic Policy Research, April 1992), p. 15.
29. See D. Greenaway, T. Hyclak and R. Thornton (eds), *Economic Aspects of Regional Trading Arrangements* (New York: New York University Press, 1989), Introduction and Chapters 8 and 9, and World Bank, Trade Policy Division, *Strengthening Trade Policy Reform, Vol. II, The Full Report* (Washington, DC: 1989).

PART III DEBT & INTERRELATED ISSUES

7

ISHRAT HUSAIN

Trade, Aid & Investment in Sub-Saharan Africa

Introduction[1,2]

Sub-Saharan Africa (SSA) has experienced almost a decade of falling per capita incomes. Thirteen African countries, comprising a third of the region's population, are actually poorer in per capita terms today than they were at independence. Poverty has grown and the natural environment has deteriorated. The region has lost a substantial part of its share in the world market for its exports. Most countries have had balance-of-payments difficulties and have suffered a loss of foreign exchange and the ability to import the goods necessary for growth and development. Some African countries have surrendered many of the gains made earlier in human resource development. And in many countries open urban unemployment is a growing problem and poses a threat to stability.

In Africa, more than other developing regions, trade, aid, debt and investment are inextricably linked. African countries are especially dependent on **exports growth** as it generates the scarce foreign exchange needed to import the goods and services required for growth and development. Rising exports lead to rising imports. And, given their importance in the production structure of most African economies, the level of imports (other factors remaining constant) has a direct bearing on national income. **Foreign aid flows** can supplement export-earned foreign exchange and enable recipient countries to enhance their import capacity and achieve a higher rate of per capita income and consumption growth than would otherwise be possible. In a dynamic multi-period setting this would double or triple per capita incomes faster than if domestic resources alone were relied upon. New borrowings on concessional terms can also reinforce this effect, provided the debt-servicing payments on the existing stock of debt are lower than the new debt flows. Unfortunately, the severity of the debt problem in more than half of SSA countries has limited this option. Finally, **foreign private investment**, an increasingly important source of capital flows to developing countries, has several added advantages for Africa.

This paper attempts to bring together these three elements of the external sector – trade, aid and investment – and to assess their effects on growth and sustainable development in Sub-Saharan Africa. The first section examines trends in export performance and imports and evaluates some of the main hypotheses that are advanced to explain Africa's relatively weak performance in foreign trade. The second section raises issues about the sustainability and effectiveness of development assistance. The final section explores determinants of private investment in Africa and asks: What needs to be done to attract domestic and foreign investment?

Trade

The notion that African countries should follow an outward-oriented trade strategy for growth and development has yet to find wide acceptance among either intellectuals or policy-makers in Sub-Saharan Africa and elsewhere. Several disparate strands of argument against trade liberalization are found in the literature and in policy discussions. They can be summarized as follows:

(a) Efficiency gains from reforms are small as domestic producers cannot quickly reallocate resources to efficient sectors owing to weaknesses in the human resource base, in infrastructure and in institutions;

(b) Even if producers can reallocate resources quickly into traditional primary exports, export revenues may not rise commensurately because Africa's primary exports face a long-term trend decline in real prices and considerable price instability; or simultaneous expansion of such exports by Sub-Saharan African countries in the face of inelastic world demand will depress rather than enhance export revenues (this has been called the fallacy of composition argument);

(c) Similarly, if African countries succeed in reallocating revenues to manufactured or non-traditional agricultural commodities, growing protectionism in the OECD countries will prevent rapid expansion of African exports;

(d) Liberalization of imports undermines economic growth by:
- crowding out imports of raw materials and capital goods in favour of consumer and luxury goods;
- widening trade deficits and undermining macroeconomic stability; and
- de-industrializing African countries, because domestic manufactures cannot compete with cheaper and dumped goods from other parts of the world.

These objections to trade liberalization in SSA have been intensely debated for several years. Their conclusive testing is beset with difficult conceptual, methodological and data availability problems. Nonetheless, recent studies have utilized improved analytical methods, measurement techniques and data to test the validity of these arguments. Although these studies may not provide definite answers to settle the controversy, they enhance our understanding sufficiently to cast doubt on objections to trade liberalization in Africa. What is the empirical evidence from these studies?

Export performance

During the 1960s, the volume of exports from African countries grew at an annual average rate of 6 per cent (Table 7.1). Almost all countries in the region shared in this growth. Since 1973, however, export volumes have remained stagnant or declined significantly. For SSA, as a whole, including oil exporters, the total volume of exports declined by about 0.7 per cent a year in the 1980s. In contrast, developing countries as a whole increased their export volume in the same period by 4.6 per cent per annum.

Table 7.1 *Key Trade Statistics for Sub-Saharan Africa*, 1960–90

	1960	1970	1980	1986	1990
Value of Exports ($ billion)	3.6	7.6	48.9	25.8	36.2
Value of Imports ($ billion)	3.8	7.2	42.8	27.2	36.9
Volume Index of Exports (1980 = 100)	52	99	100	77	92
Volume Index of Imports (1980 = 100)	36	54	100	69	75
Unit Value Index of Exports (1980 = 100)	14	15	100	66	80
Unit Value Index of Imports (1980 = 100)	22	25	100	92	116
Terms of Trade Index (1980 = 100)	55	54	100	72	69
Purchasing Power Index of Exports (1980 = 100)	30	56	100	57	63

Source: UNCTAD, *Handbook of International Trade and Development Statistics*, 1991.

Table 7.2. *Shares of Sub-Saharan African Exports*, 1970–90 (%)

	1970	1980	1986	1990
A. World Exports	2.5	2.5	1.2	1.0
B. Developing Country Exports	13.2	8.5	6.1	4.9
C. Primary Commodity Exports	6.2	4.5[a]	3.9	4.0
D. Non-oil Primary Exports	7.3	3.9[a]	4.1	2.7
E. Agricultural Raw Material Exports	4.9	3.4[a]	3.0	2.8
F. Minerals, Ores and Metal Exports	10.2	5.6[a]	4.7	3.7

Sources: UNCTAD, *Handbook of International Trade and Development Statistics*, 1991;*Commodity Yearbook*, 1992.
[a] Pertains to 1981.

Table 7.3. *Share in World Exports of Major African Commodity Exports* (%)

	Average 1970–79	Average 1980–89	% change between the 2 periods
Cocoa	74.2	65.2	-12.1
Copper	44.7	42.4	-5.1
Coffee	30.3	23.5	-22.1
Cotton	18.4	15.0	-18.5
Tea	17.5	19.6	12.0
Tobacco	9.6	12.3	28.1
Sugar	6.1	5.2	-14.8

Source: UNCTAD, *Commodity Yearbook* (Various Issues)

The share of African exports in world trade fell from 2.5 per cent in 1970 to 1.0 per cent in 1990 (Table 7.2). More dramatic was the relative decline of African exports among developing countries from 13 per cent to 5 per cent while other regions either maintained or increased their relative shares. Africa's share of non-oil primary commodities also declined substantially, from 7 per cent to 3 per cent; if SSA countries had maintained their 1970 market share and prices had remained the same, their export earnings would have been $20 billion a year higher in 1991–92. The difference is approximately equal to the region's total scheduled debt-service payments in this period. In practice, part of this gain might have been lost because of lower prices resulting from increased supplies. However, competitors might not have expanded their exports so much had African countries been stronger exporters.

During the 1960s, African agricultural exports grew at nearly 2 per cent a year. But since then, they have declined sharply – by more than 3 per cent a year. Africa's share of exports for most of its major crops also fell during the 1970s and early 1980s. For example, between the 1970s and 1980s, Africa's world market share for three main agricultural exports – coffee, cocoa and cotton – shrank by 22, 12 and 18 per cent respectively. Indonesia, which produced 16,000 tons of cocoa in 1980, exported more than 220,000 tons in 1990. Of seven major commodity exports, African market shares rose only for tea and tobacco (Table 7.3).

The structure of Sub-Saharan exports has remained largely unchanged since the early 1960s. The heavy reliance on primary commodities (including oil) persists; they accounted for 93 per cent of total export earnings in 1970, declining to 84 per cent by the end of the 1980s. A few countries, such as Kenya and Mauritius, have diversified somewhat out of primary products, but they remain the exceptions. The markets for SSA exports have also changed little. Roughly half the region's exports still go to the European Community. African exporters have yet to take advantage of the booming markets of Asia. For most of Sub-Saharan Africa, growth in imports has tended to outpace growth in exports, generating a major foreign-exchange constraint and impinging on overall economic growth. This constraint was particularly acute in the 1980s, the result in part of the adoption of import-substitution policy, and in part of inconsistent macroeconomic policy. While terms-of-trade deterioration played a role, such deterioration was no greater than that faced by other developing countries.

Effects of terms of trade

The evolution of the barter terms of trade varies among groups of countries and has changed significantly over time. For the SSA region as a whole, terms of trade fell sharply in the 1980s, but the decline was from the historically high level attained in 1981. Despite this fall, the terms of trade were 34 per cent higher in 1989 than in 1967. The loss in income caused by deteriorating terms of trade between 1985 and 1990 was far less than the gains up to the mid-1980s. Although declining terms of trade result in depressed levels of income, the region gained more real income from terms of trade changes after 1961 than it lost.[3]

The terms of trade losses are not unique to SSA. In fact, other developing regions experienced a more severe deterioration in their terms of trade in the 1980s, but their export volumes still grew at a rapid rate. In the period 1980–88, East Asia's terms of trade fell by about 16 per cent compared with only 8 per cent for SSA. But East Asia was able to expand its exports at an annual rate of 10.4 per cent while SSA's exports declined by 0.7 per cent p.a. during the same period. Latin America's terms of trade declined by some 14 per cent but its exports grew by 3.4 per cent a year.

It is true that several African countries are distinguished from those in other regions of the world by the fact that three commodities of which Africa is a major exporter – coffee, cocoa and copper – were severely depressed over the decade of the 1980s and their real prices dropped to historically low levels (although copper prices rebounded in the later half of the decade). Countries deriving their export revenues mainly from any of these commodities were indeed badly hurt. But it is interesting that the response of each of the affected countries was different and no general conclusions can be drawn.

Though most countries in the region suffered a significant decline in export revenues in the period 1970–85, the main cause of the decline was falling export volumes and not the declining terms of trade.[4] By contrast, in the period 1986–91 the terms of trade fell by about 10 per cent while the volume of exports increased by almost 30 per cent. In an earlier less favourable period (1954–69) in the terms of trade, export revenues grew significantly, mainly owing to increases in export volume.

Pickett[5] attempted to assess the effects on GDP growth of long-run movement in the terms of trade for a sample of twenty SSA low-income countries over the period 1966–86. In all these countries the income effects of the terms of trade were negative, but in most cases the effect was quite modest. Worst hit were three mineral exporters – Zambia, Zaïre and Mauritania. For the others, the income effects were relatively small, reducing estimated annual GDP growth by less than one-third of a percentage point.[6]

Export volume vs. export revenue: fallacy of composition

It is often argued that increases in volume of primary exports may not be accompanied by increases in export revenue if many countries increase their exports at the same time. The argument is that, with a generally inelastic world demand, aggressive increases in supply by all countries will lower world prices.

This 'fallacy of composition' argument is unconvincing. African production of most commodities (excluding cocoa, coffee, and copper) is small (less than 20 per cent of the world market). Even doubling production would have a small effect on total world supply.

Akiyama and Larson[7] have empirically tested the validity of the argument by estimating the elasticity of export revenue (ERV) with respect to volume, which is the percentage change in export revenue when export quantity is increased by one per cent. If expansion of export quantity has no effect on world prices, then the elasticity is equal to one. If world prices decline as a result of expansion of export quantity, then the elasticity is less than one. A negative elasticity means that increase in export quantity causes export revenue to decline. The estimates of ERV are higher in the long run than in the short.

The results of this study show that cocoa is the only commodity that faces a serious adding-up problem. In the short run, the ERV for cocoa is −0.19, which means that a 10 per cent increase in export quantities will reduce export revenues by 1.9 per cent. For the long run, the ERV is 0.33. Côte d'Ivoire, and to some extent, Ghana are the two countries that face this problem. The best way in the short run to address it is to impose an export tax which will discourage inefficient producers. In the long run, productivity-enhancing technologies may lower the marginal cost of production.

An argument is advanced that the structural adjustment programmes in SSA, by expanding exports of primary commodities, have depressed world prices. In only two agricultural commodities – cocoa and coffee – is SSA's share of the world market high, but in the case of coffee, no individual SSA country has a large share. Furthermore, no SSA country has expanded coffee production substantially in recent years. Most of the price-depressing expansion has been in Columbia, Indonesia and Vietnam.

The story of cocoa markets is different. As noted above, there is an 'adding-up' problem in cocoa. The question is whether exports from Ghana and Nigeria under their structural adjustment programmes are the main contributory factor to the depressed world prices. Coleman *et al.*[8] have recently analysed the impact of cocoa export increases in the major Sub-Saharan producing countries on world prices. They used a large simultaneous equation model of the world cocoa market consisting of three blocks: supply, demand and price determination. The simulation results show that world cocoa prices would have been on average 8 per cent higher and the value of world cocoa production 6 per cent higher had there not been structural adjustment programmes in Ghana and Nigeria over the period 1982/83–1989/90. The incremental exports from Ghana and Nigeria made only a small contribution to the decline in world cocoa prices in the 1980s; the major part of the decline can be attributed to the rapid production increases in other countries – Côte d'Ivoire, Indonesia and Malaysia.

In any event, Africa cannot afford to adopt a passive role and lose even larger market shares to more aggressive Asian and Latin American exporters. In negotiating commodity agreements, its loss of market share should be seen as an argument for more favourable treatment. That producers compete for markets is a fundamental reality, as true for manufacturing as it is for primary products. During the 1970s, it was aggressive exporting on the part of other developing country producers that eroded Africa's market share, compounded by agricultural subsidies in developed countries. The less efficient producers will be shaken out of the market, and, as some SSA countries have now become low-cost producers, the other competitors, who have relatively higher marginal costs, will be the ones to give up production unless the producers in these countries are subsidized by the state.

Industrial country protectionism against Africa's manufactured exports

Although most countries in SSA have found it difficult successfully to reallocate resources to manufactured exports, there is pervasive concern about industrial country protectionism against such exports. This concern and the resulting pessimism are, however, unwarranted.

A detailed study of protection facing SSA exports in EC, Japanese and US markets[9] rules out such protection as the cause of the SSA countries' relatively poor export performance in manufactures. It was found that SSA had more favourable arrangements in terms of both tariff and non-tariff barriers against their exports to those markets.

Africa is a beneficiary of the GSP under the GATT, while the Lomé Convention grants African countries virtually free access to the EC market. While African exports of primary commodities typically face low tariff rates and insignificant quantitative restrictions,[10] market access for manufactures is not a problem at all.[11] Some SSA countries benefit from protection because industrial country protectionism restricts non-SSA developing countries' exports more than those of SSA countries.

Import liberalization and exports

Despite some success in import liberalization in a number of countries, protection is still appreciably higher in SSA than in other developing regions. While the average level of tariffs and other *ad valorem* import duties is about 30 per cent, non-tariff import barriers in different forms, including quantitative restrictions, foreign-exchange controls and state trading, provide a high degree of protection to import substitutes.

It has long been recognized that restrictions on imports effectively tax exports.[12] By implicitly taxing exports and thereby reducing international competitiveness, tariffs and other import restrictions often foreclose possibilities for expanding exports. Several studies[13] of the tax incidence of import substitution on exports show that the specially administered systems of incentives that are often used to offset the tax and promote or diversify exports have generally not been very effective. In simple terms, providing greater freedom to import improves the incentives for expanding exports in the most efficient manner. A recent study has modelled the export incentive of imports for SSA. Using available estimates of trade elasticities, it estimates that if import duties are reduced to a uniform rate of only 10 per cent and non-tariff barriers are dismantled, exports increase by between 15 per cent and 33 per cent per annum.[14] The study also shows that protection in SSA inhibits the progress of African countries in achieving greater export diversification.

Country-specific evidence

Studies of adjustment policies and growth in SSA show one outcome consistently across countries and across different time-periods – that import policy reforms have contributed significantly to improving export performance. Using several estimation methods including a modified control group approach in which the initial conditions and internal and external shocks were controlled, El-Badawi *et al.*[15] found that the estimated marginal effect of adjustment programmes on SSA export performance was positive and highly significant. After controlling for other factors, adjustment programmes were estimated to have increased the export to GDP ratio of the intensive adjusters by 8 per cent compared with other countries in the region.

There is also a good deal of country-specific evidence in Africa to substantiate a positive relationship between import liberalization and export growth. Econometric studies[16] of Malawi and Tanzania show that when import liberalization reduces protection and depreciates the real exchange rate, primary exports rise rapidly. The same has been true of Ghana and Uganda. Import liberalization in Mauritius led to a rapid expansion of manufactured exports.

The recent experience of Nigeria provides another pertinent illustration of import liberalization prompting export expansion. Since 1986, Nigeria has implemented substantial import liberalization.[17] Although official export statistics underestimate the true response to these measures, Katherine Moseley[18] has documented the evidence of 'informal' exports from Nigeria to the West African sub-region.[19] She notes that 'Made in Nigeria' has become a common epithet in the region rather like 'Made in Japan' or 'Made in Taiwan' at the global level. The ultimate boundaries of this distribution network are not precisely known, but might be as far away as Zaïre, or, to the west, Conakry in Guinea.

In the early 1980s, about one-half of the annual Nigerian cloth consumption of some 200 million metres was imported. Today Nigerian cloth exports are making serious inroads into these same regional markets from where it used to import. Nigerian textiles are now estimated to supply as much as 30 per cent of the needs of low-income groups in the West African sub-region as a whole. Similar developments have been reported for other goods. Spare parts for Peugeot cars, cosmetics, medicines, cassette recordings, shoes, manufactured foods and detergents are now common exports to the region. Moseley notes that, although export production is often associated with large, multinational corporations, in Nigeria it was the indigenous small- and medium-sized firms which led the export drive to the sub-region.

Inappropriate import composition after liberalization

Concerns about the disruptive effects of import liberalization – inappropriate import composition, trade deficits and de-industrialization – are overstated. These effects are certainly not inevitable nor intrinsic to liberalization. In most cases they arise because import liberalization is not accompanied by complementary policies. For example, import liberalization accompanied by financial sector reform or by appropriate exchange-rate adjustments can avoid most of the disruptive transitional effects that are alleged.

It is often asserted that one of the pernicious effects of import liberalization is an unrestricted flow of consumer goods and especially luxury goods at the expense of the raw materials and capital goods needed for investment and growth. Where this has happened, it is either because pre-liberalization restrictions on consumer goods led to a pent-up demand or because of imperfections in the financial market.

The available evidence for a group of liberalizing SSA countries does not support the claims that intermediate and capital goods have been 'crowded out' and that import liberalization has opened the door for 'undesirable' and 'anti-development' imports. A sample survey of 27 adjusting low-income countries in SSA for the period 1988–92 shows that capital goods and intermediate goods accounted for 67 per cent of total imports, food about 16 per cent, fuel 4 per cent and consumer goods only 13 per cent. Ten years ago the share of capital and intermediate goods was only 54 per cent, followed by food 26 per cent, fuel 8 per cent and consumer goods 12 per cent. The share of consumer goods has not declined but the share of food imports has. The declining dependence of African countries on food imports during the adjustment period is largely due to the expansion of domestic food production.[20] Lower world prices of petroleum products have also led to a dramatic fall in the ratio of fuel imports. On the other hand, raw materials and capital goods imports needed to increase utilization of existing capacity and new investment have been picking up over the last five years.

Generation of trade deficits

Import liberalization, if unaccompanied by offsetting macroeconomic policies, will generate trade deficits in any economy. This is true not only if there was macroeconomic disequilibrium in the pre-liberalization period but also if there was macroeconomic stability. The reason is that import liberalization reduces domestic prices of imports and thereby raises import demand.[21] If the economy starts from a position of macroeconomic balance, either the exchange rate has to depreciate sufficiently to offset the decline in the average domestic price of imports, or monetary policy has to become more restrictive to ensure that import liberalization *does not* generate trade deficits. If the economy starts from a position of macroeconomic imbalance (e.g. trade deficit), the offsetting policy changes have to be greater. Failure to depreciate the real exchange rate sufficiently has generally been a key factor in worsening the balance-of-payments situation after liberalization.

SSA countries have often failed to implement complementary macroeconomic policies with import liberalization. For example, Kenya implemented substantial liberalization of its quantitative restrictions in 1989 and 1990, but failed to depreciate its exchange rate sufficiently.[22] As a result, there was pressure on the trade balance and an implicit reversal of import liberalization in late 1990 and early 1991 as the government tried to prevent an outflow of reserves by increasing the length of time necessary to attain import licences. Franc Zone countries have experienced a similar fate as their real exchange rate appreciated rather than depreciated after import liberalization. This experience is not unknown outside Africa, especially in the Southern Cone countries of Latin America.

De-industrialization of Africa

Many observers have expressed the fear that a liberal flow of imports will crowd out domestic manufactured products and lead to the de-industrialization of Africa. The evidence behind these assertions is at best anecdotal and spotty. In principle, it is necessary to distinguish between the short-term and medium-to-long term aspects of the question. In the short run, it is possible to minimize the disruptive effects on manufacturing firms by offsetting the decline in the average domestic price of imports with an exchange-rate depreciation. To the extent that pre-liberalization tariffs (explicit and implicit) were not uniform, the higher-than-average tariffs will experience some contraction. But the overall adverse effect on manufacturing output will be minimized by the 'compensatory' depreciation. In the long run non-viable firms will close but new firms will open. The only issue is how long before the new firms emerge.

Over-valued exchange rates, high tariff and non-tariff protection, subsidized interest rates and other incentives promoted a pattern of industrialization in SSA that was highly import-intensive and capital-intensive. This judgement is shared by critics of structural adjustment such as Stewart *et al.*[23] who state that

> while industrial output grew at a rate comparable to that of other areas in the world before the 1980s, the pattern of industrialization was, for the most part, inefficient by every measure, highly protected, highly import-dependent, with very few linkages with the rest of the economy and associated with very low levels of export.

The policy reforms initiated since the mid-1980s in many countries have tended to change the prevailing incentive structure and favour raw-material-based and labour-intensive industries. This reallocation of resources cannot take place without some transitional social costs in terms of unemployed labour, underutilized capacity, financial losses and increased indebtedness in established industries. On the other hand, the emergence of new competitive industries supported by fresh investment takes time and is often relatively slow and uneven. The factors determining investment are complex and extend to non-economic considerations such as political stability, policy credibility, etc.

Nevertheless, the buoyant growth of informal and small enterprises in Nigeria, Tanzania, Ghana, and Uganda, following import liberalization and other policy reforms, suggests that some reallocation of resources is already taking place and is in the right direction. Moseley's study of the Nigerian industrial sector confirms the responsiveness of entrepreneurs to the policy changes.[24] Sourcing of local raw materials has become the predominant mode of adjustment for most of the previously import-dependent industries. There has also been a marked shift in capacity utilization and production away from industries such as vehicle assembly, paints and chemicals, beverages, etc., to textiles, fabrics and wood products – products in which countries of SSA have a larger comparative advantage.

The empirical basis of 'de-industrialization theory' is quite shaky. If de-industrialization is in fact resulting as a consequence of structural adjustment, this could be observed by comparing the changes in the share of industrial value-added in GDP before and after adjustment and examining the growth rates. An inspection of the data for 11 adjusting countries in SSA with sizeable industrial sectors does not show any decline in these shares. And average annual industrial growth rates in the 1988–91 period have been fairly high relative to the earlier periods (Uganda 11 per cent; Nigeria 7 per cent; Malawi 7 per cent; Ghana 5 per cent; Kenya 5 per cent; Zimbabwe 4 per cent).

Openness and GDP growth

The foregoing discussion suggests that scepticism in respect of the outward-oriented strategy does not rest on firm grounds. This inference is strengthened by the results of recent cross-country analyses linking openness with GDP growth.

The cross-country evidence for SSA provides considerable support for a positive relationship between increased trade liberalization and GDP growth. Together with country-specific evidence, it undermines the traditional presumption that openness does not work in the SSA region. This cross-country evidence is of two types: one linking export growth to GDP growth and the other linking trade policy openness with GDP growth.

The evidence linking exports to GDP growth consists of two cross-country econometric studies. One study,[25] attempting to explain the GDP growth of SSA for the period 1970–86, shows that the strongest explanatory variable is the growth of export earnings; even when the import growth variable is introduced, the result is unchanged, i.e. its coefficient remains significant and with positive sign. The other study,[26] for a cross-section of 16 African countries (using period-average data) shows a strong positive relationship between export growth and GDP growth. These results demonstrate the importance of export growth in augmenting GDP growth in SSA, though it is not obvious whether they capture the fact that increased exports increase the capacity to import and this relaxes the import constraint on growth, or whether the growth of exports arises from efficiency increases generated by trade liberalization.

The second type of cross-country evidence is based on measures of actual trade policy rather than the effect of trade policy (i.e. export growth). The evidence is much more convincing because one does not have to assume that export growth is the effect of trade liberalization. A cross-country study of SSA,[27] for the period 1967–87, using an augmented production function framework and pooled time series and cross-section data, found that differences in levels of, or changes in, openness accounted for significant differences in the level and growth of GDP. The study uses four different measures of openness – index of trade liberalization, index of outward orientation, black market premium on foreign exchange and actual trade shares – to investigate the relationship between openness and economic performance. The econometric results are robust across all four measures. In addition, estimates of the coefficient on openness remain virtually unchanged when a macroeconomic policy variable is introduced in the regression.[28] These results (i.e. coefficient estimates on openness) compare quite favourably with those for developing countries in other regions.

Prospects

Since the prospects for significantly higher prices for most primary commodities are poor, export earnings must grow through increasing the supply of exports and through diversification. Diversification that is consistent with the comparative advantage of a country is an effective way to protect the country from the impact of large fluctuations in individual commodity prices, as shown by the experience of South and South-East Asian countries. However, although diversification will take place as economic growth is accelerated, in the short and medium term countries must seek to expand their traditional exports since it will take time to establish a new product as a major export. Managing the commodity price risk by using financial risk management measures will certainly help in reducing the volatility in export earnings. In any event it is best to provide neutral incentives for exports and to avoid targeted policies that may misallocate resources. Governments, after all, are generally bad at picking winners.

Encouragingly, during the past 15 years or so, some African countries have managed to find new opportunities in world markets for primary commodities such as vegetable oils, soybeans and fishery products. Kenya has had success in exporting fruits, vegetables and flowers. However, with the exception of Mauritius, countries have not diversified significantly into labour-intensive light manufacturing, and Africa's manufactured exports largely remain processed primary products with little value added.

SSA also needs to find new markets in addition to taking full advantage of its preferential access to European Community markets. While Europe has seen declining imports from developing countries (down from 34 per cent to 20 per cent in 1970–85), imports into the United States, now the biggest market for developing country exports, and Asian countries are still growing. Since the share of Asian markets and of non-traditional items in world trade is likely to grow rapidly, special efforts will have to be made to take these opportunities. Competition in international markets will remain intense, but continued economic growth worldwide could expand demand for African exports. African countries also need to expand trade with each other.

In the World Bank's scenario for SSA, the ratio of exports to GDP is targeted to rise from an annual average of about 19 per cent in 1986–87 to about 24 per cent by 2000 and 28 per cent by 2020; the growth rate of exports should improve significantly from a negative rate in 1980–87 to about 5 per cent a year, thus reversing the decline in Africa's share of primary exports.

Africa will be affected more than any other region by the likely slow growth in demand for primary commodities. Any hope of a revival of economic growth predicated on the recovery of primary commodity prices would seem to be misplaced. The price forecasts for Africa's five major primary commodity exports to the year 2000 do not show any significant increases. Except for oil, prices are now close to their long-term trend. While Africa can and must seek to expand its market share wherever it has a comparative advantage, it is clearly not advisable to divert more resources into commodities or sectors that have a long-term declining unit value.

Africa's export performance indicates the continent's unrealized potential. The average annual growth rate of exports from SSA fell from 6.6 per cent in 1965–80 to –0.7 per cent in 1980–90. The expansion of world trade during the past three decades appears to have largely bypassed Africa. If its economies are to grow, they must improve their share in world markets and diversify their exports.

Aid

Despite a resurgence in exports, Africa will continue to face a foreign-exchange shortage well into the next century. African countries have scope for using imports more efficiently as well as for reducing non-essential and food imports. As domestic production grows, domestic products can substitute for imports, particularly in high value-added goods. Nonetheless, in the 1990s imports need to grow faster than GDP to make up for the compression that occurred during the previous decade. Imports in the 1990s will need to grow by 5 to 6 per cent a year. Recent experience with strong adjustment programmes suggests import elasticity of 1.5 per cent. It is assumed that success in increasing food production will curb the growth in food imports, but that, given the projected rise in investment from 15 to 25 per cent of GDP, imports of capital goods will rise faster than income. To meet these growing import requirements, external resources in the form of aid or concessional loans will have to supplement the region's export earnings. This section examines the past trends and pattern of external resource flows, assesses the debt burden and the various initiatives taken so far and considers future prospects.

Trends and pattern of external flows

It is often asserted that the external resource flows to SSA have declined and the region is being marginalized. How far is this fear well-founded? It is true that the volume of external resources available to SSA declined in real terms until 1985, but it rose in the latter half of the 1980s (see Table 7.4). The increase in external resources as a proportion of the region's GDP was dramatic. Aggregate net resource flows rose from 6.2 per cent of the region's GDP in 1980 to 10.7 per cent in 1990.[29] If all adjustments are made for debt servicing, profits, remittances, dividends and payments to the IMF, the region as a whole received 7.4 per cent of GDP in 1990 from all external sources. This compares with 6.2 per cent in 1980 and 3.3 per cent in 1970.

The composition of external resource flows has also changed significantly during

Table 7.4 Aggregate Net Flows and Net Transfers to Sub-Saharan Africa (US$m)

		1970	1980	1986	1990
A.	Net Flows on Long-Term Debt	824	7,940	5,399	4,974
B.	Official Grants	363	3,089	4,880	11,669
C.	Foreign Direct Investment	92	20	719	669
D.	IMF Purchases (net)	-44	833	-482	-34
	Aggregate Net Flows (ANF) (A+B+C+D)	1,235	11,881	10,516	17,278
E.	Interest on Long-Term Debt	180	2,277	3,391	4,255
F.	Profits on FDI	737	2,890	1,339	1,313
	Aggregate Net Transfers (ANT) (ANF-E-F)	319	6,714	5,786	11,669
Memo Items:					
	Aggregate Net Flows (Constant 1992 $)	–	14,704	13,657	18,035
	Aggregate Net Transfers (Constant 1992 $)	–	8,309	7,514	12,180

Source: *World Debt Tables 1992–93.*

the last decade. While net borrowing through loans accounted for more than two-thirds of total resource flows in 1980, this source has been diminishing in importance and provided only 28 per cent in 1990. Of all resource flows, Official Development Assistance (ODA) has grown the fastest. Official grants (excluding technical assistance) now comprise more than two-thirds of external flows to SSA, reflecting the increasingly limited access SSA countries have to commercial funds and the growing recognition that more concessional assistance is needed. The terms at which external assistance is currently being provided are highly appropriate in view of the severe indebtedness of most SSA countries.

Net ODA disbursements in real terms, which are used in this paper as the indicator of aid flows, grew at an annual rate of 2 per cent between 1980 and 1990 for the developing countries as a whole. But for SSA, ODA has grown by almost 4.0 per cent a year over the period. Consequently, the share of SSA in net ODA disbursements rose from one-fourth to about one-third.

ODA flows from multilateral sources expanded more rapidly – 4.6 per cent annually – while bilateral ODA increased by 3.4 per cent. Among the multilateral agencies, IDA's net disbursements have risen consistently in every year since 1985. By 1992, SSA accounted for 48 per cent of IDA's worldwide net disbursements compared with 31 per cent as recently as 1985. As a result of the large increase in IDA disbursements, net flows from the World Bank to SSA grew from $1.3 billion in 1985 to $2 billion in 1992.

The relative importance of aid in financing Africa's development can be seen in comparison with other developing countries and in changes over time. In 1985–86, the year before a large upsurge in adjustment programmes in SSA, ODA receipts accounted for 5 per cent of SSA's regional GDP, but by 1990–91 this had more than doubled to 10.8 per cent. At the same time, Asia, North Africa and the Middle East received only 1 per cent of their GDP from ODA and Latin America 0.5 per cent.

Overall, ODA accounts for 1.3 per cent of the GDP of developing countries.

While the aid is necessary to finance the imports and investment necessary for growth and development in SSA, a high level of aid transfer may lead to dependence and a decline in domestic savings, overvalued exchange rates, and high wage rates. With a proper policy framework, however, such transfers can be associated with high growth rates and appropriate wage and exchange rates. In Korea, for example, resource transfers amounted to about 10 per cent of GDP throughout the 1960s and 1970s, and impressive growth rates of GDP and exports as well as high investment rates were achieved while maintaining competitive exchange rates and wages. In Africa, however, resource transfers of the same order of magnitude in the late 1980s have generated growth rates of only 3 to 4 per cent and investment rates have remained low. Efficiency in resource use leading to accelerated growth is the only viable way to sustain these high levels of aid flows to the region in the 1990s.

An important issue often raised is whether ODA flows have compensated African countries for their terms-of-trade losses. We agree with Helleiner that this issue is best examined country by country rather than by SSA in the aggregate. Helleiner[30] has analyzed the country-level data for 26 SSA countries for the period 1980–90 to examine whether the terms-of-trade losses suffered by these countries were offset by increased ODA. Twenty countries experienced terms-of-trade losses averaging 28 per cent. The average loss of the losers was 8.3 per centof GDP.[31] The study showed that 12 of the 26 countries either enjoyed terms-of-trade improvements or ODA increases that more than compensated for terms-of-trade losses over the 1980s. The countries that suffered most were four oil exporters – Nigeria, Congo, Cameroon and Gabon, which are not the recipients of ODA – and two cocoa exporters – Côte d'Ivoire and Ghana. In addition, Sudan, Somalia, Liberia, Sierra Leone and Mauritania had decreases in their ODA during this period for reasons unrelated to economic performance. It would be fair to surmise that except for the lower-middle-income countries, the donors, by and large, met the financial needs of most of the adjusting countries to cope with external shocks. The volume and timing may not have been perfect in each case but the efforts need to be recognized. The recent example of donor financing for drought-related imports in Southern Africa reinforces this observation.

This analysis broadly suggests that the international community has responded positively since 1986 to reorient its aid flows to the region, and that the increase in ODA to SSA was consistently and significantly higher than to other regions and to developing countries as a whole during the 1980s. It also suggests that the type and terms of the new commitments of aid and loans are appropriate from the viewpoint of servicing future obligations and financing current import needs; the average grant element of all new long-term loan commitments increased from less than 20 per cent in the early 1980s to 50 per cent by the end of the decade (if actual grants are included, the overall grant element of financial flows reached more than 70 per cent for SSA). Continued assistance of the same volume, type and terms has to be sustained in the 1990s.

Multilateral agencies have mobilized special additional finance for low-income African countries. Through the World Bank's Joint Programme of Action for Sub-Saharan Africa, the Special Facility for Africa mobilized almost $2 billion in non-project aid and joint co-financing of structural adjustment programmes from mid-1985 to mid-1988. The World Bank also launched a three-year Special Programme of Assistance (SPA) for low-income, debt-distressed Sub-Saharan African countries at the end of 1987, which provides highly concessional, quick-disbursing finance. To be eligible, a country must have a donor-endorsed economic reform programme with the World Bank and the IMF. By the end of 1992, 26 countries were eligible for the SPA. It has four main elements: additional disbursements from IDA, concessional adjustment co-financing from bilateral donors and other multilateral agencies, concessional rescheduling, and concessional financing of interest due on World Bank loans. Eighteen donor governments and agencies pledged an initial $6.4 billion in co-financing, about half of which can be considered additional to existing aid programmes.

In 1986, the IMF established its Structural Adjustment Facility to provide assistance on concessional terms (interest rates of 0.5 per cent, with repayments over a 10-year period including 4.5 years' grace) to low-income countries undertaking comprehensive structural adjustment programmes. To enlarge the pool of concessional resources available to low-income countries, the IMF established the Enhanced Structural Adjustment Facility, which became effective in January 1988. Donor contributions have provided new resources totalling $8.4 billion, and the concessionality of IMF resources in Sub-Saharan Africa has been increased. By 1992, 15 African countries had access to the enhanced facilities.

Debt

Any discussion of aid and external resource flows to Sub-Saharan Africa will remain partial without considering the region's burden of debt. SSA's external debt grew rapidly throughout the 1970s and 1980s. During the period of commodity boom and petrodollar recycling, commercial creditors had been able to expand credit easily and borrowers were happy to contract new loans at negative or low real interest rates. At the end of 1991, Africa's debt stood at $173 billion, more than three times the 1980 level. SSA's debt was 111 per cent of its GDP and 345 per cent of exports. In these terms, the debt burden exceeds that of any other region. Almost two-thirds of Africa's debt is owed to official creditors.

The net increase in debt stock since 1980 is largely due not to new borrowing but to the accumulation of arrears of debt service and interest capitalization. Most African countries are not fully servicing their debt. In 1991, for example, the scheduled amount of debt service due was $20 billion. Yet, African countries paid only $10 billion. This has in fact been the pattern for the last five years. Interest arrears have climbed steadily from $4.5 billion to over $14 billion between 1987 and 1992 and arrears on principal amount to a further $20 billion.

To whom do African countries owe their debt? Excluding short-term debt, the shares of the major creditors in the region's total the end of 1991[32] were as follows:

Bilateral governments	45%
Multilateral agencies (incl. IMF)	30%
Commercial banks	13%
Other private creditors	12%

The one-half of debt-service obligation actually paid was divided among creditors as follows:

Bilateral governments	22%
Multilateral agencies (incl. IMF)	38%
Commercial banks	22%
Other private creditors	18%

A large proportion of private debt is serviced because the interest rate on this type of debt is high relative to that on bilateral or multilateral debt which is mostly concessional. Also, two-thirds of the payments made to commercial banks originate from only two countries – Nigeria and Côte d'Ivoire. The same two countries pay almost 50 per cent of Africa's debt service to other private creditors. A majority of African countries make no attempt to service their debt to commercial banks or other private creditors, as they do not expect any new borrowings from them.

Tables 7.5 and 7.6 show the difference in the debt burden of SSA as a whole and of the group of 26 low-income debt-distressed SPA countries which are the main focus of donor assistance and which benefit from larger concessional flows and debt relief. The debt structure of the region as a whole is shifting towards more concessionality but the change is not as dramatic as in SPA countries, where the proportion of concessional debt has risen from 39 per cent in 1980 to 60 per cent in 1991. The debt-servicing ratio for these countries has declined to about 20 per cent from 28 per cent in 1987. Net transfers from all sources to SPA countries amounted to 240 per cent of debt service paid in 1991. Debt servicing paid by these countries as a proportion of their export earnings and aggregate net transfers taken together was only 15 per cent. Hence this group has been able to increase its imports of goods and services by 6.2 per cent annually between 1987 and 1992.

The aggregate figures of Sub-Saharan African debt mask the concentration among countries of debt stock and debt service paid. Ten large countries – Nigeria, Côte d'Ivoire, Sudan, Zaïre, Zambia, Kenya, Tanzania, Cameroon, Congo and Ghana – account for two-thirds of the debt stock outstanding. Five countries – Nigeria, Côte d'Ivoire, Kenya, Zambia and Zimbabwe – pay two-thirds of the region's actual debt service.

Almost all the ten large borrowers are severely indebted countries and some of them are not yet eligible for concessional debt relief. Nigeria, Côte d'Ivoire, Cameroon and Congo are still considered lower-middle-income countries. If the bilateral official and private debt stock of these ten countries were reduced by one-half, the debt outstanding of SSA would decline from $178 billion or 111 per cent of GDP to $140 billion or 86 per cent of GDP.

Mistry[33] has argued that African debt service to multilateral institutions such as the IBRD has made these institutions 'the problem' rather than the solution. The facts and analysis hardly support this assertion. In assessing the role of the Bank Group, the entire range of the lending instruments should be taken into consideration. The first instrument is the IBRD, the loans of which are 'hard-window' or non-concessional in nature. Very few countries in SSA are current borrowers from this window. The second, and the most predominant source of financing for SSA, is the concessional arm, the IDA. Finally, the Bank introduced in 1988 a new instrument in the form of the 'fifth

Table 7.5 Structure of Debt Stock, end 1991 ($bn)

	Sub-Saharan Africa		SPA Countries	
	Amount	Share	Amount	Share
A. Official	110	61.8	45	76.3
Multilateral	40	22.5	22	37.5
Concessional	26	14.6	19	32.2
Non-Concessional	14	7.9	3	5.1
Bilateral	70	39.3	23	39.0
Concessional	34	19.1	16	27.1
Non-Concessional	36	20.2	7	7.8
B. Private		21.9	5	8.5
Commercial banks	21	11.8	2	3.4
Other Private	18	10.1	3	5.1
C. Short-term debt	22	12.3	4	6.7
D. IMF	7	3.9	5	8.5
Total	178	100.0	59	100.0
Memo item:				
Concessional Debt – 1980		26.9		39.1
1991		33.8		60.0

Source: *World Debt Tables 1992–93.*

Table 7.6 Structure of Debt Servicing Actually Paid, end 1991 ($bn)

	Sub-Saharan Africa		SPA Countries	
	Amount	% Share	Amount	% Share
Multilateral	3.7	35.9	1.8	56.2
World Bank	2.0	19.4	0.8	25.0
IMF	0.8	7.8	0.5	15.6
Bilateral Official	2.2	21.3	0.5	15.6
Commercial Banks	2.2	21.3	0.4	12.5
Other Private	1.7	16.5	0.3	9.4
Short-term Debt	0.5	4.8	0.2	6.2
Total	10.3	100.0	3.2	100.0
Memo items:				
Net transfers from[a] *the World Bank*	0.5		0.9	
Aggregate net transfers	11.4		7.7	

Source: Ibid.

a Net transfers in 1991 were lower than the average because of the large payment of accumulated arrears by Zambia. The net transfers from the World Bank in 1988–90 to SSA and SPA were $1.1 billion and $1.0 billion p.a. respectively.

dimension facility' to help IDA-eligible countries refinance their IBRD payments. The Bank Group's assistance is closely linked to the recipient country's policies and performance.

In response to the debt crisis of the 1980s and the growing financial difficulties of most SSA countries, the Bank has made a conscious shift from hard-window lending to concessional lending. In the early 1970s, there were 24 SSA countries that were IBRD borrowers but by 1992 the number had dwindled to only six and most countries were receiving concessional IDA loans. Consequently, net disbursements from IDA have risen five-fold from about $400 million in 1980 to almost $2 billion in 1990, and are being made to 37 SSA countries.

The Bank has also been providing a portion of IDA reflows under the 'fifth dimension' programme as supplementary adjustment credits to countries that are currently IDA-only borrowers and that have outstanding IBRD debt. Through annual allocation, the supplementary IDA credits have helped ease the debt-service burden of eligible borrowers who are undertaking adjustment programmes. A total of SDR 400 million has been allocated since 1988. In the financial year 1992, the allocation amounted to SDR 118 million, equivalent to approximately 90 per cent of the eligible IBRD interest payments due.

The total 'hard-window' or non-concessional multilateral debt of SSA at the end of 1991 was about $14 billion, or 8 per cent of the total debt stock; of this, the IBRD debt was $9 billion, or 5 per cent of the total debt. Debt service on multilateral debt is about $2.0 billion or 10 per cent of total debt service due and 3.7 per cent of the region's exports of goods and services. On an aggregate basis, the servicing of non-concessional multilateral debt may appear onerous, but the burden is in fact limited to a handful of countries which are relatively better-off in terms of their export earnings, are capable of improved economic performance with better economic management and can service this debt without much difficulty. Four countries – Nigeria, Côte d'Ivoire, Kenya and Cameroon – hold three-fourths of the IBRD debt stock.

Debt servicing on IBRD loans claims only 4 per cent of Nigeria's exports of goods and services. On the other hand, Nigeria's scheduled debt service to its other creditors amounts to 45 per cent of exports. Its major problem is the net negative transfer of $2.5 billion made mostly to bilateral and private creditors and not the small amount of debt service it makes to the IBRD. For Côte d'Ivoire, the debt service on IBRD loans is 8.6 per cent of its exports, while the debt service actually paid to all other creditors is about 32 per cent of exports. Nigeria and Côte d'Ivoire have already become eligible for IDA financing. In Cameroon, debt service to IBRD hardly exceeds 5 per cent of exports. Kenya is now receiving its assistance entirely from the IDA and has not contracted any new loans from IBRD since 1986. Its debt servicing to IBRD is therefore steadily declining and 90 per cent of its interest payments to IBRD have been refinanced through concessional IDA reflows since 1988. In 1992, Kenya paid $162 billion in debt service to IBRD but received $257 million in new flows from the World Bank Group.

The stock of IBRD debt in SSA countries in fact declined between 1987 and 1991. For the low-income SPA countries, the reduction in the IBRD debt stock is much larger as they are no longer receiving any new funds from the hard-window of the Bank and all new commitments are in the form of highly concessional IDA money. Their debt servicing[34] to the Bank Group – at about $150 million – is 6 per cent of the total debt service paid or 1.4 per cent of exports of goods and services. Disbursements from the World Bank Group to SPA countries in 1990 were $1.7 billion. Net transfers from the Bank Group to these 26 countries in the period 1988–90 exceeded $1 billion annually – more than half the total debt-related net transfers. But it needs to be emphasized that net transfer is not a particularly appropriate and meaningful concept as countries could not receive net positive transfers in perpetuity. In the case of low-income Africa, the continued positive transfers indicate the protracted nature of the economic difficulties that these countries face and the response of the Bank Group to their need.

Debt relief: a menu of options

Africa cannot escape its present economic crisis without significantly reducing its debt burden. Several important initiatives have been taken in recent years to provide debt relief, and many new proposals are under consideration. Together they provide a menu of options for keeping the actual debt-service payments within manageable limits. They fall into two broad categories: debt reduction and flexible and concessional debt rescheduling, which postpones debt-service payments or reduces long-term debt burdens, and debt swaps.

Debt reduction and debt rescheduling

Several donors including Canada, Finland, Germany, the Netherlands, Norway, Sweden, and the United Kingdom, have converted concessional bilateral loans to low-income countries into grants. Sub-Saharan Africa has also been the target of about two-thirds of the worldwide cancellations by creditors, far higher than its share of global concessional debt. ODA forgiveness accelerated during the 1989–91 period, with some $10 to 11 billion of concessional debt being written off by the major creditor countries. France wrote off concessional debt owed by 35 of the poorest African countries, resulting in the cancellation of some $3.4 billion of debt. Belgium has also decided to cancel its government-to-government debt owed by 13 African countries. In 1989, Germany cancelled $1.2 billion or 19 per cent of the debt owed to it by African countries. In the same year, the United States announced that, beginning in the fiscal year 1990, it would forgive development assistance (DA) and Economic Support Fund (ESF) debt owed by Sub-Saharan African countries undertaking reform programmes. To be eligible, the debtor country must have in effect an IMF standby, an enhanced structural adjustment facility, or a World Bank structural adjustment programme. The total amount forgiven in the years 1990 and 1991 was approximately $3.7 billion. To date, creditor countries have cancelled 11 per cent of SSA's concessional bilateral debt.

The scope for further relief through concessional debt cancellation is limited, however, since scheduled payments on bilateral ODA debt are small. The bilateral concessional debt owed by 26 low-income adjusting countries at the end of 1991 was about $15 billion, but at least one-fourth of this belonged to non-Paris Club creditors who have not taken a lead in writing off or cancelling debt. As this debt is not being serviced by most of the countries anyway, the accumulation of arrears is adding to the debt stock.

The main vehicle for restructuring bilateral official debt has been the Paris Club, where agreements are reached on a consensual basis consistent with equitable burden sharing among the creditor countries. This restructuring includes both inter-governmental loans and private export credits guaranteed or insured by a creditor country agency. The Paris Club has divided the debt into two categories, pre-cut-off date and post-cut-off date, and restructures only the former. The post-cut-off debt represents about 11 per cent of total non-concessional bilateral debt owed to Paris Club creditors.

Traditionally, bilateral debt restructuring has had short consolidation periods – at most, two years. It was intended to provide an adequate amount of cash-flow relief under adjustment programmes. This approach was found suitable for countries facing liquidity problems but was not appropriate for most African countries faced with a severe solvency crisis. The initial response of the Paris Club was to restructure previously rescheduled debt up to 100 per cent of current maturities and arrears, with a consolidation period up to three years. During the second half of the 1980s, the maximum repayment terms were extended to 20 years including a ten-year grace period. But this was also found to be inadequate. In an attempt to explore more generous terms of debt relief for low-income countries, it was agreed at the June 1988 Toronto summit of the G7 that the debts of IDA-eligible countries could be rescheduled by individual creditor countries choosing among three options:

- Forgiving one-third of the debt service due on obligations rescheduled through the Paris Club;
- Rescheduling all eligible obligations at market interest rates, but over a very long time period (25 years' maturity and a grace period of 14 years);
- Rescheduling all eligible obligations at concessional interest rates with long maturity (14 years, including 8 years' grace).

By September 1991 the Toronto initiative had been applied to 18 low-income African countries which obtained reschedulings on a consolidated debt of some $6 billion. The average grant element was more than 20 per cent on non-concessional debt. The Toronto Terms achieved a debt reduction of about $1 billion in present value terms.

The debt relief offered by the Toronto Terms was insufficient to restore external viability to many severely indebted countries. In December 1991, a further step was taken to implement concessions – the 'Enhanced Toronto Terms', which were essentially two options providing for deeper debt reduction and a non-concessional option of rescheduling over 25 years at market interest. The two concessional options amount to 50 per cent forgiveness in present value terms on debt-service payments falling due during the consolidation period. In addition, the new agreements provided for deferred consideration of potential debt reduction. Creditors indicated that they would be willing to consider restructuring of the remaining stock of pre-cut-off debt after three or four years. Twelve countries have so far benefitted from these new terms, and the consolidated amount is about $2.5 billion.

In 1989, US Secretary of the Treasury Brady called on the IMF and the World Bank to support and encourage efforts aimed at commercial debt reduction for major developing countries by catalyzing new financing. Subsequently, the World Bank and the IMF agreed that for the following three years a proportion of their lending might be earmarked for debt reduction. Among SSA countries, the Brady Plan has benefitted only Nigeria.

Impact of debt relief measures

The Enhanced Toronto Terms are a step forward but they fall short of the terms proposed by John Major at Trinidad. Under the 'Trinidad Terms' two-thirds of the debt stock would be cancelled and followed by a period of interest capitalization to provide further cash-flow relief and possibly by a graduating of later payments, depending on the debtor's ability to pay. An assessment of the impact of alternative rescheduling terms can be made by measuring the reduction in the present value of debt-service obligations they are expected to produce. This measure captures not only outright debt forgiveness but also the larger degree of concessionality of rescheduled debt resulting from lower interest charges. The impact is expressed by the ratio of the present value of debt to exports. When simulations were made to assess the impact of alternative terms on the severely indebted low-income countries, it was found that, even after the application of Trinidad Terms and assuming the forgiveness of all bilateral concessional ODA loans, the debt to export ratios remain unsustainable for some of these countries such as Mozambique, Sudan and Somalia.[35] This suggests that the restoration of external viability may require even further measures by official and commercial creditors.

Another evaluation of the alternative debt-rescheduling proposals – the Toronto Terms, the Trinidad Terms and a Dutch proposal (full forgiveness of bilateral official debt owed by the least developed and other low-income countries which face severe debt problems and are implementing sound economic policies) – was carried out by Abbate and Tran-Nguyen.[36] This study concluded that for the 26 low-income countries, assuming a 5 per cent annual growth rate of exports, the debt relief under the Dutch proposal was, on average, most favourable, although for a few countries – Mozambique, Guinea-Bissau, Somalia, São Tomé, etc. – additional debt-service reduction beyond the terms of the Dutch proposal would be required. The important difference between the Dutch proposal and the Trinidad Terms lies in the inclusion of the post-cut-off debt in the former.

All of the debt-rescheduling initiatives are designed principally to benefit only low-income African countries; there are no comparable schemes for middle-income African countries with acute debt problems. Yet the middle-income countries face long-term development problems not significantly different from those of the low-income countries. And, indeed, when the correction of overvalued currencies – Nigeria's, for example – places some of these countries in the low-income category, they should be considered eligible for the same debt relief measures as those granted to low-income African countries.

There are a number of technical and legal problems to be resolved in determining the adequacy of debt relief measures. Each debtor country has a specific debt profile and special circumstances, and the solution to its debt problem must be decided on a case-by-case basis. As a general principle, debt relief should be given only to countries that are both debt-distressed and willing to adopt reforms to improve their capacity for growth and future debt service. Truly to benefit debtor countries, special finance for debt relief or concessional rescheduling should be genuinely 'additional' and not taken out of the aid budgets already allocated to the beneficiary countries. In countries with severe problems of arrears, bridge financing may be needed to make use of debt relief facilities.

Africa's debts, although a burden for the region, are only a small part of the global portfolio of creditors. Significant debt relief from new money cannot be counted on in the near future, and conventional debt restructuring is unlikely to generate the relief required to restore growth. For most African countries the predominant problem is the official debt and although the Enhanced Toronto Terms are a step in the right direction, clearly more far-reaching relief is needed.

Debt swaps

A large number of proposals have been made to relieve the pressure on foreign-exchange resources by swapping local assets – physical or financial – for debts. Nigeria has already used debt swaps to reduce some of its external debt burden. But in other countries the practice has been neither widespread nor highly successful.

Debt swaps vary greatly, but there are some common features. Most arrangements enable the debtor to share part of the market discount on debt, determine the sectors of the economy in which equity can be purchased, and place restrictions on the dividends and principal that can be repatriated. The simplest form of swap – debt for equity – has very limited application in Africa because of the lack of perceived investment opportunities and developed markets for financial instruments.

Although debt-for-nature swaps have received a lot of publicity in recent years, the total amount converted in this way has remained small. In SSA, only Madagascar, Zambia, Nigeria and Ghana were able to convert about $6 to $7 million of face value. Some initiatives in debt-for-nature swaps have been prepared by the official sector. The new Paris Club terms for lower-middle-income countries, granted since September 1990, have authorized various types of debt conversions, such as debt-for-nature, debt-for-aid, debt-for-equity and other local currency debt swaps. Provisions for voluntary bilateral swap arrangements have been inserted into the Paris Club agreements, stipulating that ODA and inter-governmental loans are eligible for such debt conversions without limit and that export credits are eligible up to 10 per cent of the debt stock. This clause has been inserted in the rescheduling agreements of Congo and Nigeria.

Similar to debt-for-nature swaps, debt-for-development swaps support projects in education, health and agriculture. UNICEF has converted $20 million of face value for its development projects in Sudan.

Another variation is for a donor to purchase debt (at a discount) and then to pass the loans to a non-governmental organization, on the understanding that the debtor government will redeem the loans in local currency or bonds. The NGO will subsequently exchange or swap the debt and use the proceeds for development purposes. Such local currency swaps are useful only when the country has domestic savings available for that purpose; otherwise they may result in inflationary pressures. In the CFA Franc Zone, the scope for such swaps is particularly limited because of the convertibility of local currency with the French franc. For a debtor country to benefit, such schemes must provide additional resources.

Prospects

The momentum of aid generated in the past few years will have to be maintained during the 1990s for several reasons. The World Bank's long-term perspective study estimated the external capital requirements that would translate into one per cent average annual growth in per capita consumption for SSA in the 1990s. As the first two years of the decade have seen a decline in per capita consumption, the updated requirements of external financing amount to $30 billion (1990 prices) annually, consisting of debt relief of $12 billion and new money flows of $18 billion.

Donors will have to consider a number of developments in setting aid policy in the 1990s. First, countries will have to continue the difficult economic reform programmes initiated in recent years. Those that have not yet embarked on reform will need to do so. Unless these programmes are funded adequately, they cannot be effective or sustained.

Second, there are some major new entrants to the list of IDA-eligible countries. Nigeria has already become eligible and will increasingly depend on official development assistance to meet its external resource gap. In the past Nigeria has received a negligible amount of ODA ($0.6 per capita in 1986). If by the year 2000 it were to receive the same level of per capita ODA as Cameroon, another oil-exporting African country, it would account for about $2.5 billion of ODA a year; this would mean a 17 per cent increase in ODA. In addition, Angola can be expected to join IDA.

Third, special efforts are needed in the 1990s to correct the backsliding that has occurred in areas such as food security, human resource development and infrastructure, and to fund initiatives in family planning and the environment. For human resource development, additional expenditures of about $10 billion (1990 prices) a year will be needed by 2000. The backlog of road maintenance itself is estimated to cost $5 billion on top of the $700 million needed annually during the following decade to avoid further deterioration. Large initial efforts are needed to give momentum to programmes for family planning and environmental protection.

The World Bank estimates that a net annual transfer of resources of about 9 per cent of Sub-Saharan GDP will be required to achieve sustained growth during the 1990s. The ODA required to meet this target will depend on such variables as debt relief programmes, non-concessional capital inflows from private and public sources, and reserve requirements – all of which are subject to uncertainties. With sustained policy reforms, private capital inflows could improve significantly through remittances, reverse capital flight and foreign private investment. Evidence from several countries (such as Ghana and Senegal) suggests, however, that restoring private sector confidence takes time and that during the next decade only moderate progress can be expected. Moreover, given deteriorating creditworthiness, non-concessional borrowing will be lower than in the past. It is estimated that the net receipts from these sources will be moderate, probably about $6 billion a year.

The external resource requirement of Sub-Saharan Africa during the 1990s could be met if donors achieved two related targets. First, gross ODA must continue to increase during the 1990s at about 4 per cent a year in real terms. Second, debt relief mechanisms must be put in place so that the actual debt-service payments for countries with strong reform programmes are kept within manageable limits. For the region as a whole it is estimated that adequate debt relief will be available to keep the debt-service payments in the 1990s around the level of the 1980s (that is, about $9 billion a year). If this does not occur, higher levels of external assistance will be necessary. Alternatively, if debt relief exceeded the above estimate, external assistance requirements would be correspondingly reduced.

A more permanent solution to SSA's external debt problem will be one of the most important development challenges of the 1990s. Without a return to a reasonable degree of external viability – the ability to service external claims without recourse to rescheduling and arrears – the necessary adjustment, investment and modest growth in per capita incomes that Africa requires to recover and get on the path to sustainable development will remain elusive.

The scope for the expansion of other alternative sources of external capital for SSA such as commercial bank lending, FDI and the return of flight capital is limited. The only viable option is for a continued flow of ODA.

However, SSA must help itself by raising its domestic savings rate. Foreign resources need to become less of a substitute for, and more a complement to, domestic savings. The region, with the help of donors, must also use its external resources more efficiently. Finally, the quality and efficiency of overall domestic investment needs to be improved. It is to these issues that we now turn.

Investment

The ratio of gross domestic investment to GDP in SSA has not recovered from its historical level of 23 per cent in the 1970s. Investment has remained depressed even in countries which have intensively adjusted their economies. Although there was a slight recovery in the period 1986–90, the overall ratio of 16 to 17 per cent is much lower than the 25 per cent average for developing countries as a group (see Table 7.7). The gross national savings rate in SSA of less than 10 per cent is also in stark contrast to the 24 per cent achieved by the developing countries as a group. It is often thought that poor countries with a low level of per capita incomes cannot save very much. The evidence from South Asia, a region with almost identical per capita incomes to SSA, contradicts this belief. The differential in the savings rate between the two regions in the 1970s was insignificant, but between 1986 and 1990 the average national savings rate in South Asia was almost 20 per cent, about twice as high as in SSA. The collapse of saving in SSA is partly responsible for the region's low investment ratios. However, the doubling of external resource flows during the same period should have enhanced investment.

The average ratio of total investment to GDP in SSA masks the variance among countries in the region, ranging from 2 per cent to 50 per cent. It is noteworthy, however, that during 1986–90 the nine countries with the highest per capita incomes in the region had lower investment ratios than the region's nine lowest-income countries. This reflects the fact that decline in investment seemed to continue for the higher-income group during adjustment, while there has been some recovery of investment among the lower-income group, providing some optimism for an improved outlook for investment growth.

Table 7.7 SSA: Key Savings and Investment Indicators (% of GDP)

	1970–80	1981-85	1986–90
Gross Investment Ratio	20.8	15.7	16.8
Private Investment Ratio	-	10.4	10.2
Foreign Direct Investment Ratio	-	0.7	0.8
Gross National Savings Ratio	14.6	9.3	9.7
Memo Items:			
Gross Investment Ratio for Developing Countries	24.7	24.1	25.3
Gross National Savings Ratio for Developing Countries	22.2	22.1	24.0

Source: World Bank data.

Private investment

Private investment in SSA remained stable at around 10 per cent of GDP during the later 1980s and was concentrated in the higher-income countries of the region. A review of determinants of private investment will help us understand why levels of private investment remain depressed. A survey of the literature reveals that several factors influence private investment.

A certain amount of macroeconomic stability – such as low and predictable inflation, external and internal balance – are of paramount importance in ensuring a strong response of private investment to economic incentives. The recent literature has emphasized the key role of uncertainty in investment decisions. The uncertainty follows directly from the irreversible nature of investment expenditures. Empirical studies have also found that fiscal deficits and foreign debt have a strongly negative effect on private investment.

An overvalued exchange rate can also be a factor, because it reduces the returns in local currency received by exporting farmers and manufacturers. Real interest rates and policies affecting them can influence private investment, but there is no empirical finding supporting this relation for developing countries. This is because of repressed financial markets in these countries, where credit policy (and not interest rates) directly affects the investment level. The impact of public investment on private investment depends on whether they are complementary or substitutes. The most important effect that the public sector has on private investment in developing countries is through institutions and regulations. Investors, local and foreign, are frequently hampered by legal and bureaucratic impediments, as well as by underdeveloped capital markets.

A case study of Zimbabwe[37] confirms the importance of government policies in stimulating private investment and concludes that one of the key issues to be tackled by public policy should be to raise expected future profits by reducing the perceived risk of investment. In most African countries, the perceived risks are fairly high and the response of potential investors can be positive only if these risks are minimized or shared.

A study of sixteen SSA countries was carried out for the period 1980–90 to examine how adjustment has affected private investment in Africa.[38] Its findings suggest that determinants of private investment in SSA countries do not follow the same pattern as in other regions. In Africa, real effective exchange rates are found significantly to affect private investment – a finding not borne out by the studies of other regions and the developing countries as a group. This outcome is consistent with an interpretation that a real depreciation of local currency expands exports, raises real incomes, and consequently stimulates aggregate investment expenditures. The study also shows that long-term debt in SSA does not have any statistically significant effect on private investment in the region. As is true for other developing countries, real interest rates also do not have any significant effect on private investment. Inflation has a positive effect on private investment but the effect is statistically insignificant.

Why is private investment not responding to the policy changes taking place in adjusting countries? Prior to adjustment, the pattern of investment in Africa was oriented towards import-substituting industries under high protective barriers. A reduction in protection and exposure to competition from imports has squeezed the profits and lowered sales in these industries. Significant devaluation makes imported inputs more expensive,while higher interest rates erode opportunities for cheap local borrowing, which had encouraged foreign investors. Higher prices for energy, transport and other services have the same adverse effect on current and expected profit flows. Thus the immediate response of investors to policy changes is how best to manage these disruptions.

The immediate effect of adjustment policies on investment has called into question the credibility and sustainability of these policies in some countries. The World Bank's third review of adjustment lending (RAL III),[39] completed in 1992, addresses this issue systematically. Its major findings can be summed up as follows:

(i) The response of private investment to adjustment programmes has taken longer than initially expected. However, private investment has begun to recover in some adjusting countries, especially middle-income countries.

(ii) In fact, the pattern of investment response to an adjustment programme seems to have two phases. In the first phase, there is an initial contraction and then stagnation of the share of private investment in GDP. This is the phase of 'investment pause' caused by necessary stabilization measures. Reducing aggregate demand through fiscal and monetary contraction reduces the demand for output and thus the readiness of firms to invest. Phase two sees the sustained increase in the share of private investment in GDP. Once distortions are removed and stabilization attained, the private investment ratio begins to rise in response to economic incentives that lead to export expansion and output growth.

(iii) Although some sort of 'investment pause' in response to adjustment is common, the length and intensity of the pause differs among countries. The difference is due to the fluctuating intensity in adiustment efforts, the varied initial conditions from which adjustment programmes started, and a changed business environment. In most middle-income countries, the investment pause lasted 3–5 years. In low-income adjusting countries, export and output growth has been weaker, and private investment has not yet recovered.

(iv) Efficiency of investment allocation improved with adjustment programmes even during the period of the 'investment pause'. Adjustment programmes generally succeeded in bringing prices more into line with economic costs, and exposure to increased international competition also resulted in stronger cost discipline, greater technological capability, and increased productivity. These gains in efficiency from adjustment programmes helped to generate greater output growth from existing levels of investment.

(v) The varying nature of investment response to adjustment programmes depends on economic predictability, the legal and regulatory framework, the physical infrastructure, and the functioning of factor markets. Investor confidence about the stability of the macroeconomic environment and the permanence of structural reforms seems most crucial. Strong investment recoveries in middle-income countries after a pause are explained by sustained adjustment efforts and measures that have improved the business environment, including good regulatory and financial policies, adequate and well-maintained infrastructure, efficient factor markets and a supportive legal and administrative framework. A lack or weakness of these conditions explains the poor investment response to adjustment programmes in developing countries.

(vi) Adjustment programmes have generally succeeded in reducing distortionary trade and financial and exchange-rate policies, but have had limited success, especially in low-income SSA countries, in encouraging measures needed to improve the business environment. Where implementation of adjustment programmes has been tentative, economic uncertainty has played a major role in causing private investors to defer investment decisions. Even after adjustment programmes started, continuing barriers to the entry and exit of firms and uncertainty regarding the legal and regulatory framework for private investment continue to constrain private investors in many SSA countries.

To sum up, adjustment programmes in the short run may have a negative effect on private investment because of reduction in aggregate demand and contractionary fiscal and monetary policies. However, as structural reforms are carried out, private investment can be expected to recover in response to a new set of incentives. But this later recovery and growth of private investment depend on a congenial business environment.

Foreign Direct Investment

Foreign Direct Investment (FDI) has been a dynamic and growing source of capital flows to developing countries in recent years. FDI net flows to developing countries increased from $500 million in 1965 to slightly over $10 billion in 1985, and then more than tripled to almost $34 billion in 1991. Until the mid-1970s, the level of FDI in SSA was similar to that of other developing regions. In the 1980s, however, there was a marked decline and FDI now plays a small role in overall investment and total external resource flows. In the period 1977–93, the share of African countries in total FDI flows to developing countries has remained stagnant at $1.3 billion. Nigeria is the only country which has attracted large sums of FDI, mainly for its oil and gas sectors.

As noted earlier, policy-makers and others in Africa have a sceptical view of the benefits that can accrue to national economies from FDI. The conventional view has been that multinational corporations invest in Africa primarily to exploit the natural resource wealth of African countries in order to maximize monopoly rents. Evidence from other developing countries suggests that these fears are not well-founded. FDI should become an attractive source of capital flows for SSA also. The two major obstacles to higher growth in this region are low investment and shortages of foreign exchange. Foreign direct investment could address both problems. It brings in foreign exchange, supplements domestic savings and raises investment. Foreign investment could also increase the efficiency of the domestic economy.

FDI also offers a number of advantages over commercial borrowing,[40] which has proved costly to African countries in terms of the debt crisis. First, equity financing requires payments only when the investment earns a profit, while debt requires payments irrespective of a country's economic and balance-of-payments situation. Second, payments on FDI can be regulated by the host country while debt repayments are outside its control (affected, as they are, by interest rates set in the international market). Third, because much of FDI consists of reinvested earnings, only a portion of the returns on investment is repatriated. Debt, on the other hand, requires full repayment of interest and principal. The reinvestment also involves less constraints and has an almost built-in rollover mechanism, compared with the fluctuations in commercial bank lending. Fourth, FDI permits a closer match between the maturity structures of earnings from an investment and the required payments on the capital used to finance it, thus avoiding the mismatch created when developing countries borrow short-term to finance long-term investments. FDI also offers externalities, which borrowing does not. FDI flows help in easing capital shortages and financing balance-of-payments deficits but their long-term benefit lies more in the transfer of technology, human capital creation, the development of managerial skills and foreign market penetration. SSA has to diversify its limited production and export base and these attributes of FDI can play a vital role in this process.

Questions have been raised about whether investment can be attracted on the basis of advantages such as cheap labour. A recent survey[41] concluded that the ability of countries to attract investment in manufacturing on the basis of the availability of cheap, unskilled labour has diminished in recent years. The need for such labour in the manufacture of many products is simply much less than it was a decade ago, and this trend will surely continue. Given the current pace of development in products and processes, most export platforms will require technological (including human) upgrading to remain competitive. Developing countries that have more highly skilled labour available at relatively low wages can more favourably influence plant location decisions. Nevertheless, some types of products (apparel, shoes) have thus far remained largely unaffected by the declining dependence on labour in manufacturing. For investors in these industries, there will continue to be a motive for locating production in poorer countries.

It is unlikely that most African countries can compete favourably with other developing regions in the production of unsophisticated goods, but there are at least seven or eight countries which have relatively better prospects than most developing countries. Many of them are in the process of transition from a highly controlled and command economy to creating a more liberal policy and business environment. Currently, investment in these countries does not yet appear attractive. However, as the IFC noted:[42]

> The reform programs often make the business environment more difficult in the short to medium term by introducing the need to adapt to more competitive circumstances. Furthermore, measures aimed at reducing deficits often result in restrained overall demand and depressed local markets. Many businesses find it difficult to adjust to trade reforms and industrial restructuring measures and to absorb increased input and debt service costs caused by local currency devaluations. In this kind of environment, investors adopt a wait and see attitude before making new investments or expanding operations. *In the long term, however, the success of such reforms should increase the scope for private sector activity.*
>
> There have been important changes in capital movements at a global level – the growing integration of capital markets across borders, institutions and financial markets. Traditional markets have matured. Businesses have become international in perspective, looking beyond their national borders for new products, customers and inputs. Improved transport and communications have facilitated this as has technological change and innovation.
>
> Such changes suggest that long-term external structural reasons exist for continued flows of capital to developing countries. Much depends on better economic management and greater political stability in SSA. In a global market place there is a sharply-reduced tolerance for poor policies.

Prospects

Africa faces a real dilemma. To meet its requirements of external capital a number of lower-middle-income African countries will have to rely increasingly on FDI as other types of traditional flows such as ODA, commercial bank lending, and non-concessional official finance become relatively scarce. On the other hand, the image of Africa among prospective investors is not very favourable at present and the perceived political and economic risks are high. Growing competition for foreign investment from Eastern Europe and the republics of the former Soviet Union has further limited opportunities for Africa. Thus, even if African countries succeed in implementing the reforms and changes necessary, it is not obvious that they will succeed in attracting substantial new FDI. The expectation of FDI should, then, remain modest and realistic. It would be unwise to pin too much hope on foreign investment flows to bridge either the foreign-exchange or domestic savings gaps.

This does not imply that African governments should not resolve their ambivalence about the role of FDI in their countries and strive to create an enabling environment which is conducive to foreign investment. The difficulties faced by existing investors in Africa have not diminished and an active effort to attract FDI to the region has not yet been made. Foreign investors already engaged in business in African countries should be encouraged to stay and expand. This can have a positive demonstration effect for potential new investors. Companies can also be actively offered specific investment proposals, briefed about economic and political conditions and provided with the information needed to make decisions. Foreign investors can also be exposed to business opportunities by offers of management contracts, plant and technology licensing agreements, production sharing agreements, and international subcontracting. In the end, the results will depend on the successful implementation and liberalization of domestic and foreign trade regimes in African countries and an improvement in the perceived political and economic risks of doing business.

Conclusions

Our survey of the prospects for trade, aid and investment in Sub-Saharan Africa leads to the following broad conclusions:

(a) The relative pay-off from orienting outward, improving competitiveness and recapturing lost share in world markets is higher than any other strategy for growth and sustainable development in SSA countries. Had SSA maintained international competitiveness and retained its 1970 share in world exports, successfully defending against 'new' entrants, its 1990 level of exports would have been at least $50 billion higher than actual earnings. This calculation assumes that the composition of African exports would have changed in consonance with the growth in world trade. Had SSA continued to rely on primary commodity exports alone, the relative gains would have been much smaller. Care should be taken not to allocate resources for further expansion in commodities and minerals in which the relative share of SSA exceeds the elasticity of world demand.

(b) Although the dependence of SSA on external resource flows for investment, imports and development has increased in the last decade, budgetary constraints in the OECD countries, competing demand from new claimants and the insistence on new types of conditionalities by bilateral donors, such as democratization, reduced military spending, and improvement of human rights will make it difficult to sustain a high level of aid. Almost all African countries will have to mobilize domestic resources and increase domestic saving rates by reducing public sector dissavings, financial losses of public enterprises and other non-productive expenditures. While a group of lower-middle-income African countries is capable of attracting a significant amount of foreign direct investment, most resource-poor countries, especially in the Sahel and Horn of Africa, will continue to be dependent on foreign aid.

(c) There is a consensus on economic grounds for finding a more durable solution to Africa's debt problem. The fact that only one-half of the debt service due can be paid suggests the urgent need to reduce the stock of debt and thus debt-servicing obligations in alignment with debt-servicing capacity. Many of the current proposals, if implemented, can bring considerable relief.

(d) Productive investment levels in most African countries have remained depressed, and even where economic policy reforms have been implemented, the investor response – both domestic and foreign – has been poor. Uncertainty, lack of policy credibility and continuity, fears of policy reversals, the contagion effect of Africa, and more attractive opportunities elsewhere, reinforce structural weaknesses such as poor infrastructure, a weak human resource base and inefficient services to deny Africa new investment. Nevertheless, there are several countries which can succeed in attracting significant amounts of investment because of their domestic market size, location in the region, low labour costs and natural resource endowments.

(e) More fundamentally, the impetus of Africa's growth and sustainable development will come only by investing in and accelerating the education, training and skill development and capacities of its human resources and by improving the means of linking these skills and capacities to the world market through trade, capital flows, technology and investment.

Notes

1. The author is grateful to Kazi Matin for useful comments on the original draft of this paper.
2. The author is Chief Economist, Africa Region of the World Bank. The views expressed in this paper are the author's and should not be attributed to the World Bank, its management or the Board of Directors.
3. World Bank, *Sub-Saharan Africa: from Crisis to Sustainable Growth* (Washington, DC, 1989), p. 24.
4. Peter Svedberg, 'The Export Performance of Sub-Saharan Africa', in J. H. Frimpong-Ansah, S. M. Ravi Kanbur and Peter Svedberg (eds), *Trade and Development in Sub-Saharan Africa* (Manchester: Manchester University Press, 1991).
5. James Pickett, 'The Low-Income Economies of Sub-Saharan Africa: Problems and Prospects', in J. Pickett and H. Singer (eds), *Towards Economic Recovery in Sub-Saharan Africa* (London: Routledge, 1990).
6. A similar conclusion is reached in Hania El-Farhan's study, 'Analysis of the Growth Performance of Sub-Saharan African Countries 1960–85', forthcoming Ph.D. thesis, School of Oriental and African Studies, University of London, cited in Tony Killick, *Explaining Africa's Post-Independence Development Experiences* (London: Overseas Development Institute, Working Paper 60, 1992). Although a positive association is found between the terms of trade and GDP growth, it is generally not significant.
7. T. Akiyama and D. Larsen, 'Adding-Up Problem – Strategies for Primary Commodity Exports in Sub-Saharan Africa' (World Bank, draft, 1993).
8. J. R. Coleman, T. Akiyama and P. N. Varanges, 'Impacts of Policy Changes on Cocoa Sectors in Major Sub-Saharan Producing Countries' (World Bank, draft, 1992).
9. Refik Erzan and Peter Svedberg, 'Protection Facing Exports from Sub-Saharan Africa in the EC, Japan and the US', in Frimpong-Ansah *et al.*, *Trade and Development in Sub-Saharan Africa*.
10. However, African countries do encounter obstacles to trade in some agricultural commodities in which they could be competitive, such as beef.
11. It is estimated that the protectionist Common Agricultural Policy of the EC benefits SSA, as a net importer of cereals and sugar. Liberalization of the CAP would reduce welfare in the food-importing countries. See Ulrich Koester and Malcolm D. Bale, 'The Common Agricultural Policy: a Review of its Operation and Effects on Developing Countries', *World Bank Research Observer*, 5, 1 (January 1990).
12. A. P. Lerner, 'The Symmetry between Import and Export Taxes', *Economica*, August 1936; K. W. Clements and L. R. Sjaastad, *How Protection Taxes Exporters* (London: Trade Policy Research Centre, Thames Essays 39, 1984).
13. World Bank, *World Development Report 1987* (Washington, DC, 1987), p. 80.
14. Dean DeRosa, 'Protection and Export Performance in Sub-Saharan Africa', *Weltwirtschaftliches Archiv*, 128, 1 (1992).
15. I. El-Badawi, D. Ghura and Uwujaren, 'World Bank Adjustment Lending and Economic Performance in Sub-Saharan Africa in the 1980s', (World Bank PRE Working Paper 1000, October 1992).
16. Ramon Lopen, 'Trade and Macroeconomic Policies and Agricultural Exports' (World Bank, PRE Working Paper 921, 1991).
17. Nigeria abolished import licensing, removed nearly all quantitative restrictions on imports, lowered average tariff rates, devalued its currency substantially, allowed non-oil exporters 100 per cent retention

of foreign-exchange proceeds, decontrolled all output and input prices (except petroleum products and fertilizers), and allowed agricultural producer prices to be determined by the market.

18. K. Moseley, 'Seizing the Change: Economic Crisis and Industrial Restructuring in Nigeria', in J. Nyang'oro and T. M. Shaw (eds), *Beyond Structural Adjustment in Africa* (New York: Praeger, 1992).
19. These exports are made 'informally' because of overvalued exchange rates, high tariffs and import bans in neighbouring countries and the corruption and red tape encountered at customs even in legal trade.
20. Food aid to SSA has almost halved from 4.8 million tons in 1985 to 2.5 million tons in 1990. The volume data on total food imports for the same period shows a similar trend – down from 11.0 million tons to 7.7 million tons.
21. Under a monetary model of the balance of payments, a decline in the domestic prices of imports reduces the domestic price level (price level decline is greater, the larger the state of imports in GDP). This raises the real supply of money balances and, for any given money demand, results in an outflow of reserves.
22. Kazi Matin *et al.*, 'Kenya: the Challenge of Promoting Exports', UNDP/World Bank TEP Report, December 1992.
23. F. Stewart, 'Alternative Development Strategies: an Overview', in F. Stewart, S. Lall and S. Wangwe (eds), *Alternative Development Strategies in Sub-Saharan Africa* (London: Macmillan, 1992).
24. Moseley, 'Seizing the Change'.
25. El-Fahran, *Analysis of the Growth Performance.*
26. A. Fosu, 'Exports and Economic Growth: African Case', *World Development*, 18, 6 (June 1990).
27. Kazi Matin, 'Openness and Economic Performance in Sub-Saharan Africa' (World Bank PRE Working Paper 1025, October 1992).
28. In several cross-country studies of *all* countries from all regions the positive coefficient on openness was found to disappear when controls for macroeconomic policy were introduced.
29. The above estimates do not include technical co-operation grants which amounted to $4.5 billion in 1990. Including these grants the aggregate net flows rose to $21.8 billion or 13.4 per cent of the GDP of SSA.
30. G. K. Helleiner, 'Trade Policy, Exchange Rates, and Relative Prices in Sub-Saharan Africa: Interpreting the 1980s' (Paper presented at a Conference in Gothenberg, Sweden, September 1992).
31. If those countries which gained from terms of trade are included, the average loss for the whole sample of 26 countries dwindles to 5.9 per cent.
32. World Bank, *World Debt Tables 1992–93* (Washington, DC, 1992).
33. P. Mistry, 'African Debt: Options for the Future' (Paper prepared for UNICEF Meeting on Debt in New York, March 1993).
34. Figures of debt servicing paid in 1991 are exceptionally high since they include Zambia's payment of past accumulated arrears of $344 million.
35. *World Debt Tables 1992–93* (World Bank, 1992).
36. F. Abbate and Tran-Nguyen, 'Official Debt Reduction: A Comparative Analysis of the Toronto Options, the U.K. Proposal and the Netherlands Initiative' (mimeo 1992). In this study, a normative 20 per cent debt-servicing ratio was posited as the benchmark against which the debt relief resulting from the application of each of the three proposals could be judged.
37. M. Dailami and M. Walton, 'Private Investment, Government Policy and Foreign Capital in Zimbabwe', in A. Chibbier *et al.* (eds), *Reviving Private Investment in Developing Countries* (Amsterdam: North Holland, 1992).
38. R. Faruqee, 'Private Investment in Sub-Saharan Africa' (World Bank, Africa Regional Office, 1992).
39. World Bank, *The Third Report on Adjustment Lending: Private and Public Resources for Growth* (Washington, DC, March 1992).
40. C. Michalopolous, 'Private Direct Investment, Finance and Development', *Asian Development Review*, 3, 2 (1985).
41. Robert Miller, 'Determinants of U.S. Manufacturing Investment Abroad', *Finance and Development*, 30, 1 (March 1993).
42. International Finance Corporation, *Annual Report* 1989 (Washington, DC, 1989).

8

N. N. SUSUNGI

The Origins of the Debt Crisis & its *Aftermath* in *Africa*

Whence Came the Debt Crisis?

A mere thirty years after independence, the African continent finds itself saddled with debt of unbelievable proportions. Most of it was contracted during the 1970s when rising prices for nearly all commodities led many a government to prepare ambitious development plans on the assumption that prices would continue to rise. The bankers obliged because the oil shocks of 1973 generated excess liquidity in the international banking system which needed to be recycled somewhere. Governments continued to borrow in the late 1970s and early 1980s when price declines of these same commodities were thought to be temporary. The price bounce-back never took place and all the borrowing nations sank into the depths of economic misery where they have been ever since.

The Third World debt crisis has shattered two important myths, thereby providing the world with a dose of bitter reality. The first myth is that sovereign states do not go bankrupt and the second is that no country ever goes to jail for not repaying its loans.

The first myth was attributed to Walter Wriston, the former chairman of Citicorp, parent to Citibank, the world's largest commercial bank. The quadrupling of oil prices in 1973 triggered the most massive and sudden transfer of income ever known, to oil-producing countries which were physically unprepared to absorb the resources. This was equally true for heavily populated countries such as Nigeria, Indonesia and Mexico as for smaller countries such as Kuwait, Libya and the United Arab Emirates. Even in cases such as Nigeria, absorption of the resources required carefully prepared projects and plans that corresponded with the true needs of the teeming population. Such plans and projects could not be identified and prepared overnight. In the meantime what was to be done with the billions of dollars that were flowing into the countries' overseas accounts? The large banks in the money centres of the United States suddenly found themselves with ballooning short-term deposit accounts in 1974 and 1975, without having given any serious thought to how and where such large volumes of capital could be lent for profit. The last thing that a commercial bank wants is to accept interest-paying deposits without being able to find somebody ready to borrow the money at an interest rate which enables the bank to earn a decent margin.

But the recession which was triggered by the oil price increases in the oil-importing countries of the OECD, and particularly in the United States, made it difficult to find enough corporate borrowers to absorb by way of new borrowings the mountain of cash surpluses which the oil-producing countries were accumulating in deposit accounts. The logical place to lend the money was therefore the cash-short Third World oil-importing countries whose foreign-exchange reserves were being cleaned out by their oil import bills. That is called recycling. Coming at the top of the list were countries like Brazil and Argentina in Latin America, and Côte d'Ivoire and Morocco in Africa. These countries borrowed large volumes of cash from the commercial banks, which were only too happy to find takers ready and willing to pay some of the highest lending spreads in the history of world banking. What could be more sensible than financing the huge Itaipu hydroelectric project in Brazil, which cost some $15 billion and which was aimed at providing OPEC-proof energy to this energy-starved economy? Similarly, the huge sugar complexes in Brazil were aimed at producing gasohol in order to reduce the country's dependence on imported crude oil. That is clever. In Africa, the Ivorian miracle was unfolding very rapidly and the *Caisse de Stabilisation* was flush with huge revenue surpluses generated during the coffee and cocoa boom years of the 1970s. It would have been ridiculous even to think of any of these countries going bankrupt.

When the price of oil collapsed in 1981, a new category of sovereign borrowers suddenly appeared on the market. They were the heavily populated oil-producing countries which had prepared development plans based on oil price forecasts which went as high as $50 per barrel in 1980 and were sometimes projected to reach $75 by 1990. As it was found sometimes politically easier to borrow from the market to fill the budget deficit than to scale down development plans, countries such as Nigeria, Congo, Gabon, Angola and Algeria in Africa, and Venezuela, Mexico and Peru in Latin America, quickly moved into the market with a voracious appetite for capital sharpened by their ambitions. In no time they mopped up the excess liquidity that had built up in earlier years. The bankers were only too glad to oblige because, after all, the loans were secured by the underground oil reserves in these countries and, besides, the spreads were juicy. How could such countries possibly go bankrupt? The outlook for the banking world could not be better, since the fall in oil prices spelled good news for the big borrowers in the oil-importing countries.

This myth was finally shattered when officials of the Mexican Finance Ministry boarded a flight for Washington in August 1982, to tell US Treasury officials that Mexico had gone bankrupt as a country. The Chairman of the Federal Reserve Board and officials of the Treasury Department had hastily to arrange for a bail-out package involving contributions from the US Government itself and from 100 banks that met in New York City from 19 to 21 August 1982. The banks agreed on a 90-day moratorium on a payment of $10 billion in principal but not on interest. The Bank of International Settlements agreed to provide emergency short-term credit of $1.6 billion, to be syndicated by a consortium of central banks around the world.

On 20 August 1982, the US Government announced an aid package consisting of $1 billion to be made as advance payment for further purchases of Mexican oil that would go into US strategic stocks. At the same time, an additional $1 billion in credit guarantees was to be provided by the Commodities Credit Corporation of the Department of Agriculture to finance the purchase of US farm products. The world's banking system had just had a close shave with disaster, but this was only the first act of the international debt crisis.

Five years later, in one of his rare press conferences, the Chairman of Citicorp announced that Citicorp had decided to increase its loan loss reserves by the enormous sum of $3 billion. This was going to result in a net loss of $2.5 billion for the second quarter of 1987, and would bring the total loan loss reserves of Citicorp to $3.5 billion, representing 24 per cent of its total exposure in Third World countries, by which it was owed some $14.7 billion. As at the end of 1986, Brazil owed Citibank $4.6 billion, Mexico $2.8 billion and Argentina $1.4 billion.

In increasing his loan loss reserves by $3 billion, John Reed, the man who won his spurs at Citibank by building the consumer loan portfolio when Walter Wriston was recycling petrodollars to Third World countries, was in effect saying that he did not expect that 24 per cent of the loans that Citicorp had made to Third World countries would ever be repaid. This was a telling message, that sovereign nations, like companies and individuals, can go bankrupt, if they do not manage their finances wisely.

Wall Street concurred! Even though the $3 billion bad loan provision resulted in the largest quarterly loss in US banking history, the stock price of Citicorp rose by 2⅜ points on 20 May 1987 to close at $53 per share. As the share prices of the other large banks declined in response, the message from investors was that any bank that did not increase its loan loss provisions to a level comparable to that of Citicorp was probably carrying fictitious reserves.

The second myth is attributed to Kwame Nkrumah, the former President of Ghana. This myth has now been shattered because many countries now realize that the penalty that the world's financial system inflicts on those who fail to honour their international obligations is worse than a jail sentence. The cutting off of credit lines by international banks has triggered shortages more severe than anybody could possibly have imagined when the economy was still functioning satisfactorily.

The situation in Zaïre, which has been in the sick bay of the IMF for over a decade, finally came to a head on 23 September 1991, when soldiers went on a looting rampage that plunged the country into despair. As early reports estimated more than 100 people dead in the first wave of violence, France and Belgium flew in paratroopers to protect their nationals and organize the evacuation of some 20,000 foreigners. Meanwhile hundreds had already escaped the violence by fleeing on their own initiative to places like Rwanda, Zambia, Zimbabwe, South Africa and Congo Brazzaville, fearing a repetition of the events that followed in the weeks after the independence of the Congo in 1960. Many of the foreign nationals left managerial jobs in key enterprises such as Gecamines, Societé Nationale de Chemins de Fer du Zaïre, ONATRA and the Inga Shaba power line which was maintained by Italian technicians.

As President Mobutu and opposition leader Etienne Tshisekedi Wa Malumba haggled about whether French and Belgian troops should remain – Thsisekedi was in favour of their remaining, Mobutu wanted them out – the Congolese authorities closed their border to Zaïrian nationals wanting to cross over to Brazzaville by ferry. The growing sense of isolation and despair makes Zaïrians feel as if they are in a maximum security prison in which all 26 million of them are condemned to serve a life sentence. While the situation in other countries is not nearly as desperate as that in Zaïre, all African countries that have borrowed more money than they are now able to pay are discovering that the national boundaries are increasingly taking on the allure of a prison wall.

The first puzzle is about the magnitudes involved. First of all, the measurement of Third World loans in billions of American dollars is a mere abstraction to most ordinary people. What is a billion in the first place? It is a figure followed by 9 zeros. What difference would it make if it was one zero less or one zero more? In the final analysis, the figures concerned are mere abstractions which make sense only to computers which have made it possible for the amounts to be transferred from, say, New York to Tokyo at speeds faster than blinking. However, the ordinary man in the street has some idea that a billion is a large number.

The incredulity of the ordinary man is further strengthened by his inability to identify the investments in the debtor countries which justify the magnitudes which are mere abstractions to him. This fact alone explains the difficulty with which the ordinary man accepts the idea that economic austerity, of which he is the principal victim, is the solution to the debt problem.

Another puzzle is the inability to understand how intelligent bankers could have gone on lending so much money to Third World countries. The traditional image of the banker is that of the conservative penny-pinching individual who can assess the creditworthiness of a potential client the minute he walks through the door. The present magnitude of Third World loans leaves most people wondering whatever became of those bankers.

The puzzlement of ordinary people, including officials in the debtor countries, is the greater because it was not so long ago that the loan officers of these large commercial lending institutions pursued ministers of finance through the hallways during annual meetings of the World Bank, the African Development Bank, the Inter-American Development Bank and the Asian Development Bank, seeking to sell another loan to them. In many cases, the bankers believed more in the economic future of the country than the officials of the country did themselves. In spite of this, the unanimous opinion of the banking industry since May 1987 has been that these countries are bankrupt. Why did opinion change so quickly?

Another interesting puzzle is the manner in which the Mexican debt has been handled in comparison with that of Poland. Whereas the instinctive reaction of the US Government and the world banking community was to do everything possible to avoid default by Mexico, opinion was not so unanimous on how to proceed in the case of Poland. On 29 January 1982, the Reagan Administration decided to pay over $70 million in delinquent Polish debt service due that month on loans made during the last two years of the Carter Administration under the Commodities Credit Guarantee Scheme, by which the US Government guarantees principal plus 6 per cent interest to banks willing to participate in the scheme.

In deciding to honour its guarantee by making payment on the defaulted amount, the Reagan Administration by-passed a procedure which would have required Poland to be officially declared in default. Fearing the unpredictable consequences of such a declaration, the Administration decided to invoke the guarantee and honour the loan repayments to the banks. There was, however, strong opposition from officials of the

Pentagon, notably the Secretary of Defense, Caspar Weinberger, who publicly indicated his preference for Poland to be declared in default. He was one of the members of the Reagan Administration who believed that debt is a strategic weapon and that, by a declaration of default, the Soviet Union would have been forced to assume its responsibility in Poland. But does this mean that the Secretary of Defense did not consider the possible consequences for the world banking system of Poland being declared in default?

If anybody had any doubt that the debt crisis epitomizes the struggle between rich and poor nations, it would have been quickly cleared by looking at the manner in which the US government responded to the threatened default of Mexico in August 1982. First of all, it should be borne in mind that there is a special relationship between Mexico and the United States because of the shared physical boundary between the countries. The threat of unemployment, social disorder and, eventually, communism in Mexico was the most important consideration determining the manner in which the US reacted to the Mexican crisis. While there was disagreement within the Reagan Administration on how to deal with the debt of Poland, which is thousands of miles away, there was absolutely no doubt as to the need to take prompt action to defuse the debt crisis in Mexico. That is why, since August 1982, it has become clear that the battle line separating rich and poor nations in the debt war is along the Rio Grande River, and the final peace will have to be settled on that border before it is settled anywhere else in the world.

As champagne was being popped each time following the successful conclusion of another loan syndication in favour of a developing country, nobody on either side really gave serious thought to what would happen in the event of the borrowing country being unable to repay the loan according to the contractual timetable. No loan agreement ever includes a specific clause spelling out what the two parties undertake to do, should the economic fundamentals considered as the basis for justifying the loan proposal change for reasons lying beyond the control of either party. If the essence of lending money is getting repaid, and the making of a loan is usually based on an assessment of the present and the expected state of financial well-being of the borrower, how, then, does one explain the silence of loan agreements on contingency plans to be triggered in the event of the financial situation of the borrower deteriorating suddenly and irreversibly?

The company law of most nations makes such provisions under the bankruptcy code, so that it is not necessary to make any specific provisions in the loan agreements themselves. In the United States, individuals as well as corporate entities that find themselves in financial distress can opt for voluntary bankruptcy under a body of law that was enacted precisely to offer possibilities to financially strapped companies and individuals either to work their way out of trouble or to throw in the towel. Under Chapter XI of the Bankruptcy Act, for instance, a financially insolvent entity can file for the protection of a court under an arrangement whereby the court grants the distressed company protection against all its creditors, and even suspension of all collective bargaining agreements with labour unions, while the company enters into negotiations with these creditors on new terms and conditions under which it can once again resume servicing its obligations. The restructuring of the productive assets of the entity and the various agreements with its creditors quite obviously need to reflect the new economic realities to which the entity is exposed before the bankruptcy court can issue its quietus, allowing resumption of 'going concern' status to the distressed entity.

When the entity in question is a sovereign state which has borrowed from consortia of commercial banks all over the world, the financial system unfortunately finds itself without any body of law that can play a role similar to national bankruptcy laws. It is for this reason that international finance has been described as a jungle unregulated by any laws or governments; its phenomenal growth during the petro-dollar boom obeyed only the laws of electro-magnetism that governed the rate at which funds could be moved electronically around the world so that they appeared on a screen in Hong Kong and disappeared on the one in New York.

A recent report issued by the United Nations Centre for Transnational Corporations referred to the need for an international bankruptcy law for sovereign nations that might be modelled on the US Bankruptcy Act. Such a law would enable a sovereign nation that was financially distressed to declare voluntary bankruptcy and seek the protection of some court, such as the International Court of Justice, to put its financial house in order under the supervision of the Court. It would presumably be given the time to prepare a more realistic plan for servicing its external debt, one that was more reflective of its new economic circumstances, and to submit it to the creditors for approval. This is precisely what private companies do when they run into trouble. So why can't it be done for sovereign borrowers?

The view of the world's powerful nations, who call the shots on financial matters, is that, although such an international law does not exist, the international financial system already provides adequately for due process for any country that is in financial distress. Such a bankruptcy court already exists by virtue of the Paris and London Clubs. The two clubs consider debt service relief for official and commercial credits respectively, on condition that the country first signs an agreement with the International Monetary Fund and the World Bank for an economic stabilization programme or a structural adjustment programme. The recent confusion in the minds of many observers over the exact difference between the roles of the IMF and the World Bank is quite understandable. In fact, the two institutions were stepping on each other's toes so often that it became necessary for them to sign a formal agreement to settle the jurisdictional dispute. According to the agreement, which was signed on 2 April 1989, the IMF was given primary responsibility for assessing the macroeconomic performance and the economic policy conditionality and performance targets to be met by debtor countries. Meanwhile, the World Bank would continue to have responsibility concerning structural economic reforms in debtor countries.

What is important for debtor countries, however, is that, if the economic conditions of a country have changed to the point where debt rescheduling is needed, the country of its own volition can apply for debt service relief from the Paris or London Club, depending on the nature of the loans that need to be rescheduled, provided that it accepts subjection to the diagnosis and economic prescriptions of the World Bank and/or the IMF. In effect, the Paris and London Clubs and the two Bretton Woods institutions have constituted themselves a pseudo-bankruptcy court for sovereign borrowers, particularly for Third World countries.

The Aftermath in Africa: Aid and Disinvestment

While there is evidence that effective action was taken to solve the debt problems of Mexico, by way of the debt reduction that was the core of the Brady Plan and the signing of the North American Free Trade Agreement, the debt problems of Sub-Saharan Africa are virtually intact. In fact, the debt of this region increased from $72.5 billion in 1982, when the debt crisis began, to $173 billion in 1991.

Commercial lending to Africa has all but dried up as most of the banks with any exposure to Africa have not only written down their loans by 100 per cent, but have also successfully recapitalized their balance sheets with new rights issues and are announcing strong profits, having redirected their operations back to the more familiar turf of their home countries. Whatever can be recovered from Third World borrowers, either by way of direct debt service or through debt for equity swaps, is merely icing on the cake.

The ball is now in the court of the official donors, who provide loans and grants under the general heading of aid. Aid budgets are themselves on the decline as a result of the recession that has persisted in the aid-donating nations.

The big difference between aid and commercial debt is that, whereas the commercial banks lent to any sovereign borrower who was thought to have the capacity to repay by way of some exploitable resource, aid is still provided on the basis either of ideology or former colonial relationships. This is hardly surprising as aid has become part of the foreign policy of all aid donors. The aid agencies in nearly all cases are embedded in the Ministry of Foreign Affairs.

Another feature of aid is that it tends to be provided to countries that run a large trade deficit with the donor country. The aid therefore tends to a mechanism for financing the deficit. However, there is no attempt to remove the structural deficits which many African countries have with their former colonial masters; in some cases, such as the Franc Zone, institutional arrangements have been deliberately designed in order to perpetuate the structural deficits. The tying of aid to procurement in the country of the donor serves also to perpetuate the trade deficit.

In February 1992, the *Caisse Française de Depôts* announced its aid budget for Africa for the financial year 1992/93 of 3 billion French francs, undoubtedly a very generous package. Leading recipients of French aid in 1993 will be Cameroon (600 million FF), Côte d'Ivoire (550 million FF), Angola (533 million FF), Gabon (327 million FF), Mauritius (150 million FF), Senegal (100 million FF), Ghana (90 million FF), Mali, Djibouti and Guinea. Most of the aid, as might be expected, will be directed toward countries of the franc zone, which all run structural trade deficits with France. However, this aid masks the existence of a powerful back-current of capital flows from the same countries towards France as a result of the rapidly changing political and economic landscape in Europe.

The problem is that private investors are responding to other signals. The creation of trading blocs in Europe, North America and Asia is the emerging shape of the new world economic order. European investment is currently pulling out of Africa on a scale that is as frenetic as the pace that was witnessed during the initial wave of investment between 1870 and 1930. The prospect of a single European market which came into effect on 1 January 1993, and the possibility of a consumer boom in Eastern Europe in the near future, offer much brighter prospects closer to home than Africa does at the moment with its problems of poor governance and natural disasters.

Disinvestment from Africa is being encouraged by the policy of maintaining high real interest rates throughout Europe. In France, for instance, real interest rates are currently the highest in the European Community and at their highest level since the Second World War. This is for two reasons: (i) during the last ten years, successive French governments have maintained a policy of keeping the franc strongly aligned to the Deutschmark as a central tenet of their strategy for achieving European economic and monetary union; (ii) the reunification of Germany has turned out to be extremely expensive, but so far the German authorities have decided to finance its cost through borrowings rather than through taxation. In order to keep inflation down and attract the necessary capital on the financial markets, the Bundesbank has decided to maintain high interest rates which have been exported to other countries linked to the Deutschmark through the Exchange Rate Mechanism.

The effect of this policy, as a result of the continued existence of monetary arrangements which link African currencies to the French franc, is to magnetize capital from poor African countries, not only from foreign investors who are no longer interested in Africa, but also from indigenous capitalists who are only too ready to exploit the rules of free capital movements within the Franc Zone by exporting their savings toward the attractive yields now available in France. Thus a fortuitous set of circumstances has led poor African countries, the world's leading recipients of aid, which can hardly cope with their external debt, to be among the bankrollers of German reunification.

9

RAYMOND ZATE ZOUKPO

African Debt & the Need to Borrow More

Investment is the key to economic growth, and investment has to be financed by savings, domestic or foreign. The supplementing of domestic by foreign savings in order to accelerate growth is not exceptional, either historically or in the contemporary world. It is even more necessary where increases in domestic savings would jeopardize minimum levels of consumption. So African countries that borrowed externally in the 1970s were not behaving abnormally, and in the short term their borrowing was quite rewarding, accompanied as it was by impressive economic growth.

Nevertheless, the debt of African countries is now a major obstacle to economic recovery and the resumption of growth. How has this happened? One reason is inefficiency in investment: borrowings were not always used in ways that would generate sufficient income to service the debts. Another reason is the deterioration in the external economic environment in the 1980s, manifest in falling African export prices and earnings and rising real interest rates. The capacity to meet debt-servicing obligations to foreign creditors diminished, and as a consequence the stock of debt inevitably grew. The growth of external obligations weakened the incentive to improve economic performance, since gains from improvements tended to be absorbed by larger payments of debt service.

The shrinking of incomes in Africa led to declines in the aggregate saving ratio (from 20 per cent of GNP in the 1970s to the current level of about 15 per cent) and in investment rates. Aggregate net resource inflows, including official development assistance and foreign direct investment, have stagnated at around $20 billion a year, after having grown steadily in the 1970s. Particularly striking is the fall in net FDI from about $2 billion a year at the beginning of the 1980s to only some $200 million currently. In other developing regions, FDI has become an increasing proportion of total resource inflows, but in Africa it has fallen from 10 per cent in 1980–82, before the eruption of the debt crisis, to only 1 per cent in 1991.

Most African governments have embarked on macroeconomic and structural reform programmes with a view to encouraging investment. While in the long term these reforms should considerably increase the scope for profitable private activity, in the shorter term they make the business environment more difficult (through increased foreign competition and contraction of domestic demand), leading to a wait-and-see attitude among prospective investors. The prospects for attracting additional FDI to Africa (and additional ODA as well) are also adversely affected by current economic and political changes within the European Community and in Eastern Europe and the former Soviet Union.

Several debt relief proposals have been advanced or implemented. The concessionality of Paris Club reschedulings has been increased by the Toronto Terms, now enhanced to provide reductions of 50 per cent in debt and debt service over the consolidation period. Some bilateral donors have cancelled part of the debts owed to them. In a few countries (Madagascar, Morocco, Mozambique, Niger, Nigeria), debt conversion or buy-back operations have been concluded.

There is still a strong need for further relief, for instance by building on the proposed Trinidad Terms. The measures taken so far have clearly been inadequate. Indeed, the frequency with which new relief initiatives appear is an indication of the failure to bring the African debt crisis to an end. The ultimate objective must be to reduce the debt-service payments that are due to the real capacity to pay.

International schemes to reduce the African debt burden to sustainable levels remain ineffective. It is indeed paradoxical that the impact of the current official relief options should be much less than what market-based options would have given. The resolution of the debt problem calls for more comprehensive measures that address the entire debt outstanding. Such measures would grant maturities stretching over 20 years and interest rates far below market rates.

Beyond debt relief *per se*, the question of appropriate terms and conditions for future borrowing is also of key importance, if prospective debt service is to be kept manageable. Mechanisms to reduce the cost of loans contracted on non-concessional terms would help.

Debt relief is the only means to attain economic recovery and sustained growth. The case of Mexico illustrates how well-targeted debt relief can enhance growth prospects. Following application of the Brady Plan, Mexico regained access to private lending from abroad for the first time in years. FDI has also increased, and some $4 billion of funds held by Mexicans abroad have been repatriated in a reversal of capital flight. These are the fruits of removing the perils of the debt overhang that had brought the economy close to collapse only a few years earlier.

Notwithstanding the Mexican experience, some people will argue that African countries, especially those already labelled as debt-distressed, would be ill-advised to contemplate further external borrowing, which would only make a bad situation worse. But to accept this argument is to accept continuing economic decline in Africa. On the contrary, African countries need to borrow even more, on terms appropriate to their situation, if the difficult circumstances in which they find themselves are to be changed for the better. This is the conclusion to be derived from a careful assessment of the experience of international development. African policy-makers were not misguided in believing that gains could be made from prudent external borrowing.

According to various estimates, including those of the African Development Bank, Africa needs to mobilize external resources amounting to about $60 billion a year in the 1990s, as well as to raise domestic savings to levels in excess of 20 per cent of GNP, if it is to sustain growth in GDP of about 5 per cent a year during the decade

– growth that would be barely enough to maintain increases in income per head. The priority is therefore to establish the preconditions for a resumption of successful borrowing by African countries.

What might such conditions be? First, the best projects and investment options should be selected, so that loans contracted would finance, not merely investment, but those investments that are most productive in the long term. Second, since even good projects will go to the bad in an unfavourable policy environment, there must be stringent appraisal of domestic fiscal and monetary policies, financial institutions, investment incentives, minimum wages, administrative and legal machinery, and so on; in other words, the process of broadly-based structural adjustment and economic reform already begun by many countries needs to be consolidated.

Next, action is required in the following important areas: multinational economic integration and policy co-ordination, trade policy, promotion of the private sector, and resource mobilization. Brief comments will be offered under each of these headings.

Integration

It is regrettable that attention has so often been limited within national borders when development goals have been defined and strategies for achieving them implemented in Africa – sometimes in ignorance of the vast potential lying beyond the borders. There have been numerous schemes of integration, but their practical effects have been far from satisfactory. As a case in point, multilateral financing institutions, including the ADB, often encounter great difficulty in finding bankable multinational projects. Similarly, it is difficult to observe effective policy co-ordination and harmonization among countries, save in a few cases. Economic integration is not a panacea, but it does offer enormous opportunities for regional self-reliance, economies of scale, more efficient economic decision-making, and greater shock-absorptive capacity. In order to come to grips with the related issue of external debt and finance for development, Africa must make a stronger effort to integrate its disparate economies, such that the dream of a Pan-African Economic Community – stretching from the Mediterranean littoral to the Cape of Good Hope – becomes a living reality.

Trade policy

African exports are predominantly of primary commodities, and it is impractical to suppose that this pattern can be greatly changed in the short term. Instead, recent experience has shown the necessity to become more efficient and competitive in the traditional lines of export production. Africa needs to recapture lost market shares and to carve out new niches in world markets. Needless to say, the penetration of markets, particularly those of the industrialized countries, requires an international trading environment conducive to free competition.

Promotion of the private sector

Notwithstanding the current vogue for privatization, the public sector still dominates economic decision-making in Africa, particularly in the production of services. The opportunity must be taken, in the present atmosphere of adjustment and reform, to build on the long African tradition of private initiative and enterprise. An active private sector, working in collaboration with the public sector, offers the best chance to find and exploit investment opportunities and to secure the transfer of technology. Reflecting on the current debt crisis and how it may be resolved, one should not simply look to governments for solutions. Governments do have a responsibility, however, for creating environments in which private investments can freely flourish.

Resource mobilization

Not only must domestic resources be mobilized (since offshore finance can never be more than supplementary to domestic efforts), but also the capacity of our economies to retain resources must be enhanced by making them more attractive and remunerative places in which to do business. This is crucial if capital flight is to be reversed and the level and quality of domestic investment raised. It must be added that investment is especially sensitive to political instability and the uncertainties usually associated with shortcomings in governance. Good governance and popular participation are of critical importance in resource mobilization.

These and no doubt other preconditions must be satisfied if borrowing by African countries is to resume successfully. Given the current low rates of saving and the imperative of faster economic growth, it is beside the point to debate whether external development finance should be sought. Development finance institutions, including the ADB, have an important part to play in helping secure these external resources and putting them to the most effective uses. In this respect, it is gratifying to note the recent initiative of the ADB to extend increased technical assistance in debt management to its African member-countries. Such practical assistance needs, indeed, to be incorporated in the overall strategy to revive growth on a long-term basis.

Support by other multilateral agencies is required. For instance, increases in the resources of the IMF's Enhanced Structural Adjustment Facility and the Compensatory and Contingency Financing Facility would be steps in the right direction, as was the recent increase in the resources of the Special Programme of Assistance for Africa (SPA-2). It would also help if procurement and other conditionalities on financial aid and technical assistance were relaxed, so as to increase the multiplier effects in recipient countries. And measures need to be taken in the international community to settle outstanding issues relating to global trade and tariffs, and to remove practices that frustrate the efforts of developing countries to promote exports, particularly of manufactured products.

To conclude. In spite of the strains of the current debt crisis, future borrowing by African countries is necessary, and we in Africa can satisfy the conditions for successful resumption of this borrowing – not alone, but with the support of the wider international community, including development finance institutions such as the ADB.

10

A.C. FARAJI

Tanzania: Debt, Aid & Foreign Investment

Introduction

This paper examines Tanzania's external debt problem, donor assistance, and the climate for direct foreign investment. While the debt burden is serious, aid appears to have been rather ineffective. Both debt and aid levels are unsustainable, and urgently demand policy and institutional reforms. Aid must be more effectively used, and the growth of debt obligations must be limited. Vital ingredients for increasing the pace of economic growth while reducing external dependence are greater reliance on domestic resources, better utilization of productive capacity, mobilization of domestic savings and a heightened export orientation. Steps have been taken to improve conditions for foreign direct investment, but the results have been disappointing and further policy and institutional reforms are required.

Debt and Aid

The total of Tanzania's external debt is alarming. As a percentage of GDP it rose from less than 20 per cent in 1970 to 250 per cent in 1991. In current dollars, the total increased from $250 million in 1970 to about $2 billion in 1980, $4 billion in 1987 and $6 billion in 1991. Per capita, Tanzania is one of the most indebted countries in Sub-Saharan Africa.

Debt service (the sum of interest payments and repayment of principal) averaged over $250 million per year in 1985–90 and has followed an upward trend (Chart 10.1). The debt-service ratio has risen to over 50 per cent and constitutes a major constraint on economic growth and development.

Tanzania is among the top recipients of external assistance in Sub-Saharan Africa. Between 1986 and 1990, it received an average of US$850 million per year (Chart 10.2).

These aid inflows grew by over 9 per cent per year between 1986 and 1990. They represent a yearly per capita level of about US$40. In terms of national output, external

Chart 10.1 Tanzania – Total External Debt Service

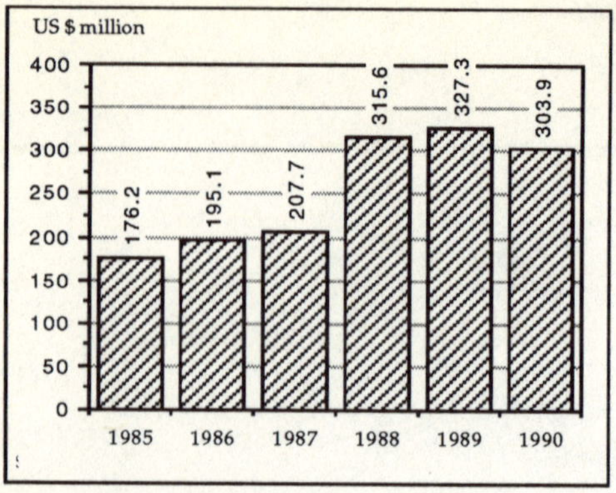

Source: Bank of Tanzania

Chart 10.2 Tanzania – External Assistance Flows

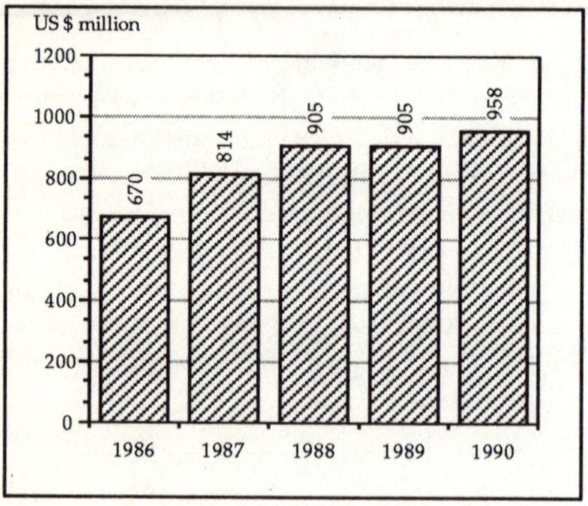

Source: UNDP, Tanzania 1990 Report

Chart 10.3 Tanzania: External Assistance by Type

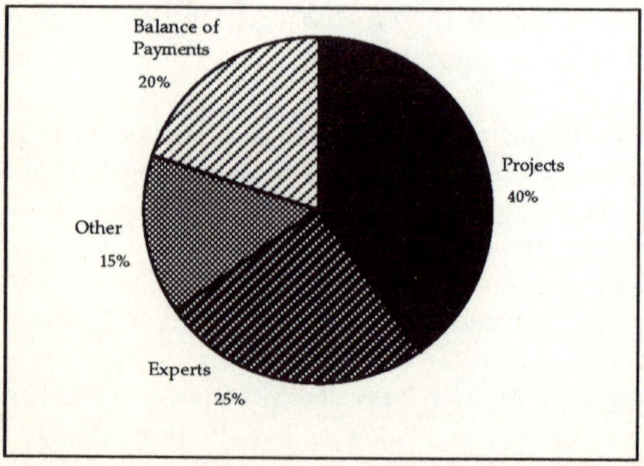

Source: UNDP, Tanzania Country Program Report, 1990

assistance rose from 35 per cent in 1987 to 48.4 per cent in 1990. Thus, Tanzania has become increasingly reliant on aid to finance its development and more recently even a considerable percentage of the government's recurrent expenditures.

The distribution of external assistance by type is depicted in Chart 10.3. Donors allocate roughly 40 per cent of their assistance to Tanzania to investment projects; 20 per cent to programme or budgetary support (balance of payments); and 25 per cent to pay technical experts. The remainder is used to fund food aid, to meet emergency and relief needs, and to provide other support requested by the government from time to time.

The terms of this external assistance are favourable. Almost 80 per cent is in the form of grants, while the remaining 20 per cent is in the form of concessional loans. On average, the terms of these loans provide for amortization over 30 years with a 10-year grace period, while interest rates range between 0.5 and 9.5 per cent.

Bilateral donors account for about 70 per cent of the total external assistance and the UN system for over 20 per cent. Non-governmental organizations account for very little inflow of assistance, less than 2 per cent in any year. The major donors are depicted in Chart 10.4. The Scandinavian countries continue to be the major bilateral donors, with Italy and Japan becoming important in recent years. Among multilateral donors, the World Bank (IDA) continues to be the largest contributor, followed by the European Community.

Studies conducted by some donors and the World Bank indicate that Tanzania is not a good user of aid.[1] The remarkable increase in external assistance in the period 1973–81 seems largely to have been *wasted*, since at the end of the period the economy entered into a period of decline. Per capita output dropped and earlier achievements in the provision of social services were eroded. What went wrong? Many explanations have been given: external shocks were to blame; domestic policies were weak; poor weather conditions played a part; weak institutions and lack of administrative capacity were to blame; projects were not correctly identified, designed or implemented. Whatever the cause, Tanzania did not reap the benefits of the generous external assistance.

Chart 10.4 Tanzania – Major Bilateral Donors (in % of total disbursements)

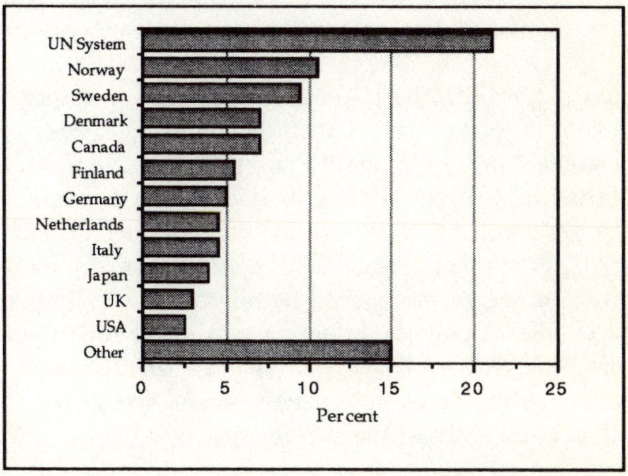

Source: Ibid.

Improving aid effectiveness

First, the efficiency of aid allocation must be improved. A thorough review of aid uses should be made in order to show the most effective channels of import support and the most productive economic sectors. Donor commodity import support has outlived its usefulness and should be replaced by tailor-made programmes.

Technical assistance needs to be reduced, and the funds previously allocated to this purpose used instead to build indigenous capacity for managing economic growth. Foreign consultants and experts may be highly skilled, but because of the shortness of their stay they may overlook local issues which are in practice important in deciding the success or failure of a project or programme. They are paid handsomely by the criterion of their plans and reports, rather than by the viability and sustainability of the projects. At the end of the day, Tanzanians pay the costs of any failure.

Second, improvements are needed in the design of projects and programmes. Design is largely donor-driven. Donors devise the project and the government is simply invited to the signing ceremony. Worse, implementation is dependent on donor initiative and technical inputs. As a consequence, some projects or programmes neither accord with Tanzanian priorities nor contain a realistic view of Tanzanian capabilities. Making matters worse are the *laissez-faire* attitude of Tanzanians and a government planning structure that does not effectively articulate local requirements, nor realistically assess the capacity for implementation. If donor assistance is to be effective, the government must take the initiative and be actively involved in design and implementation.

Third, improvement is needed in the financing side of donor-assisted projects and programmes. It is not enough to have taken care of the development expenditures. Recurrent costs need also to be taken into account. It is useless to spend millions of shillings rehabilitating roads if the subsequent funding for maintenance is lacking. A worrying observation is the tendency of government to request donors to support recurrent expenditure by means of counterpart funds. Such a system, apart from being potentially inflationary, cements the already deepening dependency relationships. Instead, there should be a taxation system that is both transparent and capable of raising the recurrent revenues needed for a limited set of government-provided goods and services – such as provision of infrastructure, high quality administration, maintenance of law and order and social services. So far as is feasible, the goods-producing and distribution sectors should be left to private enterprise and market discipline.

Last, but not least, for aid to be effective it must be supplemented by domestic savings, not be a substitute for them. If there is no domestic effort, it is very likely that aid will be wasted. During the 1960s, Tanzania was able to build up its capital formation on the basis of domestic savings. At one time in the early 1970s, domestic savings rose to 24 per cent of GDP. But as aid rose, savings declined to deplorable levels, reaching a negative 6 per cent of GDP in 1987. The low levels of public and private capital formation were compounded by private capital flight and unsupportive government macroeconomic policies. Improvements in the mobilization of domestic savings, particularly through a reformed taxation and financial system, greater reliance on market forces to determine economic activity and an accelerated pace of parastatal restructuring, will make external assistance more effective.

Addressing the Debt Problem

The first step in addressing Tanzania's debt problem is for the government to limit future obligations. Since 1987, the government and those public enterprises not directly involved in production have been required to refrain from contracting or guaranteeing any borrowing with maturities of less than 15 years that is not on concessional terms, except for normal trade credits. Aggregate non-concessional borrowing with a maturity of less than 15 years for public production enterprises has been limited to US$50 million per year. These guidelines are useful, but more needs to be done.

Each individual loan must be justified on its own economic merit, taking into account the aggregate levels of inflows and debt. How much ought Tanzania to borrow? The sustainable rate of borrowing depends on the rate of growth of the nation's income, and in particular its exports. To minimize the likelihood of liquidity problems, it will be necessary for the rate of growth of exports to exceed the rate of interest on borrowings; that will ensure that the proportion of export revenues required to service the debt will not continually rise. Thus export orientation of the economy, with a particular emphasis on non-traditional exports, holds the key to the future sustainability of debt.

Tanzania could adopt more stringent rules for international borrowing. For example, the government could limit foreign borrowing by stipulating that debt-service payments in any given year may not exceed 20 per cent of the foreign-exchange receipts (including capital inflows) of the preceding year. This rule could be agreed with the World Bank and the IMF in the country's policy framework as an integral component of debt management. To operationalize the rule, the Bank of Tanzania would need to be strengthened and equipped with computer facilities capable of providing monthly reports, and all borrowers would have to be mandated to report in detail on their debts. With close co-ordination of the Planning Commission, the Treasury and the Bank of Tanzania, guidelines could be established on the uses and terms of foreign borrowing. This co-ordination is vital because debt management must be fully integrated with economic management.

Some economists argue against imposing formal ceilings on the grounds that market forces do a better job. Certainly in a world where all decisions were made by market forces alone, governments would not be involved in deciding how much their countries should borrow from abroad. But in Tanzania, as in most less developed countries, formal ceilings on borrowing are useful. First, they encourage discipline and help to focus official attention on central macroeconomic questions. Second, official borrowing ceilings which include arms supply have the important advantage of curbing unwarranted growth in this destructive industry. Third, and probably most importantly, uneconomic projects which are so often approved in Tanzania for political reasons would be curtailed. Borrowing for consumption purposes would also be minimized.

The level of control over external borrowing increased in the 1980s for most developing countries. Increased controls were required mainly because of the inadequacy of key economic policies. To the extent that the government can adhere to fiscal and monetary policies that are consistent with a sustainable balance-of-payments position, controls are less necessary. In addition, interest rates and exchange rates have to reflect opportunity costs. If both conditions obtain, there will be less need actively to control the level of borrowing. But for a country like Tanzania, it would still be desirable to control the composition of borrowing.

Managing the Composition of Capital Inflows

Tanzania's future debt-servicing obligations are determined by the composition of past and anticipated future external borrowing. To be on the safe side, the country's debt managers need to make appropriate decisions on a number of key issues:

- striking a balance between debt and equity capital flows;
- assessing the relative roles of official and commercial sources of funds;
- determining the appropriate maturity structure of the debt (the longer the grace period and maturity, the better);
- assessing the proportions of debt at floating and fixed rates of interest (the interest to export ratio is a useful indicator of vulnerability);
- determining the appropriate currency composition of borrowing (i.e. the currency composition which minimizes the exchange risk of borrowing).

Balance between debt and equity

Equity funds have two major advantages over debt. First, the foreign investor bears both the commercial and the exchange-rate risk. This lowers the overall risk facing Tanzania, so that the country can sustain larger capital inflows and a higher level of investment. Second, direct foreign investment is normally accompanied by management and technology which are in short supply, thus benefiting the country while raising the rate of return on the investment project.

Balance between official and commercial sources of funds

A good strategy for Tanzania to follow would be to maximize the use of highly concessional funds before resorting to the commercial market. Given the blessing Tanzania enjoys through obtaining inflows in the form of grants, it might even be plausible to limit commercial borrowing to those activities that have proven high rates of return in foreign currency terms.

Debt forgiveness

Tanzania cannot escape its present predicament without reducing its debt burden substantially. The first option is for the government to seek debt cancellation from friendly donors. A few donors (e.g., France, Finland, Sweden and the United States), recognizing the slim chances of Tanzania's ability to repay its debt, have written off part or all of their debt holdings. To date a total of US$300 million or more has been forgiven. In addition, several donors (e.g. Canada, Finland, Germany, the Netherlands, Norway, Sweden and the United Kingdom) have converted some of their debt into grants. These are highly commendable gestures and the government should implore other donors to give such debt relief.

Debt rescheduling

Tanzania is a major beneficiary of the Paris Club debt reschedulings. Following the Toronto summit agreement of the G7 in June 1988, Tanzania benefited from a rescheduling of US$520.6 million in arrears and US$188.4 million in principal due in 1986, followed by US$225.1 million of rescheduled arrears and US$211.3 million in principal due in 1988. The IMF estimates that Tanzania will benefit from annual reschedulings of about US$300 million in the period 1989–94. In January 1992, Tanzania was granted a comprehensive rescheduling of its external debt obligations under the Paris Club's new menu of 'enhanced concessions'. The rescheduling covers all debt service falling due up to June 1994.

Debt rescheduling offers only a temporary relief during which a country needs to move quickly to get its house in order. But in Tanzania the debt relief accorded in 1986 fell due in 1992 and the economy in the meantime was still constrained, with a continued precarious balance-of-payments position. In the absence of key policy measures and investment programmes that effectively utilize the period offered by reschedulings to generate foreign exchange (e.g., through enhanced exports), there is likely to be little gain from rescheduling – in part because such relief only postpones the day of reckoning. While Tanzania would be well advised to use the period under rescheduling more appropriately to enhance its capacity to service the debt, the government ought to ask the Paris Club members to eliminate all moratorium interest obligations on rescheduled debt.

Debt conversion

In January 1991, the government established a Debt Conversion Programme managed by the Bank of Tanzania. The aim of the programme has been to reduce the stock of outstanding debt denominated in foreign currency, which would eventually result in a reduced debt-service burden. The proceeds of the swap are to be used to stimulate economic activities, particularly in export-oriented industries, transport, tourism and environmental protection. At least US$40 million is available each year for conversion at the rate of US$0.25–$0.40 per dollar of debt.

Debt exchanges can relieve the pressure on foreign-exchange resources. However, such exchanges of debt for domestic currency are useful only when the country has adequate domestic savings. Thus, one condition for the country to benefit from debt swaps is a concerted effort in the mobilization of domestic savings. Second, the proceeds of debt swaps should as much as possible be utilized in value-added activities which are export-oriented. The generation of foreign exchange using the shillings exchanged for debt helps to reduce the future debt burden.

Building capacity to service future debt

Accelerating economic growth provides the only sure means for Tanzania to become less dependent on external resources. But sustained high rates of growth are not dished out painlessly on a silver plate. Donors cannot be expected to carry out the development of the country on behalf of Tanzanians. It is the responsibility of Tanzanians themselves to make development happen. This entails fundamental changes in the way the economy is managed; the way we prioritize and implement key programmes; the way external finance is used and, more importantly, the way human resources are developed and used.

Economic management. If Tanzania is to have a chance of reducing its excessive dependence on external assistance, a new outlook is needed in the way the economy is run. In particular, the economic policy framework must be designed and implemented by Tanzanians with realistic expectations of achievement, having regard for domestic resource availability and manpower. Market forces must be allowed to play a greater role, complemented by a transparency in government, the maintenance of law and order and safeguarding private property. In addition, public administration must be drastically overhauled to provide room for competent leadership concerned with promoting development rather than with controls and regulations. This also entails a complete overhaul of the incentive structure so that hard work and initiative are rewarded and poor performance dealt with accordingly. The current system does not distinguish good from bad performers and sometimes those who have performed poorly in one job are moved to other organizations or departments with better pay! This is not only bad management but has important disincentive effects which can affect work performance and slow down economic growth.

Priority government programmes and their implementation. The government cannot be expected to carry out all the development of the economy, given its limited resources and lack of sound implementation capacity. Prioritization in favour of a few activities with the largest backward and forward linkages in the economy is an urgent matter. This priority action programme will entail the formulation of low-cost, efficient and well-targeted programmes in education, health, family planning, agriculture and infrastructure.

The thrust should be towards fuller and more efficient use of both domestic and external resources, with greater attention being paid to design and implementation in order to avoid underfunding and unsatisfactory management. New investment must help fill the resource gap by adding value to economic activity rather than being a burden to government and society.

External finance. Tanzania is dangerously dependent on external finance for both recurrent and development expenditure. Even for minor expenditure such as transporting maize from a surplus region like Rukwa to a deficit area like Mara, the government turns to donors for help. To remove silt from the roads and to keep the urban sewage system working, donors are called on for assistance and we often see Kajima or Konoike task force keeping the roads clean! Such a passive attitude on the part of the country's economic managers is not only dangerous for the continued existence of Tanzania as a country but may make it difficult in the future to adopt any meaningful form of self-reliance independent of donor assistance. Thus, major changes in attitudes and in the way external assistance is used are of paramount importance if the available resources are to generate rising levels of per capita income and reduced dependence.

Human resource development. Tanzania is blessed with a large number of educated and technically-skilled people. The current predicament is that some of these brains are wasted in jobs which bear little relationship to their training, others are unemployed and others have left the country to look for greener pastures. One result is the country's dependence on foreign experts, not only to plan but also to implement government policies and programmes. Thus, about one-quarter of the country's external assistance is used to pay these experts. To begin to address this problem, Tanzania needs not only to produce literate, technically and analytically skilled graduates but also to deploy them effectively and to retain them.

The Foreign Investment Climate

Tanzania is one of the many African countries that for years followed what came to be known as an inward-looking model of development, emphasizing the creation of a local industrial base, and using quantitative controls and other barriers to restrict competition in foreign trade. From the mid-1960s to the mid-1980s, the Tanzanian economy drew little benefit from the technological progress disseminated through international trade and private direct investment. Furthermore, because of the protective barriers that surrounded them, industries had little incentive to increase efficiency and profitability. Industrial and commercial enterprises became notable for high operational costs and losses, with severe repercussions on the government budget, monetary stability and the balance of payments.

In response to these difficult economic conditions, and to the wave of market-oriented economic liberalization sweeping the developed world, from 1986 the government of Tanzania moved to implement wide-ranging policy changes including those aimed at creating an enabling investment environment.

Some of the measures taken were the following:

(i) The promulgation of an Investment Promotion Code, and the establishment of an Investment Promotion Centre as a one-stop investment shop offering advice on the security of investments, incentives to investors, modalities and assurances regarding repatriation of investment income, and the other services and institutional arrangements needed by investors. In order to improve the insurance climate for investors, Tanzania has joined the Multilateral Investment Guarantee Agency (MIGA), an affiliate of the World Bank.

(ii) The launching of the financial sector adjustment programme, including the active encouragement of the establishment of private-sector banks and financial institutions. A new legal and regulatory framework has been put in place to govern the development of a commercially oriented financial sector in Tanzania.

(iii) Liberalization of the exchange and trade regime. Exchange-rate policy has become progressively responsive to market forces, while quantitative restrictions on international transactions are being removed through the relaxation of exchange controls. A system of *bureaux de change* has been established, buying and selling foreign exchange at freely determined rates, for purposes including the remittance of profits, dividends, royalties, share certificates, etc.

(iv) The establishment of the debt conversion programme mentioned above.

(v) Reform of the parastatal sector. Changes in the legal framework have been introduced to assist the development of the private sector and the transition to a market-oriented economy.

(vi) Rehabilitation of the physical infrastructure, including roads, railways, harbours, communications, etc.

In adopting these policies, the government hopes to attract foreign investment to Tanzania either in sole ownership or in joint ventures with local investors.

However, the flow of private foreign investment remains very low relative to the country's potential. Even local private investment is not commensurate with expectations following the policy reforms initiated since 1986.

Tanzania is a country with enormous untapped resources. Its natural resources endowment is richer than that of many neighbouring countries, and the potential for rapid economic growth is considerable. This factor should be attractive to private investors, especially in tourism, agriculture, mining and industry. The explanation of the dismal flows of private investment to date is that the advantages which could be offered through policy have not been maximized. The main considerations include conditions for profitability, risk, and the legal, regulatory and administrative environment.

Opportunities for profit certainly exist in Tanzania, but the economic system is still distorted, so that many of these opportunities are not apparent. Risk is seen as high because one of the most important variables that affect profitability – economic instability – has not been removed. Economic stability judged by a perceived government commitment to policies which have a direct impact on private investment has still to be attained in Tanzania. Perceived risk is influenced by, among other factors, the lack of a stable real rate of exchange, the high transaction costs of export business, and taxation policies. The liberalization of policies that are important to private investment is incomplete. For instance, investors are reluctant to commit funds if there is a probability that the currency will be devalued in the near future. There is therefore a need to speed up the process of exchange-rate unification and removal of the remaining foreign-exchange controls, particularly for current account transactions. This will reduce the uncertainty about the returns on investment. The requirement that exporters surrender a substantial part of their foreign-exchange earnings at the official exchange rate needs to be reviewed, since it represents a tax on exports. This is important, because investors shift funds to countries where the risk-adjusted rates of return are higher. Foreign investors would like to be able to buy Tanzanian shillings at the market exchange rate and be able to use them to buy foreign exchange at the same exchange rate for a wide variety of payments abroad. This can be possible only if there is a single, market-clearing exchange rate with a minimum of controls.

The *bureaux de change* system established since April 1992, which permits access to foreign exchange at the market-determined exchange rate, has been a useful step in the process of moving to a unified exchange market. The bureaux do now serve as an indicator of a market exchange rate and are gradually becoming a conduit for foreign exchange, not only for importers but also for investors. To serve these purposes fully, however, a number of improvements need to be made. It is, of course, clear that, even if the bureaux operate well, they will not be a substitute for a modern and efficient banking system capable of handling international transactions. The existing commercial banks are far from adequate, given the business potential in Tanzania.

The administrative and regulatory environment also requires substantial improvement. There seems to be a lack of clarity and specificity in the laws and regulations that affect investment in Tanzania. There are ambiguities in the Investment Promotion Centre's rules and procedures for granting incentives. Standards for granting or withholding incentives need to be made clearer. The incentives are also too discretionary and there are no clear guidelines by which either the investor or the government can tell in advance whether an investment will or will not be granted incentives. This degree of discretion generates delays and ill-will on the part of investors, and could be open to abuse – inviting corruption. If incentives are to be given to investors, they should be as automatic and transparent as possible. Criteria for eligibility should be clear, explicit and operational – leaving very little room for discretion.

The physical infrastructure, including transport, utilities and communications, remains an important factor that needs concerted attention. Equally important is the legal infrastructure, including company law, land tenure legislation, patent and copyright laws, property rights law, disclosure laws and so on. The creation of this infrastructure would provide the foundation for an attractive private investment environment in Tanzania.

Notes

1. For example, a World Bank evaluation of its rural sector support to Tanzania found that 12 out of 17 of the projects had a negative Economic Rate of Return (EER); two industrial projects had a negative EER; some industries had capacity utilization as low as 4 per cent. (e.g. Morogoro Shoe Factory).

PART IV POLITICAL LIBERALIZATION

11

STEPHEN ELLIS

Democracy in Africa Achievements & Prospects

Most people with an interest in African politics have probably at some time or other been party to a discussion about the extent to which democracy ever existed in Africa in pre-colonial times. During the days of one-party rule, it was indeed quite common to hear apologists for ruling parties assert that in Africa there existed a tradition of communal organization and government by consensus in which notions of permanent minorities and majorities were quite foreign.[1]

These days it is quite easy to comment decisively on this sort of assertion regarding pre-colonial Africa. Professional historians of the last 40 years or so have performed a considerable feat in illuminating aspects of African history which were previously regarded as unknown and even unrecoverable. We now have quite a good idea of the general outlines – and sometimes much more than that – of the continent's history over the last couple of thousand years.[2] Before colonial government was imposed upon it, mostly in the second half of the nineteenth century, Africa had a great variety of political systems, including so-called stateless societies, kingdoms, military dictatorships and other arrangements. Which of these, if any, could be called democratic depends crucially on one's definition of 'democracy'. One thing, however, is absolutely clear: there are abundant examples of pre-colonial African polities in which the rule of law obtained and the various rights and obligations of both rulers and ruled were defined by constitutions. At a time when very few Africans were literate, such constitutions were not, of course, generally written, but they existed nonetheless. We can, therefore, state with confidence that the concept of constitutional government, in which the power of the executive is subject to rules and in which governors are accountable for their actions to representatives of other elements in society, is old in Africa. Constitutional government is therefore not a modern import from elsewhere. If we define the word 'democracy' as it is generally understood in modern Europe and North America, to mean the activity of two or more political parties competing for power within the framework of a nation-state by means of periodic elections for which the whole adult population is eligible, then democracy did not exist either in Africa or Europe until the twentieth century, although its institutional origins in Europe may clearly be traced to earlier times. Let us recall that women acquired the right to vote in Britain, for example, only in 1918.

Although it is interesting to refer to pre-colonial African history with a view to identifying the various constitutional arrangements which existed before European colonization, such inquiry is of only limited relevance in establishing whether or not particular forms of government are authentically African. For as the French scholar Jean-François Bayart has eloquently argued,[3] Africa has assimilated both the colonial and modern periods into its own history. Forms of government which may originally have been imposed by force, or which may in some sense be considered aberrant or degenerate forms of their original model, have become part of Africa's historical fabric. Modern Africans, like other people, live with the heritage of their past.

In point of fact, even in its conventional modern sense, democracy existed in Africa before the late 1980s. Most of French-speaking Africa, for example, knew multi-party activity, in competition to elect representatives to the National Assembly in Paris, between 1945 and 1960. Many British colonies also had multi-party activity before, and for some years after, the declarations of independence. The era of one-party rule in Africa really began only in the mid-1960s. Even then, some countries, such as Botswana and The Gambia, never adopted one-party systems at all, or, in the case of Senegal, returned to a multi-party system at an early stage.[4] Even at the height of the one-party era there were attempts to establish opposition parties, such as the *Mouvement de redressement national* (MORENA) in Gabon, which was crushed in 1981–2.[5] One could also cite the short-lived multi-party systems which were created in Ghana, Nigeria and Sudan in the 1970s and 1980s, or various attempts in Cameroon to revive the *Union des Populations du Cameroun*. Thus, while it is reasonably accurate to refer to the period from the mid-1960s to the late 1980s as the age of one-party states in Africa, it is important to bear in mind that there existed a memory of formal multi-party systems and that there were important attempts to revive or restore such systems before the current wave of democratization.

Recent works by leading Africanist scholars have thrown considerable light on the workings of African governments and states since independence, and provide us with a better literature than previously for analysing current developments.[6] These recent works have the merit of not only examining and reinterpreting the recent history of Africa, but also of emphasizing that Africa's politics are best analysed in the same terms as are usually applied to the politics of any other continent, by using such universal notions as sovereignty, nationality, civil society and political accountability. In recent years the most penetrating insights into Africa's current situation have come from this approach rather than from emphasizing Africa's 'otherness'. As well as reading the best anthropological and historical literature available, analysts of modern African politics find much of relevance in the works of Machiavelli, de Tocqueville, Gramsci and others.

The Origins of Current Democratization in Africa

Taking these considerations into account, it is possible to make some broad generalizations about both the longer-term and the more immediate reasons for the rapid demise of the one-party state in Africa and its replacement in many places by a formal multi-party system of a type which many people in Europe and North America instinctively label 'democracy'. One of the most pressing reasons for the decline of the one-party state in Africa was, as is well known, the change in the international climate. In late 1989 two events with enormous significance for Africa occurred within a few days of each other. One of these was the opening of the Berlin Wall, leading to a collapse of the one-party states of Eastern Europe. Particularly important for Africa in this process was the massive international publicity given to the fate of the most prominent Eastern European opponent of democracy, Nicolae Ceausescu. Both African heads of state and their publics followed these events closely, and did not fail to see the parallels with their own situations.

A second key event which occurred at almost the same time was the publication of the World Bank's report *From Crisis to Sustainable Growth*, in which the Bank for the first time linked aid flows to the question of what it termed 'governance', which it defined as 'the exercise of political power to manage a nation's affairs'.[7] Although the World Bank, and most of the donor governments which adopted the Bank's approach with alacrity, were careful to avoid connecting good governance explicitly with multi-party systems, it was a clear implication of their argument, as they referred to the desirability of freedom of speech, transparency of decision-making, and open political debate. Most African heads of state, who had become highly sensitive to the whims and sensitivities of the Western donor countries which had been on the winning side in the Cold War, and which were the source of much of their foreign exchange in one way or another, were quick to seize upon the implications of the arguments which they began to hear about the connection between politics and economic recovery.

It is thus accurate to refer to the role of external actors as one of the immediate causes of the current wave of democratization in Africa. But the deeper and more important causes undoubtedly lie in Africa's own experience over the past few decades. Pressure for a new form of political accountability had been increasing over the years, long before 1989, as one-party regimes showed themselves unable to give a satisfactory account of themselves to their constituents. This was not always apparent to outside observers because one of the main elements shoring up the one-party regimes by the 1980s was superpower support; in the context of the Cold War, Western governments reasoned that a one-party state which was stable, and controlled by a strong individual who could be dealt with on a personal basis, was preferable to the uncertainties of multi-party competition. Behind this impression of stability, Africans were pressing for new forms of political accountability. As Chabal points out, this was one of the reasons for the development of the prebendial systems of Africa in the first place, as in the first years after independence Africa's governing elites sought to satisfy their constituents through patronage and clientelism.[8] These systems, which worked after a fashion, proved more difficult to operate as economic conditions worsened after the oil-price rises of the 1970s. One may therefore see today's democratization as the latest in a series of attempts made by Africans since independence to find a form of political accountability which would serve the needs of African states. The model most widely followed in the 1970s and 1980s, that of patronage politics, had become increasingly difficult to operate as a result of the economic misfortunes which followed the oil-price shocks of the 1970s.

Once the Cold War had ended, and donor countries had begun to demand 'good governance' – a process in which 1989 will be a key date in history-books of the future – time had run out for the one-party state. Some of the more far-sighted African leaders had already sensed the pressure for change long before it was made explicit by the World Bank. That leading apostle of the one-party state, Julius Nyerere, the former President of Tanzania, had actually begun to experiment with reform measures after 1985, when he renounced the leadership of the state to concentrate on reforming a party which had become arthritic. Partly in consequence of having made an early start, his CCM party has been able to dictate the pace of political reform in Tanzania with little pressure from outside. Another great apostle of the single-party state but of very different character, President Mobutu Sese Seko of Zaïre, showed no signs of doubting his belief in the single-party system until after the political earthquakes of 1989. Thereafter, his political antennae, highly sensitive to international events, detected warning signals. In April 1990, before President Mitterrand's speech at La Baule in June 1990 had signalled a new mood in the francophone world, Mobutu announced the end of Zaïre's single-party system and the inauguration of an arrangement in which three made-to-measure parties would compete for power. Every Zaïrean recognized that Mobutu proposed to control all three parties. In the face of popular pressure for greater change, he was obliged to scrap this scheme. The wily Mobutu, having initially tried to limit the number of new parties in the interests of control, promptly went to the other extreme and encouraged the creation of as many parties as possible in order to create a system known to the ever-inventive public of Kinshasa as 'multi-Mobutisme'.

Responses to Change

By and large, the responses of African governments to the irresistible forces of change may be categorized fairly simply. By the late 1980s a handful of countries, such as Senegal and Botswana, already had systems in which the ruling party contrived invariably to win elections, multi-party competition notwithstanding. After 1989 such governments could feel still more secure in their legitimacy and under no pressure to change the system of political representation. Elsewhere, some heads of ruling parties to which there was no legal opposition conceded to demands for multi-party rule by attempting, generally unsuccessfully, to create parties by administrative means. As we have seen, President Mobutu's attempt to do this in Zaïre failed. In the majority of countries, heads of state realized that they could not hope simply to create new parties by decree and that they were obliged to permit the exercise of more or less free political activity. At the same time, incumbent heads of state have used their power in an attempt to control this process, generally with considerable success. One technique widely employed has indeed been that of encouraging the formation of as many parties as possible in an attempt to divide and rule. Zaïre is now said to have over 250 political parties, and some other countries boast dozens. Another stratagem used by nervous governments has been the framing of a law forbidding the formation of ethnic parties, on the grounds that they would constitute a danger to public order, or imposing other conditions to prevent the easy formation of opposition parties. Such techniques have been used effectively in Tanzania, Nigeria, Chad and elsewhere to ensure that opposition parties remain small and subject to administrative restriction.

Only a small number of governments explicitly refused to change at all in the face of international and national demands for democracy. One of the most prominent in the French-speaking camp, President Habré of Chad, paid the price when French troops refused to defend him against his domestic enemies. More successful were Presidents Moi of Kenya and Banda of Malawi. After stubborn attempts to resist all change, both have finally been obliged to move in the direction of multi-party elections, leaving only Sudan, Swaziland, Uganda and Nigeria as countries which can be said to have made little or no effective moves in the direction of democratic government. Uganda is a peculiar case, in the sense that political parties have existed for over thirty years and are even represented in the government, though their activity is restricted. It can also be claimed to be a special case by reason of its particularly difficult heritage. Nigeria too, it can be argued, is a special case in the sense that its heavily qualified attempts to instal a multi-party system must be seen in the context of a long period of alternation between civil and military rule.

The signs are that the many heads of state who felt so challenged in the period 1989–92, and who were essentially on the defensive in those years, may now feel that the tide has changed in their favour. By my estimation five heads of state – Kérékou of Benin, Kaunda of Zambia, Sassou-Nguesso of Congo, Pereira of Cape Verde and Da Costa of São Tomé – have conceded power more or less gracefully as a result of defeat in democratic elections. Moussa Traoré of Mali brought humiliation (and, later, conviction in a court of law) upon himself by his mistaken belief that he could sit tight and resist. His violent overthrow sent shock-waves throughout the ante-rooms of power but in the end proved to be an isolated case. Elsewhere, heads of state have shown themselves able to navigate the turbulence of multi-partyism and even to turn it to advantage. Presidents Houphouët-Boigny of Côte d'Ivoire, Bongo of Gabon and others can now feel themselves under less pressure than before, secure as heads of state in multi-party systems after elections which were widely viewed as imperfect but which were grudgingly accepted by the international community. President Moi is trying to follow the same route, having been re-elected in a multi-party election which international observers considered to have been marred but which nevertheless – so Commonwealth observers maintained – represented the will of the Kenyan people. President Moi is now able to argue that he has followed the route set for him by the donor community and that the donors should therefore reciprocate by recommencing payment of the aid money which they had earlier withheld from Kenya.

Consolidation, Challenge, Collapse

For a number of reasons, the flawed Kenyan presidential and legislative elections of December 1992 probably represent a landmark in the process of democratization throughout Africa. In the first place, Kenya is one of the most important African countries, and therefore events there have a wide impact on attitudes in both the donor community and other African countries. This effect has been magnified by the fact that President Moi had very publicly defied the donor countries, and was the subject of outspoken and remarkably undiplomatic attacks by the US Ambassador to Kenya, Smith Hempstone, a political appointee of President George Bush. Once the donor community had suspended aid to Kenya, Moi was obliged to stage a multi-party election, but was able to win it with a minority of the votes cast. No doubt this was in part due to fraudulent practices by the ruling KANU party, but it may also be attributed to Moi's skill in dividing the opposition, aided by the short-sightedness of opposition leaders. Having been re-elected as president in a multi-party election, Moi now appears determined to humiliate both the opposition and the donor community, by behaving much as he did in previous times, banning opposition newspapers, harassing opponents and demonstrating his contempt for the parliamentary opposition. Athough singularly lacking in diplomatic skills, Moi has demonstrated that a determined head of state with an intimate knowledge of the workings of politics in his own country can use multi-party elections to relegitimate himself in international terms.

A key asset of heads of state who, like President Moi, are fighting a defensive action against popular and international demands for free elections has been control of the national army and security services. In the cases of Togo and Zaïre this has clearly been the crucial factor permitting Presidents Eyadéma and Mobutu to remain in power, although at the price of losing their international legitimacy. A more considered use of armed force has been in South Africa, where the ruling National Party appears to be succeeding in using its control of overwhelming force to improve its political bargaining position: a bloody process, and also a dangerous one, since it could equally easily lead either to a collapse of political negotiations or to a concentration of politicians' minds on the difficult task at hand. We must hope that the latter reaction prevails. President de Klerk has been far more astute than Eyadêma and Mobutu in dissociating himself from the violence exercised by some in his armed forces, while at the same time using that violence to attain specific political goals.

If President Moi has frustrated many Kenyan democrats by beating them at their own game, and President de Klerk may be said to be doing the same in more subtle and, perhaps, sustainable fashion, there are also examples of heads of state who refused to make any compromises at all and whose entire countries have paid a terrible price. In the case of Liberia, there is a case to be made that the country's tragic collapse into civil war may be dated to the United States' acceptance of the blatantly rigged presidential and legislative elections of 1985. This acceptance encouraged President Doe to believe that he could remain in power indefinitely and retain his international legitimacy in defiance of public opinion in Liberia. In the case of Somalia, the process was still more stark. President Siad Barre, having refused any form of political solution or political compromise, could not prevent his eviction from power by military means. This fall led to the complete collapse of the Somali state. There remains a risk of Zaïre following the same path, although it could be that Zaïreans have become so used to enduring a government which appears permanently on the brink of collapse that the eventual departure of Mobutu will in fact cause less hardship than in Somalia or Liberia. We must hope so. In the more complex cases of Angola and Mozambique, renewed civil war also looms. In Mozambique much patient negotiation now seems to be in jeopardy as a result of the tardiness and penury of the United Nations. In the case of Angola, the international community has also failed to play the role demanded of it, and the US Government is revealed to have utterly misjudged one of its more important Cold War allies. In Angola any hope of peace, not to mention democracy, now seems to be moving tragically out of reach.

What of those countries where some form of democratic transition may be said to have taken place, and which provide more grounds for optimism than the horrors of Somalia and Liberia? In Mali, where hundreds lost their lives fighting against tyranny in a manner no different from the crowds in Bucharest, the international community – and France in particular – has failed to produce even a gesture of support. At least in the first year after Moussa Traoré's overthrow, Mali received no extra financial aid from France to help its reconstruction, and French ministers conspicuously avoided any symbolic gesture of solidarity. It appeared as though the French Government, which continues to have very close relations with most of its former African colonies, had been in favour of some measure of reform but not of the overthrow of a tyranny, an example which could have worrying implications for French interests if it were allowed to spread. In fact, since President Mitterrand's measured statement in favour of democratization to the assembled francophone African heads of state at La Baule in June 1990, France's Africa policy generally appears to have lost all coherence. The question of the value of the CFA franc remains unresolved, while French Africa policy remains more than ever in the hands of lobbies and special interest groups in Paris.[9] This pattern is strikingly similar, in fact, to the colonial lobby in nineteenth-century Paris.[10] No doubt it has much to do with the decline in the fortunes and health of President Mitterrand, who began his ministerial career in the 1950s as the minister for colonies and is an old Africa hand if ever there was one.

The World Bank and the Absence of Political Choice

Benin, more encouragingly, appears to have passed its transition smoothly and to be enjoying a degree of economic progress, attributable in the main to its economic relationship with its giant Nigerian neighbour. The new government in Cotonou seems to have been successful in picking up the threads in the country's former multi-party fabric from the days when it was still called Dahomey. President Soglo, a former World Bank official himself, has committed himself to an orthodox World Bank economic reform programme. And this is one of the most striking observations to be made about political parties, new or old, all over the continent: virtually all of them, explicitly or implicitly, are committed to World Bank policies. They simply have no other choice if they are to aspire to power, since donor governments all take their lead from the World Bank, which is itself closely associated with US policy decisions.

The fact that African politicians are unable to articulate any original or critical view on economic policy, if they are to be taken seriously by local and international power-brokers, contributes to a sense that there is little to choose between rival parties, other than the moral characters and competence of the people who lead them. It follows that political parties tend to compete for the same social constituencies as their rivals and find it hard to identify and represent any social or economic interest group which has been previously under-represented, unless, of course, such a group is ethnically defined. Hence the tendency for rival parties to recruit ethnic constituencies, just as the barons of the old ruling parties tended to do. One of the few obvious exceptions to this generalization is South Africa, where rival parties clearly do represent differentiated social and economic interest groups and different ideological aspirations, in spite of the pressures from some quarters towards ethnic representation.

The relative failure of new parties to find new types of constituency is well illustrated by the contrasting cases of Kenya and Zambia. A comparison between them is particularly instructive because the government of the former has been regarded as Africa's most vociferous opponent of a multi-party system, while the latter succeeded in smoothly voting an incumbent out of office. The different course of events camouflages some interesting common features. In both Kenya and Zambia, opposition parties contesting for power had virtually no programme or manifesto beyond the ousting of the incumbent head of state. In Kenya, moreover, so great was the lust for power on the part of opposition leaders, uncomplicated by any articulation of alternative views of the national interest, that they were unable even to form an anti-Moi or anti-KANU alliance, thus allowing President Moi to win the election on a minority share of the vote. Had the Zambian opposition similarly been unable to unite, Kenneth Kaunda would still be president today.

In many other countries, too, the new opposition parties have displayed characteristics similar to those in Kenya. That is, they have often been led by experienced politicians, former ministers in the incumbent one-party regimes who for one reason or another have turned to the opposition. In the case of Kenya, there is no doubt that Moi virtually created the opposition by the single-mindedness with which he set about expelling his enemies from the ruling KANU party, which had traditionally been something of a broad church. Of course, all over Africa there was previously little scope for a person to build a political career or acquire experience of government other than as a member of a ruling party. No doubt many opposition leaders believe passionately that their countries need a new team in power. But even if we take a charitable view of their aims, the conversion of so many former ministers into born-again democrats can look suspiciously like opportunism.

The consequences of having an opposition posited with no programme beyond unseating the incumbent may be clearly seen in Zambia. The new Zambian President, Frederick Chiluba, is exceptional in being someone who made his political career outside the ruling party, as a trade unionist. Now, however, he gives every impression of being the prisoner of the experienced political heavyweights who financed and organized his election. The very name of his party, the Movement for Multi-party Democracy (MMD), suggests a pressure group rather than a real political party able to articulate the political demands of specific sections of society. Unlike its predecessor, the MMD has little grassroots structure and few institutional means of rallying support other than the organs of government which it controls. Its lack of grassroots make its grip on power precarious, which may explain recent allegations that President Chiluba has been the victim of a coup plot. Similar observations could be made of many other movements which have arisen in opposition to incumbent regimes. They find it hard to locate a new political base other than in the machinery of government itself or by taking over the networks, and the techniques, of the ruling parties they seek to replace.

Religion as a Political Factor

It should be noted, however, that religion can form the base for new forms of political recruitment. Hence perhaps the marked growth of politicized Islamic movements in

Sudan and Somalia, and the growing importance of religious affiliation in Tanzania. Throughout Sub-Saharan Africa, Christian churches organized on a national level, having so often pronounced themselves in favour of reform and often being the only institutions able to rival the state in the importance and coherence of their infrastructure, have played a crucial role in challenging or overthrowing one-party rule. South Africa, Namibia, Zaïre, Mozambique, Angola, Kenya, Togo, Benin, Zambia, Madagascar and many others bear witness to their importance. The churches, which had such a crucial impact on Africa during the evangelization of the nineteenth century and, in some cases, in the run-up to independence, are now regaining their political influence. It may well be that in the years to come we shall see organized religion playing a more important role in African politics generally, reflecting not only the economic power and international connections of the Church and of Islam, but also the failures of the secular political parties. Spiritual or supernatural forces have always played a role in African politics, although modern political parties constructed on a Western, secular model found it difficult to articulate or control such forces. Political organizations may now find means of explicitly harnessing for political purposes the widespread belief that supernatural forces are important in the lives of human beings.

Democracy and Governance

Some African countries, then, including Namibia, Senegal, Cape Verde, São Tomé, Botswana, Benin, The Gambia, Zambia and Mali, may be said to represent some sort of functioning democracy, no matter how precarious or imperfect. In each of these countries there are multi-party constitutions and elections which, although no doubt flawed, are much more than public-relations exercises. Nevertheless, in each of these cases a stern critic might argue that the constitutional form of democracy is used to hide a system so constructed that the ruling party can be confident of being re-elected indefinitely, or that a small political class competes for power while the mass of citizens see little relevance in the manoeuvrings of the elite. This line of criticism is rather more applicable in such cases as Côte d'lvoire, Gabon and Zimbabwe. It is revealing, for example, that in Senegal, on the face of it one of Africa's oldest democracies, separatists in Casamance express themselves with bullets rather than ballots. In Zambia, recent allegations about coup plots suggest that not everyone has accepted the rules of the democratic game, as at first appeared to be the case. Nevertheless, a more indulgent commentator may take a less purist view and say that in these and many other cases, while democracy has not yet arrived, a process of democratization has begun which, with the passage of time, could result in greater freedom, stability, and improved governance. This, for example, was the view expressed by the departing US Ambassador Smith Hempstone, when he was interviewed by the BBC World Service on leaving Kenya. One may also argue that it is wrong-headed to expect Africans to behave exactly like the ideal models of Western Europeans or North Americans. In the first place, Western political practice does not actually live up to the ideals which its theorists profess. More importantly, Africans have their own political culture, including their own ideas about political representation, which makes the political elites accountable to the masses in ways not immediately apparent to outside observers.[11]

In a handful of cases, nothing at all resembling political democratization has happened: government has collapsed entirely, and power is in the hands of warlords who rule by force alone, without serious reference to any principles of accountability or legitimacy. This seems to be the case in Liberia and Somalia. It is perilously close to being so in Chad, Sudan, Angola, Mozambique, Rwanda, Sierra Leone and elsewhere, where governments either rule by the naked use of force or where considerable areas of the country are controlled by warlords. This is not only appalling for the people who have to live under the threat of such violence, but also dangerous for neighbouring countries which cannot insulate themselves from the depredations of the warlords just across their borders and which are threatened with destabilization. For countries which have fallen into the category of anarchy or control by warlords, the future seems bleak indeed in the absence of any external intervention aimed at restoring some form of legitimate government. Somalia, in this respect, is a test case.

In other countries with enormous problems, notably South Africa and Ethiopia, there are in progress interesting and potentially important experiments with new constitutions. If these experiments succeed, South Africa and Ethiopia have the potential to become models of how governments that have traditionally been highly centralized, and where political winners take all, may be adapted to distribute power equitably among multi-ethnic constituencies, perhaps through some form of federal or regional government.

In those countries where some degree of democratization, no matter how slight, has taken place, we may ask to what extent it may lead to the improved governance and economic productivity which the World Bank explicitly states as its aim and which many Africans doubtless desire. There is no doubt that the wave of democratization has had a notable effect on freedom of speech. In countries where criticism of the head of state or ruling party was quite out of the question until very recently – Togo, for example, or Malawi – people are now able publicly to testify to their own experiences of prison, or of torture or misgovernment. In Togo in mid-1991, when a national conference was in session, there was no doubt as to the deep therapeutic effect it had, not only on the persons testifying but also on their listeners. These testimonies, as well as criticisms of the government and other political reflections, were reproduced in print and electronic media quite freely before a spellbound national audience. It would appear that, even in a case like Kenya, where an incumbent head of state contrives to have himself re-elected under a multi-party system by dubious means, the government must reconcile itself to living in changed circumstances – a development supporting the view that even an imperfect election is better than no election at all.

In most African countries there is now more freedom of speech than there was, although Amnesty International has noted that the number of physical attacks on and murders of journalists has also sharply increased, meaning that the freedom of the press is not widely accepted. Moreover, press freedom does not necessarily imply a great widening of political access. In Africa, even the most professionally produced newspapers rarely circulate outside the major cities, because of both poor distribution and prohibitive cost. And revenue from sales and advertisements is hardly enough to sustain a genuinely independent paper. The signs are that those papers which survive will have to do so largely by becoming the mouthpiece of a specific politician or political faction able to provide financial help. This may be an improvement, but it is something short of a genuinely independent press.

In regard to governance, understood to imply the ability of the state to formulate and carry out effective policies, it is hard as yet to discern any improvement. Free debate is no doubt one component of good governance, as the World Bank argues, but so too are financial resources and the competence and honesty of the government bureaucracy. To date, there are no signs that democratization has recast political constituencies in a new mode. They continue to be formed in terms of clientelism, although the forms of clientelist recruitment can change, whether based, for example, on party allegiance, ethnicity or some other factor. In any event, when combined with corruption, clientelist networks contrive to hamper the effective design and implementation of state policy.

It is quite widely agreed that the changes which have taken place in Africa since 1989 are the most momentous since the era of independence 30 or so years ago – the independence which in many respects, it is now apparent, took place in inauspicious circumstances. As always with changes of the magnitude now taking place, some of the deeper and more important changes may not be obvious for some time. It is hardly appropriate to attempt to draw more than the most vague conclusions from the present rapid survey of a period of history which is still playing itself out over a large continent. The one thing we may say with confidence is that nothing will be the same again in Africa.

Notes

1. For an evaluation of the literature on this argument, as on many other aspects of democratization, I am grateful to my colleagues Rob Buijtenhuijs and Elly Rijnierse for their paper 'Democratiseringprocessen in Afrika ten Zuiden van de Sahara (1989–1992): Een literatuuroverzicht', commissioned by the Dutch Directorate-General for International Co-operation. An English version is currently being prepared for publication.
2. One of the most recent of many general histories of Africa is Roland Oliver, *The African Experience: Major Themes in African History from Earliest Times to the Present* (London: Weidenfeld and Nicolson, 1991).
3. Jean-François Bayart, *L'État en Afrique: la politique du ventre* (Paris: Fayard, 1989).
4. These and other examples of specific countries are not intended to be exhaustive but are used only for purposes of illustration. It is also to be noted that I have refrained, for the purposes of the present argument, from referring to Mauritius, a remarkable democracy which is a member of the Organization of African Unity.
5. Amnesty International, *Gabon: déni de justice au cours d'un procès* (Paris: Amnesty International, 1983).
6. Bayart, *L'État en Afrique*; Basil Davidson, *Black Man's Burden: Africa and the Curse of the Nation State* (London: James Currey, 1992); Patrick Chabal, *Power in Africa* (London: Macmillan, 1992).
7. World Bank, *Sub-Saharan Africa: From Crisis to Sustainable Growth* (Washington, DC, 1989), p. 60.
8. Chabal, *Power in Africa*, pp. 136–49.
9. Stephen Smith and Antoine Glaser, *Ces Messieurs Afrique: le Paris-Village du continent noir* (Paris: Calmann-Lévy, 1992).
10. L. Abrams and D. J. Miller, 'Who were the French Colonialists? A Re-assessment of the *Parti Colonial* 1890–1914', *Historical Journal*, 19, 3 (1976), pp. 685–726.
11. See Chabal, *Power in Africa*, pp. 200–32.

12 ROGER TOMKYS

Implementing Africa's Second Liberation

The Case of Kenya

I address this subject from a relatively narrow African background since I am neither African nor an Africanist by long experience. This leads me to concentrate on what I know best which is one significant case study, that of Kenya. I went to Kenya at what proved to be the premature end of a career in the public service following two years as Deputy Secretary responsible for African as well as Middle Eastern affairs in the Foreign and Commonwealth Office, years which enabled me to see, somewhat superficially, a good deal of the African dilemma. Kenya is, however, the only Sub-Saharan country in which I have lived or whose condition I have had any opportunity to study at close hand.

I make no apology for this relatively narrow approach. It does not reflect 'typical FCO amateurism'. Neither my posting as High Commissioner in Nairobi nor my short stay was typical, and both reflected my own choices. Virtually all my predecessors had extensive African experience, as has my successor. So too had many of my staff. When I chose to go to Nairobi I was convinced that once in a while it is an advantage to have a newcomer with a relatively unprejudiced eye look again at established assumptions, particularly dealing with a country like Kenya with which Britain has had such close links. I have not revised that view.

Nor do I think it a bad thing now to concentrate on one country in addressing the subject of implementing Africa's second liberation. Lack of experience makes me humble about generalization from pre- and post-colonial African history. Realization of the great diversity of social, business and political patterns even within Kenya, let alone East Africa, makes me wary about the validity of political or economic solutions based upon theoretical models held to have powerful predictive capabilities applicable throughout the continent. I do not believe there is one African model any more than there is one European model applicable to Portugal as well as to Norway or the United Kingdom.

Obviously I do not seek to deny a common African heritage and some common African problems. It may be that political lessons learned in one African country may, in some circumstances, be applicable elsewhere. But I see no important political propositions that can be transposed unmodified from Ugandan to Tanzanian to Kenyan or to South Sudanese or to Somali experience, let alone to Ethiopia. This makes me the more cautious about assuming that changes made successfully in, say, Zambia would work in the same fashion in Kenya. It is on this ground that I would argue that my narrow viewpoint is a strength and not a weakness.[1]

Within this framework, therefore, let us take three hypothetical propositions corresponding to the three issues that have been identified of *governance*, *business* and *aid*, and examine how they fit the Kenyan condition.

Governance

Proposition

African one-party dictatorship and African socialism have failed. The transformation to independence over the last three decades has also therefore proved at least a partial failure. True independence, development and self-fulfilment in the region depend on the replacement of single-party systems by more plurality and accountability, probably by multi-party democracy, certainly by more open and less corrupt government.

From my perspective this proposition is largely true for Kenya but needs substantial qualification. Kenya, after all, has been a relative success story since independence. Under Presidents Kenyatta and Moi it has escaped the civil wars and turmoil that have afflicted so much of the continent. Despite its relative lack of natural resources (including that of educated manpower: as a newcomer I was astonished by the huge gap, obvious to those more immersed in African history, between the long tradition of university education in West Africa, for example, and the basic level of the African population in Kenya at independence), Kenya has prospered over three decades in material and other respects by comparison with its neighbours. For example, the United Nations Development Programme's *Human Development Report* for 1992 shows Kenya, despite having a lower per capita GNP than the Sub-Saharan average, recording higher than average life expectancy (59.7 years at birth compared with 51.8), literacy rates (69 per cent compared with 51 per cent), and levels of school attendance. Overall, Kenya is rated third among Sub-Saharan African countries in the UNDP's Human Development Index, with notably higher commitment to expenditure on health and education and much lower commitment than the regional norm to expenditure of resources, including manpower, on the armed forces.

Partly as a result, Kenya has managed a rate of real GNP growth slightly above the disastrous rate of growth of population, which is only now falling from a world high of 4 per cent per annum. It has achieved this in the teeth of the worsening terms of trade which have confronted most, if not all, African countries. A graphic illustration of these worsening terms of trade can be derived from the experience of Kenya's tea industry, which is partly in the hands of multinational companies, and partly indigenous. In 1962 it cost 2.3 tonnes of tea leaf to generate funds to purchase one of the small tractors typically used on smallholdings where tea is cultivated. In 1972 the figure was 4.7 tonnes and by the 1980s it was 11 tonnes or more. In more general terms World Bank figures show that over the twenty years to 1984 national output grew at an average of 5.6 per cent per annum but national income by only 4.3 per cent per annum: one quarter of the gains in output were lost through unfavourable terms of trade. Despite this handicap, the achievements are not negligible. They are greatly to the credit of Kenyans and Kenyan governments. They might have been held as a model for others had it not been for a population doubling every 17 years or so. There are non-economic achievements too. Thanks largely to the early initiatives taken by President Kenyatta, Kenya continues to operate as a multiracial society with relatively little friction above a certain economic level. By standards obtaining elsewhere in the Third World it is a society in which, even in the deteriorating situation of the late 1980s and early 1990s, freedom of expression and the rule of law have been intermittently abused, but not suppressed. It is not a country whose people flee its borders. The infrastructure works, there is a substantial middle class with a stake in the future and the economy functions.

Does this mean that all is well? Of course it does not, and the turmoil brought to a head by the riots of 7 July 1990 reflects the deficiencies.

First, the socio-economic situation of the country has been deteriorating in fundamental aspects. The underlying problem is the relative scarcity of agricultural land in relation to population. Less than 20 per cent of Kenya can support rain-fed agriculture. There is now no new land that can be brought into cultivation without severe environmental consequences or the use of capital-intensive irrigation. Sessional Paper No. 1 of 1986 identified a need for the creation of 7 million new jobs by the end of the century. Progress towards that goal in the six years that have followed has been pitifully slow in the face of world recession, mismanagement and corrupt administration. The consequence is the growing size of the rootless urban population, unemployment, rising crime and the human degradation that follows.

On the political plane, the defects which have helped this deterioration, and which are in themselves intolerable, grew steadily during the years to 1990. The one-party KANU system which had provided a tolerably 'broad church' within which most Kenyan political viewpoints and tribal affiliations could be accommodated was narrowed and distorted in the 1988 elections. Dissent was suppressed and corruption flourished.

Corruption is now endemic. I leave it to others to judge whether it is an Africa-wide phenomenon, but in Kenya it takes three distinct if overlapping forms, each with its own negative impact on prospects for the future. First, there is the corruption of the great men. The misallocation of major contracts and gross malpractice, unchecked by parliamentary or other public accountability, have gravely damaged the economy, the country's reputation and its attraction for foreign investment. Second, there is the apparently systemic and pervasive use of public office at all levels to syphon off substantial personal benefits for the office-holder, or for the entrepreneur in contact with such office-holders, breeding inefficiencies throughout the system and further discouraging foreign investment. Finally, and in political terms perhaps most sensitive of all, there is the corruption through which minor officials, police officers and all with the ability to give to, or withhold from, the common people their legitimate rights use their position to supplement their inadequate pay and oppress the poor. The roots of political patronage and the exchange of services for payment to the office-holder run very deep in Kenya. But abuses at the level of recent years are a major threat to political stability and economic progress.

On this basis 'partial failure', as advanced in the proposition stated, is a reasonable assessment. But is multi-party democracy with all its attendant complexities the answer? This question is indeed to be tested in the Kenyan laboratory. Since Douglas Hurd, visiting Nairobi as UK Foreign Secretary in September 1991, spoke publicly to the media and privately to the Kenyan Government about the inevitability and advisability of multi-party democracy, the situation has been transformed. Soon thereafter President Moi introduced multi-partyism on an accelerated timetable which caught the opposition unprepared and surprised foreign observers. The outcome will soon be clarified. At the time of writing this paper, however, only limited conclusions can be offered.

On the positive side there is much to be said. Multi-partyism is indeed, if it can be achieved and maintained within a stable framework, a good in itself. No one with any political sensitivity could miss the great gain in political commitment, replacing sullen hostility to the government, manifest in many Kenyan circles during 1992. Freedom of expression was vastly enlarged and repression of dissent correspondingly reduced. There was more open scrutiny of corrupt malpractice, and the heavy blanket of single-party doctrine was removed. Against these gains, however, have to be set more worrying indicators. Tribalism and inter-tribal violence, never absent from the Kenyan scene, flared up dangerously to threaten the country's cohesion as well as its economy and tourist trade. In the best case this may prove to be the temporary result of last-ditch resistance by the least enlightened of Kenya's politicians to the new era. It would be more reassuring, however, if the political debate between the parties had been conducted in terms of policies and principles rather than of vengeance and access to power. The suspicion must be that for a majority of the opposition the fall of President Moi and KANU took precedence over any positive aims.

This must change. The country's economic, social and political problems are enormous and there is little sign yet that they will be addressed. In a multi-party parliament, in a country accustomed to identify support for the government with local political patronage, there will be even greater need than hitherto for transparent systems to determine priorities in public expenditure, appointments, management of the public sector, etc. When I left Kenya in September 1992, no debate on these issues had begun. Multi-partyism could undoubtedly lead to better government than Kenya has known and afford at least a chance to make that new start that could be defined as the second liberation. There is as yet little sign that it will do so.

Business

Proposition

Successful development depends on an open trading system, rigorous financial policy, reducing the role of the state and encouraging private enterprise.

As noted above, there is much that is wrong with Kenya's economic system, despite its relative success. It is important to remember that the foundations for much of what is wrong were laid in colonial times. The transport system, the public utilities, the marketing boards, the originals of the inefficient corrupt and over-large parastatals, were founded to facilitate the development of the country by private, largely European, agricultural enterprise. The pattern by which the government and these organizations provided employment which elevated the university graduate and even the school leaver above the ordinary people, in numbers and at salaries unsustainable by an efficient private sector, long pre-dates independence. The difference now is that, as the numbers employed in the public sector have grown, so their remuneration has fallen to the point at which supplementing public sector income by private peculation or the misuse of office has become inevitable. This pattern has to be reversed. But such a reversal requires the dedicated commitment of precisely those politicians (or their democratic successors) and senior civil servants who have depended on the facilities afforded by the public sector enterprises to recoup their election expenses, satisfy their constituencies or clientele, or simply, in the case of the more lowly, to keep alive. There is no alternative cadre of upright public servants waiting in the wings.

It should be easier to achieve radical reform under multi-partyism than hitherto, because of the pressure of parliamentary criticism and because the possibility of alternation in government is an important discipline. But the test will be a severe one, not least in a period of worldwide economic recession that is hitting Kenya hard. Rigorous financial policy is indeed required, and an end to the gross underemployment of vast numbers of underpaid but unproductive workers in the public sector. Spendthrift capital schemes (largely aid-financed), devised more to benefit the political ringmaster than the common people, cannot be repeated. But belt-tightening is not by itself a sufficient answer: there has also to be more investment for more productive jobs. A democratically elected government will have to generate new confidence both overseas and within the Kenyan business community if this reformation is to be achieved.

The same applies to that other scourge of the Kenyan economy – the propensity for the wealthy, whether in business or in government, to move and hold substantial funds outside the country. But it should be recognized that, setting aside for the moment the issue of how those funds were generated, the KANU Government has in recent years done much to liberalize the exchange-rate system and to encourage the repatriation of funds held abroad. Given a more accountable system, yet more could be done, not only to eliminate the accumulation of corrupt and gross profits but also to encourage the return of those held overseas. But it would have to be through generating confidence throughout the system and in all the tribal and racial communities of the country. The importance of avoiding a cycle of retribution and revenge cannot be overstressed.

To tackle the need to get Kenya's economy moving at a faster pace, despite the continuing world recession, multi-party and accountable government therefore has in principle significant advantages. Whether they will be fully deployed must be questioned. But more fundamentally it should be recognized that the underlying medium and long-term problem of matching productive capacity in the country to the growing need for new jobs that cannot be provided within the agricultural sector is one that cannot be wished away by a change in the political system. Eliminate the evils and deficiencies inherent in one-party rule; gain confidence through the whole-hearted consent of the Kenyan people to government and authority wielded in a less corrupt fashion; end the tribal and criminal violence which threatens both agricultural production and the future of the tourist industry; ensure that Kenya remains an oasis of relative stability in the region; do all this and one might hazard a guess that Kenya could be capable of adding perhaps some 10 to 20 per cent to its Gross National

Product and employment capabilities above what would otherwise be the case over the next decade. This would be a remarkable achievement and give a breathing space within which to address the basic structural problems of population, land and employment. It need hardly be said that, were the transition to multi-partyism to fail, the consequences would be dire.

Aid

Proposition

Aid donors have the role and responsibility to press for political reform and the 'second liberation' both because it is their taxpayers' money which is at stake and because they ought to use the influence implicit in their aid funding for the good of the recipients as a whole. Just as within the Helsinki process Western insistence on human rights and political pluralism has helped bring about change in Eastern Europe and the Soviet Union, so it should be deployed in Africa.

My position on this proposition is equivocal. My experience has been as an official of the British Government and as its representative in Kenya. But this paper is written in my capacity as a private citizen. It is not for me to represent or to criticize HMG's policy or that of the other donors. I will therefore confine myself to addressing some considerations of principle and some specifically Kenyan phenomena.

It would be a caricature to suggest that British aid to Kenya has been largely dissipated through the weakness and corruption of a one-party system. The bulk of the aid has gone to projects and technical assistance which have been carefully, even laboriously, evaluated and scrutinized to insure against corrupt dealing. Despite this, the evidence is striking of the diversion of considerable sums of aid money – not necessarily British, though we may not be wholly immune – from the purposes for which it was intended. Those who wish to demonstrate that aid has meant the transfer of tax revenues from the poor (or at least the only moderately well-off) among the donor countries' populations to a handful of rich in Kenya can find material for their thesis. It is equally apparent that an accountable and properly scrutinized multi-party system could do better. Yet, very soon after the change to multi-partyism was announced, I had British consultants in my office in Nairobi suggesting that, now the pendulum had swung away from KANU's one-party government, it was time for the British aid programme to be directed to specific projects in areas opposed to President Moi's government to mark the transformation of Kenyan politics and to reconcile the opposition to HMG. Such pork-barrel politics, if implemented, will ensure that regional and tribal conflicts persist and, if anything, grow worse within a multi-party Kenya. The same is true of arguments that aid flows be regulated in the transitional period to reinforce the political advantage of this or that political group. It is the right and responsibility of the donors to work for Kenya's future under whatever government the Kenyan people elect, and for this freedom of Kenyans to express their choice. It is not for donors themselves to engage in partisan support, whether for the government of the day or for a group of successors.

It would also be a caricature to portray President Moi's change of direction at the end of 1991 and the introduction of multi-partyism as being exclusively or directly a response to the freeze on new programme aid from the donor community, dating from November of that year. Donor attitudes were undoubtedly among the factors which influenced Kenyan decisions. But many of the donors most vocal in condemnation of the KANU regime at that time were not substantial, in some cases not even marginal, providers of such programme aid in the first place. In my view, and it is a matter on which objectivity is not obtainable, the most important factor was internal pressure, generated not least by the scandals associated with, and revealed through, the inquiry into the murder of Dr Ouko and the courage shown by the judicial team at that inquiry in refusing to have it hushed up. The massive reduction in foreign support for Kenya added urgency and ensured that backsliding could not be contemplated once the decision to move to multi-partyism was announced. But a developing country such as Kenya will not find its economic salvation, whatever improvements are made in the political system, on the basis of violent fluctuations in the level of external assistance provided. Political transformation in Kenya is to be welcomed for its own sake and I believe that it is so welcomed by the majority of Kenyans, albeit in many cases with a degree of apprehension, but it would be a gross mistake to conclude on that account that turning on and off the aid tap is the right way to bring about political change in such a country. Kenya will need continuing and steady support, carefully monitored both by international financial institutions and by bilateral donors.

The sooner donors and Kenyans alike can concentrate on the effective economic use of that aid to address the systemic economic problems, the better.

Conclusion

Where does this leave 'the second liberation'? I suggest that the term is inappropriate to Kenya's situation. There have been grave political and economic defects in the way the country has been run. I understand why Oginga Odinga could address the proposition 'not yet Uhuru'. But not all has been bad in the past. Nor can Kenya's underlying weaknesses be eradicated simply through political will and the elimination of abuse. Transformation will take at best decades. If it is to be achieved it will require on all sides a will to reconciliation and an end to political patronage, particularly tribal patronage, as the basis on which the country's resources are directed. It will require common commitment to building the country as a whole. Kenya has natural advantages for the purpose. Above all, there is a substantial portion of the Kenyan population with a major stake in the stable prosperity of the country. These are people from all racial and tribal groups, poor as well as better-off, who are mortgaging their own resources for the education of their children and to build a better life. Their efforts can be strengthened and given a better chance of success if a pluralist and democratic Kenya and its leaders accept responsibility for reconciliation and for building the country as a whole. They will be destroyed if multi-partyism leads to cut-throat competition for limited resources on tribal and sectional lines. The obstacles are formidable. But if Kenyans can build upon what has been good in Kenya's past, and concentrate for the future not on prosecuting past malpractice but on making things better, then, with steady donor support (and need one add 'if only' there could be more open trading arrangements more favourable to the developing world producers) they could yet be overcome.

I have concentrated, for reasons explained at the beginning, on a single African country. It would be wrong not to note that, if Kenya is to advance, then improved regional co-operation and more stability in Kenya's neighbourhood are also important factors. I would like to think that one day I shall see not only Kenya's full potential fulfilled, but also the development of new regional institutions of quality comparable, for example, in the educational sphere to Makerere University as it was, and the renewal of effective economic co-operation throughout the region. Nothing could better underpin the success of political and economic transformation in Kenya and its neighbouring states.

This paper was substantially written at the end of 1992 and before the Kenyan general elections of 29 December in that year. It has been finalized while their outcome remains obscure. But the first indications, that they may lead to a further period of political uncertainty or worse, do not run counter to the theme of the paper: a better future for Kenya can be secured but the obstacles are great and the prospect of sudden transformation by the Fairy Godmother of multi-party democracy and free market economics is illusory. I leave it to others to judge whether or not this cautious view holds good for Africa as a whole.

Kenya: An Editorial Addendum

The elections did indeed take place on 29 December 1992. Their most conspicuous feature was the failure to unite on the part of the political opponents of President Moi and of KANU. Three opposition parties – the Forum for the Restoration of Democracy (FORD) Asili, FORD Kenya, and the Democratic Party – nominated candidates for the presidency and the national assembly. They were divided by ethnicity and the personal ambitions of their leaders. The outcomes were that Daniel arap Moi was returned as president by a minority (less than 37 per cent) of the votes cast, while KANU won 100 of the 200 seats in the assembly and, given also the twelve seats to which the President has power to nominate, secured a majority.

A second feature was that the electoral processes were patently flawed. More than 40 opposition candidates were prevented from delivering their nomination papers; as a consequence, KANU candidates were unopposed in 15 constituencies. Another 40 candidates nominated by opposition parties defected to KANU – in return, it was generally supposed, for material rewards. The radio and television services were not impartial in their coverage of electoral campaigning, but biased in favour of the ruling party. The North-Eastern Province, from which large majorities in favour of KANU were returned, was made difficult of access to the opposition parties, ostensibly on grounds of security (it borders Somalia). The autonomy of the electoral commission was in doubt, and in particular the fitness of its chairman to hold office was strongly questioned. The election results were nevertheless deemed acceptable by observers from both the Commonwealth (see the paper in this volume by Patsy Robertson) and the International Republican Institute of Washington DC; and the Commonwealth Secretary-General and representatives of Western governments persuaded leaders of the opposition parties that they too should accept the outcomes rather than try to create conditions in which the government would have to accede to demands for fresh elections. A consideration that surely weighed heavily with the observers was the unforeseeable but alarming consequences of declaring the elections *not* to have been 'free and fair'.

A third feature was the influence of ethnicity on the election results. KANU failed to win a single seat among the 25 contested in the Kikuyu homeland of Central Province, and Moi won only 2.5 per cent of the presidential poll in that province. In Nyanza Province, where the second largest ethnic group, the Luo, is concentrated, KANU won only one seat. The President and his party also fared badly in Nairobi Province, where the Kikuyu and Luo are strongly represented, and it was only on the strength of the results declared for North-Eastern Province that Moi secured the 25 per cent or more of the votes in at least five of the eight provinces that his election required. He and KANU owed their success, such as it was, to the support of his own Kalenjin people and of the smaller ethnic groups including the Somali. The cabinet of 25 ministers formed in January 1993 contained only one Kikuyu and one Luo; both had previously been ministers, had been defeated in the elections, and were now among the president's appointees to the assembly.

As is noticed in the paper by Stephen Ellis in this volume, President Moi's political conduct has not been significantly altered by the advent of multi-partyism and electoral competition in Kenya. For example, he prorogued the newly-elected assembly on the day after its first meeting.

The suspension of programme aid in November 1991, which helped bring about the multi-party elections, was intended also to stimulate economic reform, obliging the government to reduce its fiscal deficit, to abate corruption, and to privatize or otherwise restructure parastatal enterprises. The donors particularly favoured deregulation of the markets for foreign exchange and maize, and they were especially critical of a scheme for the preshipment financing of exports, a primary purpose of which had become the misappropriation of public funds; the alleged exports included diamond jewellery and gold, neither of which is produced in substantial quantity in Kenya. Ironically, one cause of a tendency toward increasing fiscal laxity and grosser forms of corruption was the anxiety of the government to win the elections, the desirability of holding which was so strongly urged by the donors.

The government considered that donor conditionalities had been largely satisfied by the elections and by a decision taken in February 1993 to float the Kenyan shilling, with an official exchange rate retained only for imports on government account and for external debt servicing; subsequently this official rate was itself devalued by 20 per cent. Since the float was not accompanied by any measures to contain liquidity, the exchange value of the shilling depreciated rapidly – by around 10 per cent per week – and inflation in Kenya accelerated. An IMF team that visited the country in February appears to have concluded that the government's economic management had worsened rather than improved since the Fund's last assessment in September 1992. Aid therefore continued to be withheld. President Moi declared that acceptance of the further reforms demanded by the donors would be suicidal, though it is not clear whether the reference was to Kenya or to his administration, the durability of which might be thought to have depended heavily on the absence of further reforms.

On 22 March 1993 the government revolted against the economic conditionalities. A reversal of economic liberalization was announced. Controls were reimposed on the sectors mainly responsible for earnings of foreign exchange – tea, coffee and tourism; they were henceforward to sell their earnings to the Central Bank at the unfavourable official exchange rate. The market in foreign exchange at a free and floating rate was effectively scrapped, and the allocations of this resource to users were again to be administratively determined.

This abandonment of economic reform may have been a tactical move, made in the hope that the conditionalities would be eased. Within a week, the Finance Minister was dismissing claims of a rift between Kenya and the donors. Dialogue with the multilateral agencies continued, and led in April to a further devaluation of the shilling at the official rate, a government undertaking to put the money supply into reverse, and an announcement that the World Bank would release some funds previously withheld. In May the shilling was devalued yet again, and the 'retention accounts', in which exporters could keep foreign exchange for sale in an interbank market at what it was worth, were reintroduced. Promises were made to reform the financial sector, within which agencies of government patronage known as political banks had been a cause of failure to control the money supply. After roaring like a lion, it was commented, Moi had signed like a lamb.

The suspension of bilateral aid appeared likely to continue until the end of 1993, during which interval the government would be required to show that its good intentions had been put into practice. Meanwhile, arrears were accumulating in external payments. Early in June they were estimated to exceed US$500 million. It appeared possible that the government would be forced to ask its official creditors for debt rescheduling, a course of action which Kenya, exceptionally among African countries, had hitherto avoided.

Notes

1. This view is reinforced for me by solid argument on the nature of Kenya's political culture and 'Kenyan exceptionalism' advanced by Dr John Lonsdale in a talk to the Royal African Society in Scotland on 27 May 1992.

13

PATSY ROBERTSON

Monitoring African Elections

Twenty years after their predecessors, meeting in Singapore in 1971, set out in a Declaration of Commonwealth Principles the fundamental values which underpin the association, Commonwealth leaders met in Harare and reaffirmed their full and continuing commitment to those principles in the context of the contemporary Commonwealth and its distinctive and enlarging role into the next century. The association reiterated its commitment to the promotion and protection of such fundamental political values as democracy, democratic processes and institutions, and fundamental human rights.

The Harare Declaration was, in effect, a blueprint for a new programme of action for the Commonwealth, and it is the basis for the increased activities undertaken in the promotion of democracy. Prominent among these activities is the monitoring of elections in member states. In the past three years, the Commonwealth Secretary-General, Chief Emeka Anyaoku, has dispatched nine observer missions to Malaysia (1990), Bangladesh and Zambia (1991), Guyana, the Seychelles (twice), Ghana and Kenya (1992), and Lesotho (1993).

The Secretary-General sets up an observer mission after a government has invited him to send one to its country and after a planning mission confirms that there is all-party support for the invitation. Prominent people from practising democracies are then asked to serve on the mission in their personal capacities.

It is important to note that, by their invitations, member states are welcoming the Commonwealth into an area which has long been zealously guarded as an internal jurisdiction and one affecting their sovereignty. The Commonwealth has been given this position of trust and privilege because of the close and informal relations between its peoples and governments, because it is non-threatening as an association and has no axe to grind, and because the observers are completely impartial and have no desire to support any of the contesting sides. The observers scrupulously carry out their mandate to observe and report on the organization and conduct of the elections, and have no executive or supervisory role in the process.

This does not mean that they are not critical or that they do not make their criticism public if publicity is required. On many occasions they have been convinced that the arrangements for the election have not been fair – when, for example, opposition parties have been denied access to the media. In all cases, they must finally determine whether, in their independent judgement, the conditions existed for a free expression of will by the electors and if the result of the election reflected the wishes of the people.

The Commonwealth's activities are not entirely devoted to observing events shortly before and on election day. As soon as a country announces that it intends to change from one-party or military rule to a multi-party system, the Commonwealth Secretariat is able to offer, upon request, technical and other assistance in planning the election. In the case of Lesotho, an experienced election official was dispatched well ahead of time to assist in the establishment of an electoral office and with arrangements for the election. In other countries, an election expert may make several visits in the months prior to election day to advise officials who have been given the task of preparing for the election on such matters as the electoral roll, the nomination process, and on all the components which are essential for the organization of democratic elections.

In some cases, Commonwealth assistance is given to ensure that the legal processes are correct and that a written constitution and legislation are in place which provide for such matters as the independence of the electoral commission, the work of a boundaries commission, the management of electoral law and the compilation of the electoral register.

During this period, the Secretary-General visits or dispatches planning missions from the Secretariat to the country concerned with a view to ensuring the existence or development of an acceptable environment for free and fair elections. In Kenya, for example, the Secretary-General paid three visits in the seven months before the December 1992 elections and a fourth immediately after the poll. He met the President and the leaders of the three opposition parties, and used his good offices to deal with the latter's complaints about what they deemed to be the unfair practices of the Electoral Commission. On his final visit to Nairobi before the elections, the Secretary-General and his team met the Chairman of the Electoral Commission and encouraged him to adopt a more even-handed approach to the opposition parties. He also made it plain that the Commonwealth would expect the election to be conducted as fairly as possible.

Another country which had problematic and potentially controversial elections was Guyana. Several advance missions visited that country in an eighteen-month period before the elections were eventually held in late 1992. Considerable changes to electoral law and regulations, and to the electoral institutions and structures, were needed, and the Commonwealth, together with other international institutions, was deeply involved in helping officials put reforms into place. The registration of voters and compilation of the electoral roll were also problem areas which the Commonwealth looked into.

Secretariat advance teams do not limit themselves to talking only to officials. They make it their business to develop close relationships with all political parties and, most importantly, with non-governmental organizations which are involved in the electoral process. Some of these groups have been set up with the specific task of monitoring the electoral process and events on polling day. In some countries, they are affiliated to churches or human rights organizations and are given training to equip them for the diverse tasks which they undertake, such as voter-education and duties in polling stations on election day.

The Secretariat thus uses all the influence it can bring to bear to encourage the holding of as properly conducted an election as can be organized. It is at the same time aware that there are many constraints which work against a completely satisfactory outcome. Lack of time properly to delink the governing party from the State is probably the most common, as governments, particularly in Africa, move from well-established, one-party regimes to democratic systems. This is an issue which has bedevilled most election campaigns, with opposition parties complaining bitterly about the ruling party's stranglehold on the public-owned media, and its access to State funds and transport. It is clear that, even with the best will in the world, it will take more than the year or so which most countries have given themselves to make legislative changes, and to organize and hold multi-party elections if they are to bring about a thorough separation of party and State.

Another problem is that many opposition parties, unfamiliar as they are with operating in an open system and unable to put their hands on the levers of patronage, cannot organize themselves properly and raise enough funds to compete in an election. They are often at a great disadvantage relative to the ruling party, and this heightens their feeling that the electoral odds are stacked against them.

The exercise to register voters and the compilation of the electoral roll are also sources of discontent. Commonwealth observers have received complaints about the state of the roll in every country – large and small – they have visited and it is clear that this is an area in which additional Commonwealth assistance is urgently needed. Maintaining as accurate an electoral roll as possible is almost a full-time occupation and the need to computerize and organize this task properly is paramount in many developing countries.

Despite any shortcomings which planning missions or observers may identify, the final decision to hold an election rests with the government and political parties in each country. The Secretary-General, in response to the government's invitation, begins the careful process of selecting a representative team of distinguished Commonwealth personalities to spend at least two weeks as official observers of the election. The Commonwealth Group assembles in London at the Secretariat's headquarters and receives a comprehensive briefing from the Secretary-General about the election. Its members also meet the Secretariat team which will support their activities throughout their stay.

On arrival in the country, the Group makes its presence known by holding a press conference, and inviting political leaders, representatives of organizations and members of the general public to meet members in special sessions. The observers offically visit the President and the Electoral Commission, and undertake a detailed examination of the arrangements for the elections. Where it is warranted, they may issue public statements. In Kenya, for example, the nomination process was criticized and the ruling party and Electoral Commission were warned that events on nomination day cast a pall of suspicion over the entire election.

An important area which commands the attention of the Group is the role of the media. All too often, the media remain servile to the ruling party, which also owns some of the newspapers. As there is not enough time to change the governance of broadcasting organizations, they still remain publicly-funded bodies and continue to serve the party in power. In some countries that have been observed, no attempt was made to come to any agreement on how the time devoted to election coverage could be fairly shared out between the parties, and this was a matter which the Commonwealth found unacceptable. Representation was always made to the Electoral Commission to take the initiative in getting agreement on fair access to radio and television for all the contending parties. Some organizations were exceptionally co-operative, while others found it difficult to change old working habits.

Well before polling day, members of the Commonwealth Observer Group are deployed throughout the country. Observers spend their days travelling around, and making their presence known to party and election officials and to voters. They devote a great deal of time in working to smooth out any irregularities which may be brought to their attention, and there is no doubt that by polling day they are well aware of the constituencies and polling stations where difficulties are likely to arise and very familiar with local problems and issues.

On polling day itself, Commonwealth observers rise before dawn to be at polling stations before they open to the public. The observers ensure that the correct procedures in voting, as laid down in law, are followed. They move rapidly from station to station, checking on procedures, listening to complaints, noting and observing. They are present at the end of the day, and spend the evening observing the count. In many countries, the count is a long and tedious process, often lasting over several days, and observers have to continue monitoring it until all results have been confirmed.

It is Commonwealth practice to come to a conclusion about the conduct of the election before a final result is obtained. This pre-empts any accusation that the Group's final verdict was influenced by the result. This initial and interim statement on the election is followed by a substantial report to the Secretary-General. This report is made available to the government and to all Commonwealth governments some weeks later, and to the media and relevant organizations.

The Commonwealth's work does not end here. At times the result of the election is repudiated by one of the contesting parties and mediation efforts are initiated by the Secretary-General with a view to seeking solutions, and ensuring that the process will go forward. In Kenya, for instance, the Secretary-General spent time after the election with the President and opposition leaders and persuaded them to agree to meet to thrash out their difficulties. In the end, Parliament was convened and the newly elected MPs were able to take their seats.

Follow-up action is also taken by the Commonwealth Parliamentary Association which has a programme of training for new parliamentarians. This programme includes special courses for Speakers, who have a heavy responsibility to uphold the dignity and stability of this most important forum of democracy.

PART V HUMAN DEVELOPMENT

14

SITHEMBISO NYONI

The Effects of & Responses to the 1992 Drought in Zimbabwe

The 1992 Southern African drought was the worst in our people's memory. The countries worst affected included Botswana, Malawi, Mozambique, Zambia and Zimbabwe. The presidents of each of these countries declared the drought a national disaster. South Africa was also affected, but not so badly. This paper will limit its discussion to the effects of, and responses to, the drought in Zimbabwe.

The Effects of the Drought

The effects of the 1992 drought were felt throughout the country, in the cities and the communal lands alike. Zimbabwe consumes over 2 million tonnes of maize per annum. In 1992 it harvested only a quarter of its total requirement. Most areas received the equivalent of two months' supply of rain over the whole year. By April there was only enough grazing to last for two months. Some communal farmers had to move their cattle onto the failed crops. The rainfall was so low that some rivers never flowed; the dams were therefore not replenished.

With such low rainfall and very little vegetation cover, one can imagine the impact on the ecosystem. The water table became very low. This affected not only the underground water supplies, especially the shallow boreholes and wells, but also plant growth and plant life. Trees were dried up. The grasses were affected even more since animals, both domestic and wild, competed for the little grass there was, giving it virtually no chance to grow. This led to land denudation and soil erosion.

By early June, 120,000 cattle were reported dead from drought-related causes in the communal lands. By December the number had risen to 270,066, and the true figure could be higher because many cattle deaths were not reported. Livestock death was attributable not only to lack of grazing and water, but also to the shortage of stock feed. Most stock feed had to be imported. The prices were beyond the purchasing power of most communal farmers. This affected the beef and dairy industry as well as small livestock such as poultry, pigs, sheep and goats.

The country's food supplies come from both commercial and small-scale agriculture.

Eighty per cent of supplies are still non-commercialized. Most rural families in 1992 were unable to produce enough food for themselves, let alone any surplus to earn cash. The entire agricultural sector produced only one third of the national needs. This led to serious food shortages. At the retail shops there were long queues of people scrambling for supplies. By December 1991 there were already shortages of almost everything including maize products which are a major part of the national diet. Other basic food requirements such as sugar, cooking oil and salt were also in short supply. The prices of meat and dairy products rose beyond the reach of ordinary people.

In September 1992 the Ministry of Health and Child Welfare conducted a study to measure the impact of the drought on the under-fives. This study compared Vitamin A deficiency in children at the same times in 1991 and 1992. It was found that in 1992 the deficiency was very much higher and that there was a marked deterioration in the health of children under five, manifest in wasting, stunting and weight deficiency. From schools there came reports of children fainting because of hunger. Some had stopped coming to school because they were too weak to walk long distances. Class performance deteriorated.

Also greatly affected were rural women as providers of food, fuel and water. Their burden was multiplied many times. Some found it almost impossible to obtain food and water for their families. Some spent many days away from home in search of food and several hours each day in search of water. I know of one case in a Zhombe village in the Midlands where a young mother went to look for food in the neighbouring town, leaving her children with her elderly mother. When she returned after a week one of her children had died of starvation. This story was told at an ORAP board meeting and provoked so much anger that a firm decision was taken to strengthen the *amalima* (family neighbourhood) approach to ensure that there were no more pockets of possible starvation.

At the same time the Structural Adjustment Programme exacerbated the effects of the drought. With the removal of subsidies, the cost of living rose further. Food, health services, education, transport and other necessities became unaffordable by the unemployed and low-income earners. No wonder the President declared this drought a national disaster.

Responses to the Drought

As other practitioners in the field have noted, by the time relief from outside arrives to help the victims of disaster, the victims are helping themselves. Especially in crises which develop gradually, such as drought and famine, the people directly affected have adopted various tactics of survival before aid agencies have even become aware of the emergency.

Responses to the 1992 drought varied from community to community. Some communities responded through government structures, some through church and voluntary organizations and others through their own traditional structures. I shall concentrate here on people's response through traditional structures and the Organization of Rural Associations for Progress (ORAP).

As early as February people were aware that a severe drought was on the way and were already making plans to deal with it. In addition, they had already started alerting the outside world through the Agritex Early Warning Unit, the churches and other organizations. It was the rural people who pushed organizations such as ORAP to study the extent of the drought and the effects of the Economic Structural Adjustment Programme. By April 1992 the ORAP study was complete, showing in addition what people intended to do about the drought.

ORAP's response to the drought was based on this study. It was divided into three programmes – food for development, food for sale and drought recovery.

Food for development entailed giving support to the local organizations through which people related, worked in development programmes and shared food. Support was directed through *amalima* and savings groups as well as to project sites, schools and pre-school groups. The idea was to ensure food security at family level as a priority, but also to ensure that whatever development work or structure existed in a village did not suffer because of lack of food.

Thus no new structures were created beyond what people already had and used. Food was made available through existing structures with the intention of strengthening rather than replacing them. Such an approach provided ORAP staff and the leadership of its member associations with an opportunity to hold development debates on the subject of food. These debates included the politics of food, people's rights to food, food distribution and food aid for empowerment. In this way people were able to use food aid in a positive rather than a negative way.

Food for sale involved making food available in the deficit areas. ORAP bought food from the Grain Marketing Board and delivered it to various points for those who could afford to buy. This programme was important in sending a different message – that no matter how bad the situation, wherever possible people must stand on their own feet. The sales were slow. But some people did buy their food.

The drought recovery programme involved water development, seed distribution, construction of grain storage, and new economic activities. The idea was to give people hope for the future as well as the opportunity to prepare for the worst, in case the drought continued. But should the next season be a good one, people needed to be prepared to move on with their development rather than allow the drought to have pushed them back.

In water development activities, people dug and deepened wells in areas such as Silobela in the Midlands where the water table was high. Seventy-two more wells were dug during 1992 than in any other single year of ORAP's operations. It was not possible to drill any boreholes because all the rigs in the country were required for government programmes. So the people did what they could with the resources they had. In other districts, in particular Gwanda and Kezi in Matabeleland South, small dams were constructed. Five dams were completed; most of these dams are full in 1993. At Inyathi an old irrigation scheme was revived and five people employed to run it. Apart from creating jobs, it also provided fresh vegetables for the community.

Communities also organized themselves to build food storage units. Small- and medium-sized granaries were professionally designed to store enough grain at family and community levels. These granaries have a capacity of up to 150 bags, enough to feed eleven or twelve families for a year or one family for five years, including some surplus they could sell for cash. One hundred and fifty village granaries were requested, but only a few could be completed due to lack of the arching grass. As in the case of water development, more granaries were requested and constructed during the drought than in any other year. Some of the food aid was stored and distributed from these granaries.

It was hard to initiate any new economic activity, not only because of the drought but also because of the structural adjustment programme. There was very little money to start or develop business. However, ORAP did its best to encourage groups not to give up. Most of the economic activities were linked to food production and distribution. The grinding mills were kept going and some of the irrigation schemes where water was available were revived.

International donors who helped with food aid also supplied seeds. ORAP runs a seed multiplication programme in which farmers multiply and distribute drought-resistant crop seeds. During the 1992 drought the programme did not succeed. Most of the seed distributed by ORAP therefore came from outside. A total of 32,415 tonnes of maize seed was distributed, plus 585 tonnes of sorghum, 112 tonnes of millet, 1,924 tonnes of groundnuts, and 423 tonnes of sunflower.

All this work could not have been completed so successfully without our friends abroad, who gave generously and freely. The relationship between aid givers and recipients is complex. Aid intended to help can do harm. But all those who gave help to ORAP can be proud that their assistance left rural people stronger and better prepared for development than is often the case during disasters. This can be attributed to ORAP's mobilization approach to development as well as its emphasis on awareness building and development education, so that such a disaster was seen as an opportunity rather than a catastrophe. Also, the donors who provided resources did so in such a way as to reinforce and enhance our efforts. They were encouraging and affirming, and in most cases the aid was as timely as the international communication systems would allow.

From this experience I learnt that it takes all sides to withstand natural disasters. It is very important for NGOs to work closely with the people, to understand and respect their survival strategies and to build on, rather than to try to replace, their efforts. It is then easier for those outside to help us with confidence and where possible on time.

Although the 1992 drought was the worst in living memory, the rural families in Zimbabwe and most of the agencies who supported them refused to be defeated by it. Together we saved lives and together we built stronger foundations for the future. For this I am most grateful to all who took part.

15

RICHARD JOLLY

Challenges & Hope for the 1990s

Africa is slipping from the stage of popular concern and public support.[1] A cloud of crisis grows over the continent – just as the actual number of crises increases: Somalia and Liberia, Mozambique and Angola, Zaïre and Rwanda, Sudan and Sierra Leone. Even for those countries not in crisis or emergency, the economic record is not encouraging. Apart from a handful of small exceptions, Mauritius and Botswana primarily, per capita growth rates have been small, stagnant or negative.[2] For Sub-Saharan Africa as a whole, agricultural production per capita declined over the 1980s, along with per capita income. Debt rose from less than 30 per cent of national income to almost 110 per cent in 1991.[3] Perhaps the cruellest cut of all, there is an increasing number of voices within the World Bank admitting that the programmes of structural adjustment are not working. Between 1990 and 1992, the World Bank increased its projection of the number of Africans in poverty in the year 2000 by 39 millions, from 265 to 304 millions.[4]

Matching these dire trends within Africa is a parallel downturn – perhaps crisis is also the more appropriate word – in aid policy and donor attitudes to Africa. The rise in support for emergencies and for the former Soviet Union and Eastern Europe is leading to a decline in aid for development, with aid to Africa being under pressure just when more is needed. Action to deal with bilateral debt is stalled, even as debt increases. The need for action on multilateral debt grows ever more urgent. Yet the international community continues to set the frame for adjustment – and policies of governance – even as the evidence mounts that adjustment is not working and earlier approaches to governance and democracy are seen to be over-simplified and often destabilizing.

Overshadowed by this record, one may too readily miss some more positive trends. In spite of general downward pressures on living standards and the quality and accessibility of social services, specific interventions in key areas of health have shown considerable progress, and have helped somewhat to reduce the still high infant and child mortality rates. Moreover, the latest survey results, admittedly from only a handful of countries, show a marked decline in fertility rates: for instance, in Kenya the total fertility rate fell from 8.0 in 1981 to 6.4 in 1991. Access to clean water increased impressively, bringing an additional 168 million of the population within reach of some form of improved well, handpump or deep tube well, a number slightly exceeding the total with such access in 1980.[5] With dehydration from diarrhoea still the largest single cause of child death in Africa, the fact that over the 1980s almost one-third of mothers learned the simple technique of oral rehydration therapy, and applied it, has contributed to an important reduction in such mortality.

Table 15.1 Immunization Coverage in Africa[a] (% DPT /OPV)

	1981	1985	1990	1991
North	58	74	85	88
West	18	16	49	40
East	16	22	62	54
South	43	45	60	57
Total Africa	27	30	60	53
Sub-Saharan Africa	20	21	55	47
Number of countries attaining 75% coverage in all six antigens	0	1	21	17

Sources: UNICEF and WHO data.

a UNICEF/WHO immunization targets refer to antigens against six major diseases – tuberculosis, diphtheria, pertussis, tetanus (DPT), polio and measles. Coverage of tetanus and polio vaccinations (DPT/OPV), which are usually given together, is taken as a good proxy for total immunization coverage.

The expansion of immunization over the later half of the 1980s was truly remarkable. Estimated DPT/OPV coverage in 1981 was 27 per cent for all of Africa and 20 per cent for Sub-Saharan Africa; by 1985, it was 30 per cent and 21 per cent respectively, as shown in Table 15.1. African Ministers of Health meeting in Bamako in 1986 set the target of 75 per cent coverage for each of the six antigens by 1990. Worthy and important as was this goal, few seriously supposed it to be attainable. Yet, by 1990, no fewer than 21 countries had attained or exceeded the goal, while average DPT/OPV coverage had risen to 60 per cent. These improvements alone accounted for a reduction of deaths from measles, whooping cough and tetanus of some 500,000 a year,[6] although some of the children whose mortality from these causes was avoided must, of course, have succumbed to other diseases.

In 1992 UNICEF undertook an analysis of the 21 countries attaining or exceeding the 75 per cent immunization goal.[7] The purpose was to assess whether these countries were also those showing positive economic performance. Interestingly, there was no correlation between them and those countries with better performances as indicated by the successful undertaking of adjustment policies, higher income per head, or growth of per capita income during the 1980s. If there was one factor that explained success in achieving the immunization target, it seemed to be clear and sustained political commitment to this goal – and backing up this commitment with clear administrative support and mobilization of the media and of non-governmental groups such as the churches. The decline from 21 to 17 countries in 1991 shows, however, the need for sustaining this commitment and action if the gains are to be retained.

Opportunities for the 1990s

This success, albeit in a limited range of health interventions, sets the stage for a new opportunity on a broader front of human development in Africa. Just as the eradication of smallpox over the 1960s and 1970s set the stage for the World Health Organization to develop broader goals for immunization over the 1980s, so now the success of immunization sets the stage for a broader programme of human development. At the World Summit for Children in New York in September 1990, 71 heads of state signed a Declaration and Plan of Action for making progress for children in the 1990s. The Plan of Action set seven major goals and twenty supporting goals for the year 2000.[8] Africa was identified as the continent of special need. The seven major goals are listed below, and the other supporting goals in the Annexe to this chapter.

Major goals for child survival, development and protection

- Between 1990 and the year 2000, reduction of infant and under-5 child mortality rates by one-third or to 50 and 70 per 1000 live births respectively, whichever is less.
- Between 1990 and the year 2000, reduction of the maternal mortality rate by half.
- Between 1990 and the year 2000, reduction of severe and moderate malnutrition among children under 5 by half.
- Universal access to safe drinking water and to sanitary means of excreta disposal.
- By the year 2000, universal access to basic education and completion of primary education by at least 80 per cent of primary school-age children.
- Reduction of the adult illiteracy rate (the appropriate age group to be determined in each country) to at least half its 1990 level, with emphasis on female literacy.
- Improved protection of children in especially difficult circumstances.

Individual governments committed themselves to adapting these goals to the specific circumstances of their countries and to preparing National Programmes of Action (NPAs) setting out strategies of implementation. By the end of 1992 some 40 in Africa had prepared NPAs or had them in good draft. Some NPAs are of impressive quality – like those of Ghana, Guinea, Uganda, Zambia and Zimbabwe. Others are less detailed but contain the broad lines of strategy for achieving the goals during the 1990s.

In November 1992, the OAU hosted in Dakar a major international conference on the NPAs and the challenge of 'mobilizing assistance to African children'. Virtually all African countries participated at ministerial level and some 13 donor countries were also represented, with ministers from France, Japan and Norway. This conference ended with the production of a 'Consensus of Dakar' which summarizes commitments and priorities for implementation of the NPAs, identifies the special problems of children in difficult circumstances and of female children and women, and ends with key sections focused on mid-decade goals and the national and international challenges of mobilizing and restructuring resources to achieve them. [9]

Mid-decade goals for Africa

- Raise Africa's average immunization coverage level against diphtheria, pertussis, tetanus, poliomyelitis and tuberculosis from the 75 per cent achieved for the Universal Child Immunization (UCI) effort to 80 per cent.
- Ensure 90 per cent coverage against measles, by far the most lethal of the vaccine-preventable diseases, and against tetanus for women of child-bearing age.
- Achieve 80 per cent usage of oral rehydration therapy in order to prevent dehydration caused by diarrhoea.
- Virtually eliminate iodine-deficiency disorders.
- Virtually eliminate vitamin-A deficiency and its consequences.
- Encourage exclusive breastfeeding for four to six months and sustain breastfeeding for up to two years of age and beyond, with complementary foods beginning at four to six months.

Pursuit of these goals in the 1990s could provide the social and political impetus needed after a decade of 'lost development', in which the economic preoccupations have been stabilization and structural adjustment. Human development could be put at the centre, with the goals serving to provide specific operational targets for mobilizing both social participation and political commitment. The goals are for the most part low-cost, and thus within the capacity of virtually every African country with a modest level of external support.

Progress in education, especially of girls, in child health and in the reduction of child mortality will also set the conditions for accelerating the reduction of fertility and of population growth. As the Plan of Action of the World Summit for Children stated:[10]

> there is an added benefit in promoting maternal and child health programmes and family planning together, in that, acting synergistically, these activities help accelerate the reduction of both mortality and fertility rates, and contribute more to lowering rates of population growth than either type of activity alone.

It is a major mistake to see human development and pursuit of these goals as primarily a matter of governmental action in the main sectors of health, education and water supply. Experience in the 1980s shows that some of the most dynamic and positive initiatives have sprung from community action – as in health, where the collapse of the formal health care system has often acted as a catalyst for local action. Often women's organizations have displayed enormous social energy in mobilizing action and achieving results. The potential for further success is large, without the need for massive injections of new resources from government or from abroad. Indeed, as in the Bamako Initiative in Health, endorsed by African Ministers of Health in 1986, the key element is community involvement and management control at the local level.

The mid-decade goals should reinforce but not replace progress towards the more challenging longer-term goals in education, nutrition, water supply and sanitation.

Conditions for Success

To support achievement of the sectoral programmes set at the World Summit for Children is estimated to require an additional $8.85 billion per year for the rest of the 1990s (see Table 15.2).[11] Such estimates can at this stage be only rough. Only when country-by-country plans and estimates are available will it be possible to assess more accurately the resources required. But it is also recognized that in many areas new financial resources are less important than prioritization and restructuring in the use of existing resources. Altogether, it is estimated that roughly half of the required $8.85 billion will need to come from within African countries and the remaining half from international sources, either through additional or restructured aid or through equivalent measures of debt relief.

Table 15.2 Indicative Annual Costs for Achieving the Goals 1993–2000 (US$m.)

Key Sectoral Programmes:	
Basic health care	1,550
Basic education	1,875
Nutrition-focused programmes	825
Water supply and sanitation	4,600
Subtotal	8,850
Targeted Cross-Sectoral Actions:	
Focused poverty alleviation programmes	900
Environmental preservation	250
Subtotal	1,150
Special Post-war and Post-disaster Support:	
Post-war livelihood rehabilitation	2,500
Post-disaster support	200
Subtotal	2,700
Total Annual Costs:	12,700

Source: OAU/UNICEF, *Africa's Children, Africa's Future – Human Investment Priorities for the 1990s* (Addis Ababa and New York, 1992), p. 53.

The 'Consensus of Dakar' embodies several commitments from participating African countries towards the goal of restructuring national resources, as follows:

(i) Adoption of specific goals for achieving by end-1995 a priority list of low-cost achievable goals for children and women, selected from the core adopted at the World Summit for Children, with special attention to those goals primarily dependent on social mobilization and national leadership rather than on major additional financial resources (for example, achievement by 1995 of 90 per cent measles and tetanus toxoid immunization, 80 per cent oral rehydration therapy, universal iodized salt, and reduction by half of the gender gap in primary education).

(ii) The principle of first call on available resources to meet the basic needs of women and children to be carried forward by restructuring allocations of government resources to favour child survival, protection and development and to support the key goals for children and women.

(iii) Consequential reallocations within existing social sector budgets and/or a shift of resources away from non-productive uses, such as military/internal security expenditures and subsidies for inefficient parastatals.

(iv) An increase of domestic resource mobilization to be supported by other actions such as national tax reform and the encouragement of community actions and contributions.

Some comments are in order on the realism of these commitments. In the first place, the commitments to restructuring (ii and iii) are in many countries a reinforcement of those already being made in relation to adjustment policy and to secure more efficient use of national resources. Though this may raise questions about the seriousness of the additional national commitments, it should be noted that restructuring in the sectors of health and education will often generate some populist local response. UNICEF has experienced many times over the 1980s demonstrations of popular support precisely because meeting basic human needs through low-cost means can be 'good politics'.

As to restructuring of military budgets, it is too easy for the jaded Western cynic to regard it as easy rhetoric without action. In fact, African experience over the 1980s provides at least six positive examples to confound the cynics. In Zimbabwe, military spending was reduced from 44 per cent of public expenditure in the early 1980s and the savings largely used to finance a three-fold expansion of primary and secondary education. Benin, Tanzania, Namibia and Uganda are other examples that might be cited. More recently, the case of Ethiopia has been carefully documented and analysed by the World Bank. Between 1989 and 1991, military expenditure was reduced from 19 to 6 per cent of GNP, and declined from almost 70 per cent of public expenditure.[12] The reduction has been used to reduce the public expenditure deficit and also to increase expenditure on education. These examples of the peace dividend, of swords being beaten into ploughshares of health, education and deficit reduction, deserve to be better known.

Domestic resource mobilization needs to encompass new approaches to local finance, not merely to central government taxation. Many countries already have examples of a growing involvement of village and district communities in mobilizing resources to meet health needs and in ensuring control of these resources by managing the health facilities they support. Sometimes the resources are raised through selling low-cost essential drugs with a mark-up that is used to finance local health workers; sometimes finance is raised through a local set fee for using health services; sometimes payment takes the form of an insurance premium, building on traditional mechanisms. Some 30 countries in Africa have variations of such approaches under way and UNICEF, under the Bamako Initiative, is supporting at least 15 of them as a mechanism for supporting health care towards the goals of the 1990s.[13]

International Action

As regards international action, donors and international financial institutions committed themselves in the 'Consensus of Dakar' to:

(i) Explore short-, medium- and long-term commitments of resources to support health, nutrition, basic education, water and sanitation as set out in specific sectors and subsectors of National Programmes of Action.

(ii) Increase and sustain the share of Official Development Assistance commitment to social priority sectors by 1995 in line with increasing commitments by African countries to sectors such as basic education, primary health care, low-cost water and sanitation systems, responsible parenthood and family planning, and nutrition programmes, bearing in mind the level of 20 per cent of total ODA for these sectors recommended in UNDP's *Human Development Report*.[14]

(iii) Formulate debt relief and conversion schemes in such ways as to make possible increased budget allocations and renewed economic growth, with at least part of the benefits being used to advance programmes for children. 'Debt relief for Children', i.e. the swapping of debt for investment in social development programmes, used on a small but encouraging scale since the World Summit for Children, to be much more actively considered by debtors and creditors. Such schemes to be considered on a case-by-case basis reflecting the macro-economic conditions of the country concerned.

The commitment to restructure international aid deserves particular attention, especially at this time when many donors stress the political impossibility of contemplating increases in their aid budgets. There was a strong note of political realism in Dakar in putting the emphasis on restructuring aid rather than increasing the total. Since only 6.5 per cent of bilateral aid goes to support the basic components of human development, there seems to be ample scope for increasing this share. Table 15.3 gives the estimates for individual donors and shows that if each bilateral donor were to increase the share of its aid for basic education, health, water, nutrition and family planning to 20 per cent, the result would be an additional $1.59 billion allocated to these priority sectors.[15] This would go some way to meet the additional international resources required.

The second measure identified at Dakar was debt relief. Here one must note the scandalous inadequacy so far of actions to tackle indebtedness in Sub-Saharan Africa. Over a period when in Asia and Latin America the major problems of indebtedness have been dealt with, Africa's debt as a share of national income has steadily increased, year by year, since 1980. By the end of 1992, the debt of Sub-Saharan African amounted to 110 per cent of GNP, and the annual outflow of foreign exchange in payment of debt service had risen to $11.7 billion. The Secretary-General of the United Nations referred to this as 'a mill-stone around the neck of Africa'. He added that 'easing the

Table 15.3 Aid to Social Priorities in Sub-Saharan Africa, 1990

Bilateral donors:	ODA as % of total GNP	Social priorities as a % of ODA	% to Sub-Saharan Africa of bilateral ODA	ODA to Sub-Saharan Africa net ($m)	Est. ODA to social priorities in Sub-Saharan Africa ($m)	ODA to social priorities in Sub-Saharan Africa if donors allocated 20% ($m)
Australia	0.34	2.0	10	70	1	10
Austria	0.25	8.1	22	70	10	10
Belgium	0.45	6.5[a]	54	300	20	60
Canada	0.44	10.9	25	430	50	90
Denmark	0.93	10.6	43	300	30	60
Finland	0.64	15.7	48	240	40	50
France	0.55	4.0	52	4,050	160	810
Germany	0.42	1.9	26	1,140	20	230
Ireland	0.16	6.5[a]	65	10	1	3
Italy	0.32	8.5	52	1,090	90	220
Japan	0.31	2.7	12	830	20	170
Netherlands	0.94	9.4	33	620	60	120
New Zealand	0.22	6.5[a]	0	0	0	0
Norway	1.17	19.7	50	370	70	70
Sweden	0.90	7.1	45	620	40	120
Switzerland	0.31	18.1	40	220	40	40
UK	0.27	8.8	37	540	50	110
USA	0.21	8.3	12	1,010	80	200
Total	0.35	6.5	30	11,800	790	2,380
Multilateral Organizations:[b]						
Int. Development Association		8.3	49	1,890	160	
African Development Fund		5.4	98	590	30	
European Community		c	54	1,560		
Int. Fund Agricultural Dev.		16.8	0			
UNDP		c	34	330		
UN			23	220		
UNICEF		78.8	36	310	250	
WFP		c	41	60		
UNHCR		c	46	180		
Other UN		c	15	140		
Arab agencies		c	0			
Other multilaterals		c	28	430		
Total				5,700	(440+)	
Arab countries		c	2	120		
Overall Total				17,620[d]	(1,230+)	

a No UNDP assessment made, average share has been applied.

b Data on assistance from individual donors to the whole of Africa are not readily available and estimates of ODA to social priorities from multilateral agencies active in Africa are only available for four agencies.

c Noticeable allocations to social priorities are likely.

d This total includes assistance to Mayotte, Réunion, St. Helena and unspecified Africa (not included in the table).

Sources: UNDP, *Human Development Report 1992*, p.43 and OECD, *Development Cooperation Report 1991* (Paris, 1991).

continent's debt burden must be a priority for the international community.'[16]

Programmes of debt conversion have been supported by the private sector for health and water programmes in the Sudan, and other social investment programmes in Madagascar. But all this on a tiny scale. What is now required is a major new initiative, built on the enhanced Toronto Terms, leading to serious implementation of the Trinidad Terms and beyond to the call made by Minister Pronk of The Netherlands for the total cancellation of Africa's bilateral debt. UNICEF believes that if such an initiative were linked in part to the generation of local resources committed to the support of health and education, not only would it be strengthened but also it would secure political appeal in all countries required to support it.

There is also need for relief with respect to debt owed by the poorest African countries to the World Bank and the IMF. Such debt, and the annual servicing payments arising from it, account for an ever-higher proportion of the total African debt burden. The fact that such payments are required from the poorest continent in the world has become a travesty of the system created precisely to encourage a more efficient and more equitable financing of world economic activity.

Some indication of the consequences is provided by the case of Burundi, a country which since 1987 has been a World Bank model of good adjustment and one where the beginnings of economic growth, reduced inflation and reduced deficit are clearly seen. Remarkably, Burundi does not lag in any of its debt-servicing payments. It has benefitted from debt forgiveness in the commercial and bilateral sectors. Yet Burundi, with clear commitments to education and health and an excellent National Programme of Action towards the goals for the year 2000, is constrained from spending more than 18 per cent of public expenditure on education and health by the need to spend over 30 per cent on debt service.

The Challenge: a Revival of Commitment to Africa

A new effort is needed within Africa and among friends outside in support of a major revival of human development in Africa during the 1990s. Such an effort could lay the foundations for a more positive and dynamic process of African development during the twenty-first century. With this effort African countries could be helped to achieve the conditions required for self-sustaining growth built on strong popular participation and strengthened national capacity. Without it, with a second decade of lost human development and retrogression or stagnation in education, nutrition and much of health, Africa in the year 2000 will be increasingly unstable and its basis for development ever more fragile and partial.

The challenge to those in the industrial countries who feel a sense of commitment to Africa is particularly strong. Africa may be slipping from the stage of public concern – but it need not do so. What is required is not merely day-to-day commitment and action to reverse these retrogressive trends but a sense of vision of what Africa could become. The continent is still rich in potential. From every one of its countries more and more Africans have demonstrated leadership and skill, though too often and perhaps increasingly outside their countries rather than within. Such are the consequences of ever greater neglect of the least developed countries and the inadequacy of existing mechanisms to offset the extreme imbalances in trade, aid and debt. Now is the moment for those who can sense the long-run opportunity to reject these tawdry, short-sighted and insular attitudes and, instead, to emphasize the need for global perspectives of a more balanced and humane world economy during the next century.

Notes

1. See also Marguerite Michaels, 'Retreat from Africa', *Foreign Affairs*, 72, 1 (1992).
2. L. Yaker, *Preliminary Assessment of the Performance of the African Economy in 1992 and Prospects for 1993* (Addis Ababa: ECA, 1992).
3. Data from World Bank, *World Debt Tables 1992–93*, as analysed in the leaflet, *African Debt Crisis: a continuing impediment to development* (New York: UN, 1993).
4. World Bank, *World Development Report 1990* (p. 139) and *World Development Report 1992* (p. 30).
5. OAU/UNICEF, *Africa's Children, Africa's Future : Background Sectoral Papers* (Addis Ababa and New York, 1992), p. 107.
6. Estimate by UNICEF using WHO projections.
7. Santosh Mehrotra, 'Immunization Coverage in an Uneconomically Unfavourable Environment', unpublished UNICEF working paper.
8. The full texts are available in UNICEF, *First Call for Children: World Declaration and Plan of Action from the World Summit for Children* (New York, 1990), and reprinted in UNICEF, *The State of the World's Children 1991* (New York: Oxford University Press, 1991).
9. OAU, *Consensus of Dakar*, International Conference on Assistance to African Children, Dakar, 25–27 November 1992.
10. UNICEF, *First Call for Children*, para. 17.
11. OAU/UNICEF, *Africa's Children, Africa's Future – Human Investment Priorities for the 1990s* (Addis Ababa and New York, 1992), p. 53.
12. Personal communication from the World Bank representative, Addis Ababa.
13. UNICEF, *Board Report on Bamako Initiative* (New York, 1993).
14. UNDP, *Human Development Report 1991* (New York: Oxford University Press, 1991), p. 58.
15. See OAU/UNESCO, *Africa's Children, Africa's Future – Human Investment Priorities for the 1990s*, pp. 60–63.
16. Quoted in United Nations, *African Debt Crisis* (New York, 1993).

Annexe: World Summit for Children Goals for Children and Development in the 1990s

The following goals have been fomulated through extensive consultation in various international fora attended by virtually all governments, the relevant UN agencies including WHO, UNICEF, UNFPA, UNESCO, UNDP and IBRD, and a large number of non-governmental organizations. These goals are recommended for implementation by all countries where they are applicable, with appropriate adaptation to the specific situation of each country in terms of phasing, standards, priorities and availability of resources, with respect for cultural, religious and social traditions. Additional goals that are particularly relevant to a country's specific situation should be added in its national plan of action. Achievement of these goals is essential to full implementation of the Convention on the Rights of the Child, which is the ultimate objective of programmes for children and development.

1. Major goals for Child Survival, Development and Protection (See text, p. 167).

2. Supporting/Sectoral Goals

i. Women's Health and Education

- Special attention to the health and nutrition of the female child, and pregnant and lactating women.
- Access by all couples to information and services to prevent pregancies which are too early, too closely spaced, too late or too many.
- Access by all pregnant women to prenatal care, trained attendants during child birth and referral facilities for high risk pregnancies and obstetric emergencies.
- Universal access to primary education with special emphasis for girls, and accelerated literacy programmes for women.

ii. Nutrition

- Reduction in severe as well as moderate malnutrition among under-5 children by half of 1990 levels.
- Reduction of the rate of low birth weight (less than 2.5 kg) to less than 10%.
- Reduction of iron deficiency anaemia in women by one-third of 1990 levels.
- Virtual elimination of iodine deficiency disorders.
- Virtual elimination of vitamin A deficiency and its consequences, including blindness.
- Empowerment of all women to exclusively breast-feed their child for four to six months and to continue breast-feeding with complementary food well into the second year.
- Growth promotion and its regular monitoring to be institutionalized in all countries by the end of the 1990s.
- Dissemination of knowledge and supporting services to increase food production to ensure household food security.

iii. Child Health

- Global eradication of poliomyelitis by the year 2000.
- Elimination of neonatal tetanus by 1995.
- Reduction by 95 per cent in measles deaths and reduction by 90 per cent of measles cases compared to pre-immunization levels by 1995, as a major step to the global eradication of measles in the longer run.
- Maintenance of a high level of immunization coverage (at least 90% of children under one year of age by the year 2000) against diphtheria, pertussis, tetanus, measles, poliomyelitis, tuberculosis and against tetanus for women of child-bearing age.
- Reduction by 50 per cent in the deaths due to diarrhoea in children under the age of five years; and 25 per cent reduction in the diarrhoea incidence rate.
- Reduction by one-third in the deaths due to acute respiratory infections in children under five years.

iv. Water and Sanitation

- Universal access to safe drinking water.
- Universal access to sanitary means of excreta disposal.
- Elimination of guinea-worm disease (dracuncutiasis) by the year 2000.

v. Basic Education

- Expansion of early childhood development activities including appropriate low-cost family and community based interventions.
- Universal access to basic education, and achievement of primary education by at least 80 per cent of primary school age children through formal schooling or non-formal education of comparable learning standard, with emphasis on reducing the current disparities between boys and girls.
- Reduction of the adult illiteracy rate (the appropriate age group to be determined in each country) to at least half its 1990 level, with emphasis on female literacy.
- Increased acquisition by individuals and families of the knowledge, skills and values required for better living, made available through all educational channels, including the mass media, other forms of modern and traditional communication, and social action, with effectiveness measured in terms of behavioural change.

vi. Children in Difficult Circumstances

- Provide improved protection of children in especially difficult circumstances and tackle the root causes leading to such situations.

Further Reading

Bjornland, Eric, Michael Bratton and Clark Gibson, 'Observing Multiparty Elections in Africa: Lessons from Zambia', *African Affairs* 91 (July 1992).

Decalo, Samuel, 'The Process, Prospects and Constraints of Democratization in Africa', *African Affairs* 91 (January 1992).

Healey, John, and Mark Robinson, *Democracy, Governance and Economic Policy: Sub-Saharan Africa in Comparative Perspective* (London: Overseas Development Institute, 1992).

Husain, Ishrat, and John Underwood (eds), *African External Finance in the 1990s* (Washington, DC: World Bank, 1991).

Killick, Tony, *Explaining Africa's Post-Independence Development Experiences* (London: Overseas Development Institute, 1992).

Moore, Mick, (ed.), 'Good Government?' (Brighton: Institute of Development Studies at the University of Sussex, *IDS Bulletin*, 24, 1 (January 1993).

OAU/UNICEF, *Africa's Children, Africa's Future: Human Investment Priorities for the 1990s* (Addis Ababa and New York, 2 vols, 1992).

Rimmer, Douglas (ed.), *Africa 30 Years On* (London and Portsmouth, N.H.: Royal African Society with James Currey and Heinemann, 1991).

Rimmer, Douglas, *Staying Poor: Ghana's Political Economy, 1950–1990* (Oxford and Elmsford, N.Y.: Pergamon for the World Bank, 1992).

Rothchild, Donald (ed.), *Ghana: the Political Economy of Recovery* (London: Lynne Rienner, 1991).

Sandbrook, Richard, *The Politics of Africa's Economic Recovery* (Cambridge: Cambridge University Press, 1993).

UN Department of Public Information, *Africa Recovery* (New York, serial newsletter).

UN Economic Commission for Africa, *African Alternative Framework to Structural Adjustment Programmes for Socio-Economic Recovery and Transformation* (Addis Ababa, 1989).

World Bank, *Accelerated Development in Sub-Saharan Africa: an Agenda for Action* (Washington, DC, 1981).

World Bank, *Ghana: Policies and Program for Adjustment* (Washington, DC, 1984).

World Bank, *Sub-Saharan Africa: From Crisis to Sustainable Growth: a Long-Term Perspective Study* (Washington, DC, 1989).

World Bank, *Governance and Development* (Washington, DC, 1992).

Index